“Tilt this country on end and everything loose will slide into Los Angeles.”

„Wenn man dieses Land auf die Seite kippte, würde alles, was locker ist, nach Los Angeles rutschen.“

« Penchez ce pays sur le côté et tout ce qui ne tient pas très bien dégringolera jusqu’à Los Angeles. »

Will Rogers

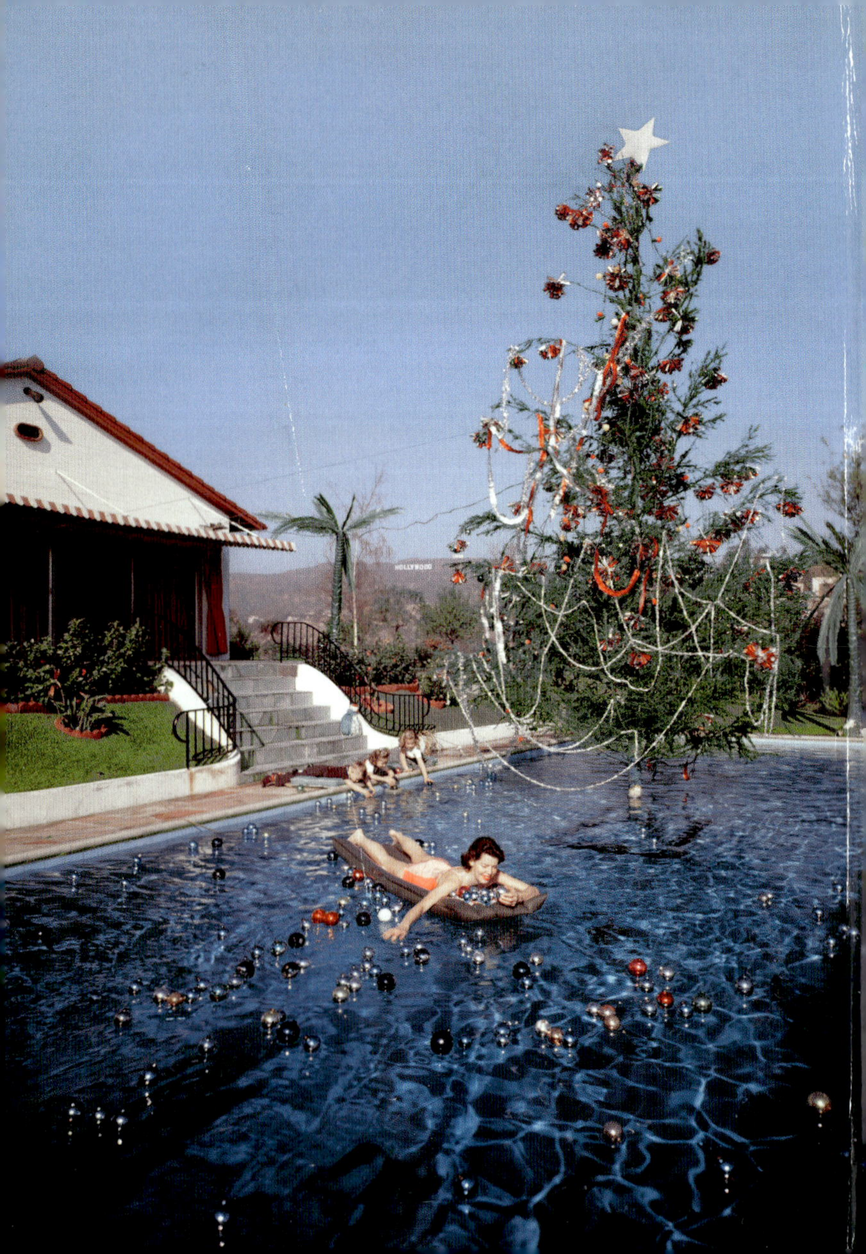
HOLLYWOOD

Jim Heimann

Captions written
by David L. Ulin

Los Angeles

Portrait of a City • Porträt einer Stadt • Portrait d'une ville

TASCHEN

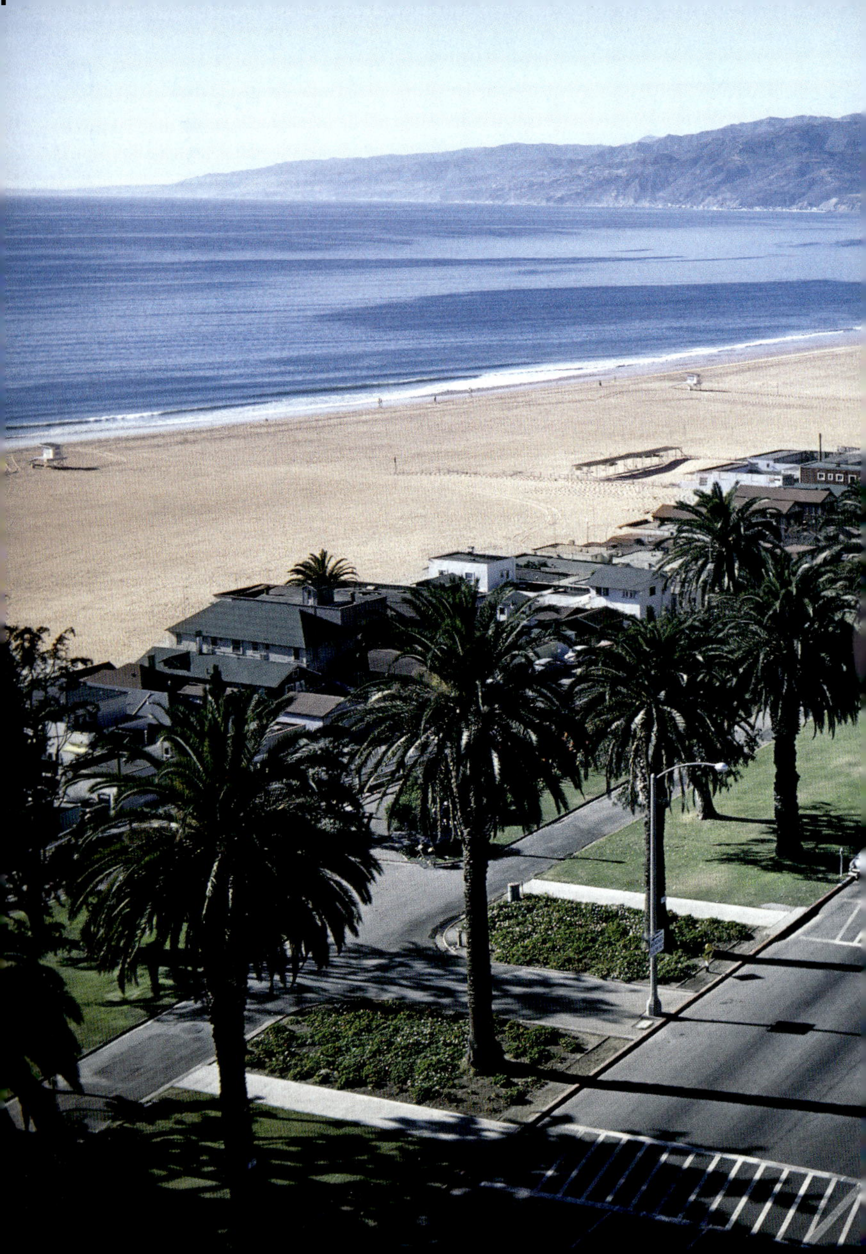

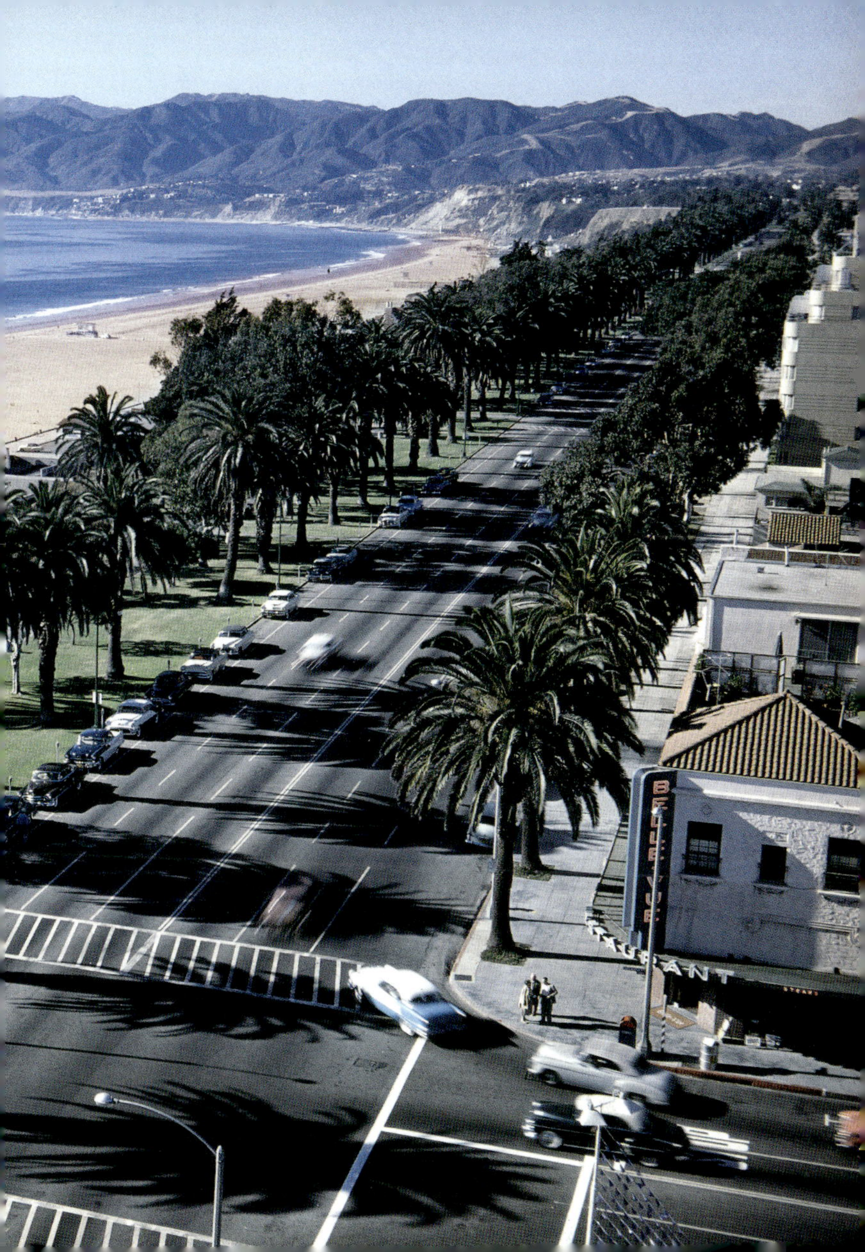
BELLEVUE

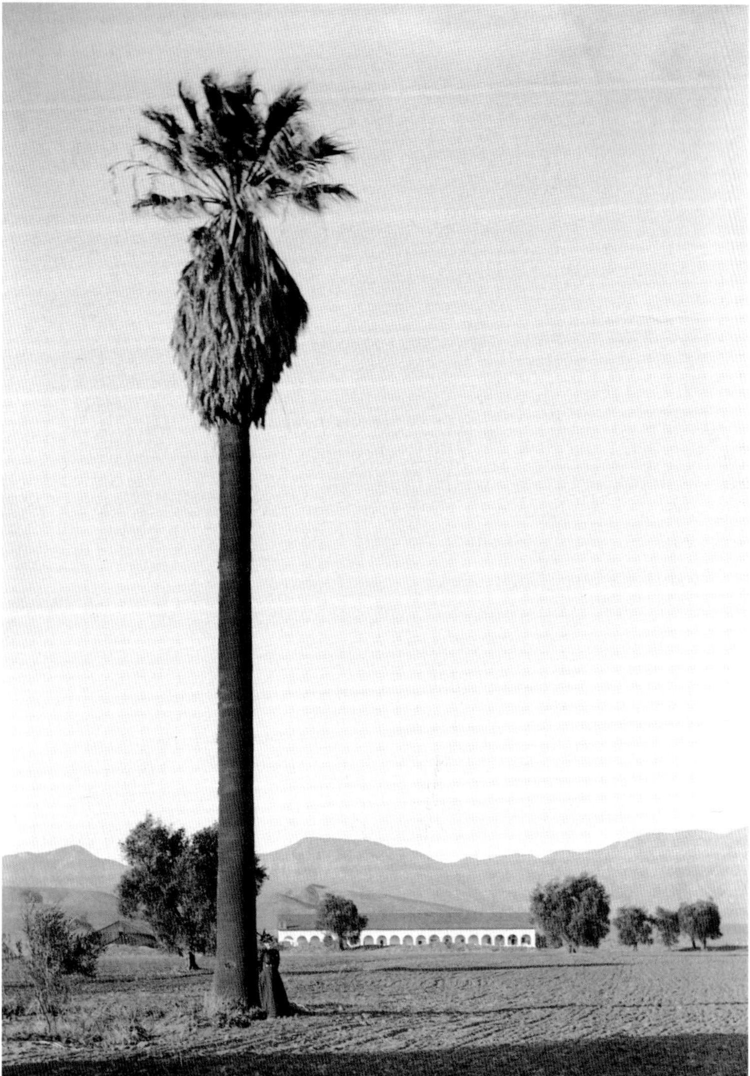

City of the Angels

by Jim Heimann

Orange blossoms. Smog. Exotic. Erotic. Strange. Familiar. Hollywood. Skid Row. Paradise. Hell. Los Angeles, a city of extremes, has been a perplexing paradox right from its start. From the natural beauty of its mountains and ocean to the fabricated beauties of the silver screen, it is truly one of the most unique—and most photographed—destinations in the world.

A Metropolis Is Born c. 1862–1900

Sailing along the Southern California coast in 1542, Spanish explorers could see in the distance the inland smoke from the native camp that was to become the city of Los Angeles. The Tongva had established their village, Yang Na, along a bend of what is now called the Los Angeles River. Here the Spaniards planted their flag, establishing the settlement of *El Pueblo de Nuestra Señora la Reina de Los Angeles del Rio de Porciuncula*, The Village of Our Lady Queen of the Angels by the Porciuncula River, in September 1781. The humble pueblo would serve as the capital of Southern California and, along with the neighboring missions of San Gabriel and San Fernando, would propagate trade and agriculture and Christianity in the region.

When Mexico won its independence from Spain in 1821, Los Angeles became part of the Republic of Mexico. Retaining its frontier status, the town slowly grew with an influx of immigrants from other areas of the Americas and Europe. This period was highlighted by vast ranchos and a cattle industry that created an elite ruling class who resisted government intervention.

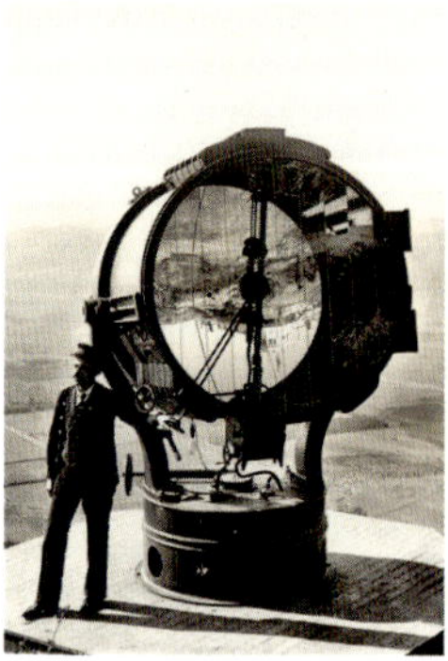

p. 6
Anonymous
The San Fernando Mission, c. 1895.

Missionsstation San Fernando, um 1895.

La mission San Fernando, vers 1895.

←
C. C. Pierce
Searchlight overlooking the San Gabriel Valley at the top of Mount Lowe, c. 1897.

Suchscheinwerfer auf dem Mount Lowe mit Blick auf das San Gabriel Valley, um 1897.

Projecteur surplombant la vallée de San Gabriel au sommet du Mount Lowe, vers 1897.

In 1846, when Los Angeles was invaded by the U.S. military during the Mexican-American War, it boasted 5,000 inhabitants. By 1850 it was part of the new State of California, and an Anglo presence began to dominate the city, diminishing the influence of the *dons* of another era. With the arrival of the railroad from San Francisco in 1876, the growing Anglo community began developing the city south from Sonoratown and the Plaza. In its wake a city of office buildings, public transportation, and suburbs began to emerge. The population boomed to over 50,000 within a few years of the 1886 arrival of the Atchison, Topeka and Santa Fe Railway, and that number would double by the century's end. As the city became more Anglicized, many of its inhabitants embraced the Hispanic influence of the region and utilized this romantic imagery in selling L.A. as a tourist destination.

Population Explosion 1900–1920

With 102,479 residents in 1900, Los Angeles was a city of optimism. In 1905 developer Abbot Kinney created a cultural and amusement playground in swampland near the Pacific Ocean and named it Venice after its Italian inspiration. Vast groves of citrus trees covered the region, adding to the agricultural abundance of the Southland. The discovery of oil by Edward Doheny in 1892 created an instant industry that surpassed all of the area's revenue generators. Most significant, however, was the securing of a reliable water source made possible in 1913 by the city engineer, William Mulholland, a feat that made possible L.A.'s tremendous growth in the 20th century.

By the end of the 1920s Los Angeles was the fifth-largest city in the United States, with over half a million inhabitants. Championed by its boosters, politicians, and developers, the city had virtually willed itself into being a major player on the national stage. A deep-water port was created to encourage international trade. The L. A. Chamber of Commerce promoted establishment of an aviation industry by sponsoring winter air meets that showcased the temperate weather as a year-round advantage. Henry Huntington's Pacific Electric Railway spanned the region with 1,000 miles of track, linking the city and its numerous suburbs with an efficient mass-transit system.

Seeking refuge from Thomas Edison's patent enforcers and relishing the climate, among other factors, the motion picture industry slowly migrated west from New York to create a vast entertainment factory by the 1920s. In an oblique way, the filming that took place in the city's streets and suburbs would serve as a visual introduction to the world of Los Angeles as an emerging metropolis.

Boomtown 1920–1945

The nascent film industry took a firm hold in Los Angeles a mere decade after some of its major players set up shop. With its cluster of movie studios, the suburb of Hollywood, annexed in 1910, became the center for this new industry. Hollywood monopolized the world's imagination, and the movie mystique drew thousands of fans to L. A. to pursue that dream, recasting their lives and discarding their past —an allure that continues right up to today.

The city was maturing, while population and real estate booms fostered growth on all levels. The arts thrived, particularly architecture, as some of the world's most innovative architects were commissioned by local residents to build structures free of conventional norms. With its growing and diversifying populace, the city's downtown took on a metropolitan air, crowned by a new City Hall—the tallest building in town at 32 floors. Suburbs exploded, filling in the vacant landscape with rows of bungalows, Tudor mansions, and miniature ranchos, imprinting the region with an endless sprawl. The automobile had become king, making L. A. the first major metropolis to rely on cars as the primary mode of transportation.

The Great Depression was a defining moment for the United States, and Los Angeles was no exception. The optimism that had carried the region through three decades of growth suddenly went stagnant, with a momentary reprieve as the city invited the world to visit for the Summer Olympics in 1932.

Adding to the city's woes, a 6.4-magnitude earthquake hit the region in March 1933. Record downpours later in the decade spurred creation of a flood control system to direct the water in a contained system of channels to the ocean. Further casting the city in a dark light were corruption scandals involving civic officials and the police department, highlighting the shortcomings of a city on the move. Writers found this criminal behavior inspiring for novels and films that explored the downside of the Chamber of Commerce image of oranges, sunshine, and snow-capped mountains.

Surviving the financial problems that plagued the rest of the country, the motion picture industry continued to thrive by providing an escape from daily doldrums and, not insignificantly, jobs for the area. As L.A. continued to expand, its buildings embraced the imagery of the future, especially the Streamline Moderne style, which incorporated itself into the polyglot of architectural styles. The Pan-Pacific Auditorium, a prime example of this style, expressed the city's optimism for embracing all that was new — including religions, evangelical movements, and cults, planting a perception that this was indeed a city of "fruits and nuts."

As the decade turned, L.A. found itself gearing up for battle as a major center for the war effort. Aircraft produced in Southern California were used on both the European and Pacific fronts. Once war was declared, the city produced planes, ships, and other matériel in record numbers. And with the war came a new population boom. Thousands of soldiers, sailors, and others who passed through would decide Los Angeles held the future for them.

Postwar Paradise 1945–1965

After the war Los Angeles became the desired destination for thousands of newcomers. In the 15 years after peace was declared, 2.5 million people were calling L.A. home, over 800,000 of them in the San Fernando Valley alone. This blast of people forced the city to grow exponentially, subsidizing an infrastructure on which freeways burgeoned, schools multiplied, and shopping centers blossomed to create a suburban middle-class utopia. Manufacturing, the aerospace industry, automobile production, an emerging apparel industry — and, to a lesser extent, oil and agriculture — propelled the postwar economic explosion.

With this blooming Arcadia came a rise in pollution (most notoriously smog) as well as crime. Impacts on the area's natural resources reached their limit, exposing the growing pains of a city struggling toward maturity. The Los Angeles

→
Anonymous
Venice amusement zone, 1907.

Vergnügungsviertel in Venice, 1907.

Quartier des attractions de Venice, 1907.

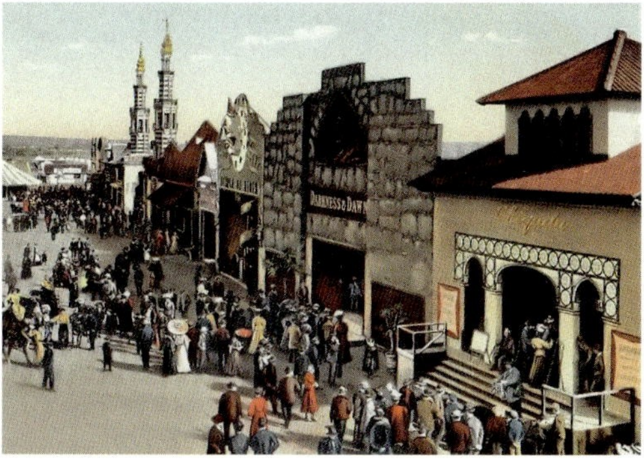

Police Department, long troubled by corruption, was mobilized into a paramilitary organization dedicated to keeping trouble at bay.

Los Angeles in the early 1960s had become a favorite focus of global media, portrayed as a source of trends and styles that dictated a lifestyle to be desired and copied all over the world. Sports such as surfing and toy companies such as Mattel projected Southland sensibilities to an international audience. Los Angeles, the super city, was set to become a global powerhouse with both positive and negative results on the horizon.

Lost Angeles 1965–1980

The view of Los Angeles as an urban Eden came to a slamming halt in the summer of 1965, when African American neighborhoods, centered in Watts, south of downtown, exploded into a racial battlefield. The growing resentment of minorities left out of L.A.'s prosperity became a theme that would continue for the foreseeable future and affect the city in myriad ways. The turbulent '60s seemed to find an epicenter in the city, with the assassination of Robert F. Kennedy and murders committed by Charles Manson's followers further drawing a black cloud over the city.

Seemingly immune to urban problems was the burgeoning music scene exhilarated by the surge of teenage baby boomers. This group, projecting an endless culture of youth, was highly effective in defining the region through obsession with cars, fashion, and leisure sports. Long considered a backwater for visual artistic movements, small groups of independent-minded artists like Ed Ruscha and Ed

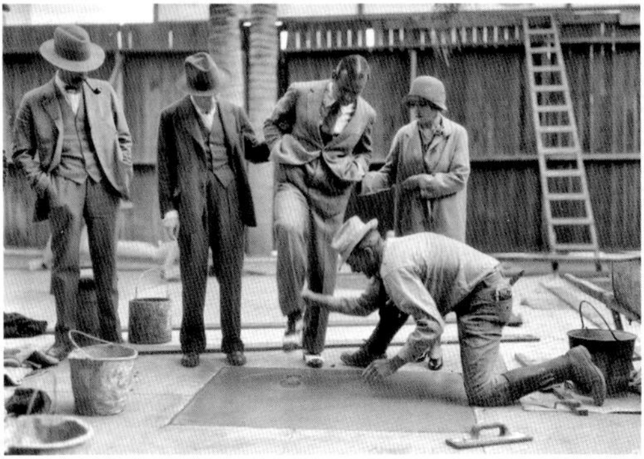

←

Anonymous

Douglas Fairbanks and Mary Pickford embed their footprints in concrete at Sid Grauman's Chinese Theatre, April 20, 1927.

Douglas Fairbanks und Mary Pickford setzen ihre Fußabdrücke in den Beton vor Sid Grauman's Chinese Theatre, 20. April 1927.

Douglas Fairbanks et Mary Pickford marquent le ciment de leurs empreintes devant le Chinese Theatre de Sid Grauman, 20 avril 1927.

Kienholz and galleries like Ferus took a refreshing approach to art that would challenge New York and Paris.

The seamless continuum of streets and buildings was fulfilled by the 1960s and L. A. became more of an idea than a city bound by physical limits. Soon "Los Angeles" would expand into an urban mass spread across multiple counties and more than 200 miles of California coast. For the first time in more than 100 years, the Anglo Saxon predominance was being edged out by a multiethnic infusion led by immigrants from Mexico and the rest of Latin America.

Financially the city was poised for change as the aerospace industry and manufacturing slowly subsided. Gone, downsized, or merged were Lockheed, Northrop, Douglas, Goodyear, General Motors, and Firestone. Houses, shopping malls, and industrial parks largely replaced agriculture and oil. Change was in the air, but change has always been the driving force that seemed to define Los Angeles as a city of the future.

Apocalypse Now 1980–TODAY

If the Los Angeles of the previous decades was a darkening city, it now seemed headed into a black hole. Mass immigration from Latin America provided a new stream of cheap labor while straining the city's infrastructure. Spreading out from East L. A. to the whole of the basin, low-income neighborhoods were transformed into communities very different from past population booms, adopting the traditions of citizens from around the world.

Perhaps the most ominous and destructive element in this period was the rise of a gang culture affecting all segments of the populace. In 1995 alone, gang-related homicides reached a peak of 807 in L. A. County. Firing guns and police helicopters became a common soundtrack.

The riots of 1992, a response to a jury acquittal of police officers in the beating of motorist Rodney King, further eroded the fragile social contract. The city burned and was looted for over three days. National Guard troops on city streets and declaration of martial law confirmed that this was an urban war zone. The resulting $1 billion in damages was a severe setback for the entire region. The 6.7 Northridge earthquake in 1994 added another blow to the recovering Southland and ended up costing more than $20 billion in property damage—economically and psychologically shaking its citizens to the core.

But the era was not all doom and gloom: One bright spot was the 23rd Olympics in 1984. City planners anticipated the worst in terms of congestion and crowd control, but the event proved to be an effective showcase for the city as an international capital. As L.A. gained confidence on the world stage, its cultural cachet beyond films and television also rose.

Local architects such as Frank Gehry continued the long tradition of innovation, eventually producing downtown's iconic Disney Hall. Museums thrived and multiplied: The Getty, the Hammer, and the Museum of Contemporary Art added to an already rich art-based landscape. California cuisine came into its own with a restaurant and food scene lauded by critics.

Entering the new millennium, Los Angeles had exceeded all expectations of the dusty pueblo some 200 years earlier. New terms had to be created to define a city that had no precedents. Its fulfillment as the city of the future was not complete, nor will it ever be. Los Angeles is a work in progress, a city maligned and admired but one that demands the attention of the world and receives it every day.

p. 14

Julius Shulman

The Beverly Hilton Hotel, Conrad Hilton's West Coast flagship, designed by Welton Becket, 1956.

Das Beverly Hilton Hotel, Conrad Hiltons Flaggschiff an der Westküste, entworfen von Welton Becket, 1956.

L'hôtel Beverly Hilton, vaisseau amiral de la chaîne de Conrad Hilton sur la côte Ouest, a été conçu par Welton Becket, 1956.

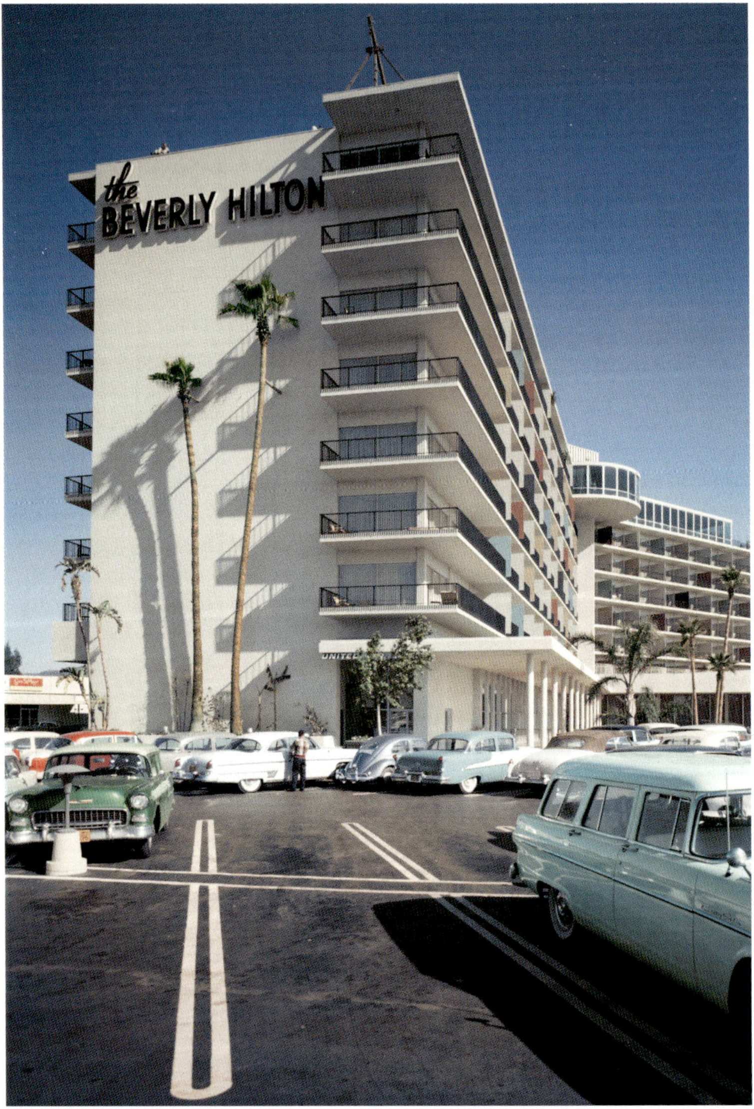
the BEVERLY HILTON

Stadt der Engel

von Jim Heimann

Orangenblüten. Smog. Exotisch. Erotisch. Seltsam. Vertraut. Hollywood. Skid Row. Das Paradies. Die Hölle. Los Angeles, die Stadt der Extreme, verblüfft und fasziniert schon, seit es sie gibt. Mit ihrer Pracht – von der natürlichen Schönheit der Berge und des Ozeans bis hin zu den künstlichen Schönheiten der Leinwand – ist sie eine der ungewöhnlichsten und meistfotografierten Städte der Welt.

Eine Metropole wird geboren CA. 1862–1900

Als spanische Entdecker im Jahr 1542 die südkalifornische Küste entlangsegelten, sahen sie von Weitem aus dem Landesinneren Rauch aufsteigen. Er kam aus dem Dorf Yang Na, das Ureinwohner vom Stamm der Tongva an einer Flussbiegung des heutigen Los Angeles River errichtet hatten. Aus diesem Dorf sollte einmal die Stadt Los Angeles werden. Hier hissten die Spanier ihre Flagge und erbauten im September 1781 die Siedlung El Pueblo de Nuestra Señora la Reina de Los Angeles del Rio de Porciuncula (das Dorf unserer lieben Frau, Königin der Engel, am Fluss Porciuncula). Das bescheidene Pueblo sollte als Hauptstadt von Südkalifornien dienen und zusammen mit den benachbarten Missionen San Gabriel und San Fernando in der Region Handel, Landwirtschaft und das Christentum verbreiten.

Als Mexiko 1821 von Spanien unabhängig wurde, fiel Los Angeles an die Republik Mexiko. Durch den Zustrom von Einwanderern aus anderen Teilen des amerikanischen Kontinents und aus Europa wuchs die Grenzstadt stetig. Geprägt war diese Periode von ausgedehnten *ranchos* und Viehwirtschaft; es entstand eine herrschende Klasse, die jede Einmischung des Staates vehement ablehnte.

Als 1846 im Zuge des Mexikanisch-Amerikanischen Kriegs US-Militär in Los Angeles einmarschierte, lebten hier bereits 5000 Menschen. 1850 wurde die Stadt Teil des neuen Staates Kalifornien – Einwanderer angelsächsischer Herkunft gewannen die Oberhand und ließen den Einfluss der ehemals mächtigen *dons* schrumpfen. Mit Ankunft der Eisenbahn aus San Francisco im Jahr 1876 begann die wachsende Anglo-Community, die Stadt von Sonoratown und der Plaza aus in Richtung Süden auszubauen, es entstanden Bürogebäude, öffentlicher Nahverkehr und Vororte. Schon wenige Jahre nach Ankunft der Atchison, Topeka and Santa Fe Railway 1886 schoss die Bevölkerungszahl auf über 50000 hoch und sollte sich bis zum Ende des Jahrhunderts noch verdoppeln. Obwohl die Stadt zunehmend angloamerikanisch wurde, wollten viele Bewohner ihr hispanisches Erbe bewahren und erschufen gezielt ein romantisch verklärtes Image, um L. A. als Touristenziel zu bewerben.

Bevölkerungsexplosion 1900–1920

Im Jahr 1900 hatte Los Angeles 102479 Einwohner und strotzte vor Optimismus. 1905 ließ der Stadtplaner Abbot Kinney auf Sumpfland in der Nähe des Pazifiks ein Kultur- und Vergnügungszentrum erbauen und nannte es nach Venedig, seiner italienischen Inspirationsquelle, Venice. Ausgedehnte Zitronenhaine prägten die südlichen Regionen und trugen zu ihrem landwirtschaftlichen Reichtum bei. Als Edward Doheny 1892 auf Öl stieß, entstand schlagartig ein Wirtschaftszweig, der alle bisherigen Profitquellen bei Weitem überstieg. Am wichtigsten war es jedoch, eine zuverlässige Wasserversorgung zu gewährleisten, was 1913 dem städtischen Ingenieur William Mulholland gelang. Damit war der Grundstein für das enorme Wachstum von L. A. im 20. Jahrhundert gelegt.

Ende der 1920er-Jahre war Los Angeles mit über einer halben Million Einwohnern die fünftgrößte Stadt der USA. Unter der Führung ihrer Politiker und Stadtplaner war die Stadt durch pure Willenskraft zu einer Macht auf der nationalen Bühne geworden. Ein Tiefseehafen wurde angelegt, um den internationalen Handel anzukurbeln. Die Handelskammer warb mit Winter-Flugshows, die die Vorzüge des milden Klimas demonstrieren sollten, für den Aufbau einer Luftfahrtindustrie. Henry Huntingtons Pacific Electric Railway überzog die Region mit einem 1600 Kilometer langen Schienennetz und verband so die Stadt und ihre zahlreichen Vororte durch ein effizientes Massenverkehrssystem.

Auch Filmschaffende, denen das Klima gefiel und die Thomas Edisons Patentwächtern aus dem Weg gehen wollten, zog es allmählich von New York gen

Westen. In den 1920er-Jahren hatten sie in L. A. bereits eine riesige Unterhaltungsindustrie aufgebaut. In gewisser Weise wirkten die Filmaufnahmen, die damals in den Straßen und Vororten der Stadt gemacht wurden, wie eine visuelle Visitenkarte von Los Angeles als angehender Metropole.

Boomtown 1920–1945

Schon zehn Jahre nachdem einige ihrer führenden Figuren übergesiedelt waren, hatte die junge Filmindustrie Los Angeles fest im Griff. Der 1910 eingemeindete Vorort Hollywood mit seinen vielen Filmstudios wurde ihr Zentrum. Hollywood bestimmte die globalen Fantasien und der Zauber des Films lockte Tausende nach L. A., die ihr Leben neu erfanden und sich von ihrer Vergangenheit lossagten, um ihre Träume zu verwirklichen – eine Verlockung, die bis zum heutigen Tag anhält.

Die Stadt reifte heran, während der Bevölkerungs- und Bauboom ein Wachstum in allen Bereichen förderte. Die Künste entfalteten sich, insbesondere die Architektur, da einige Bewohner von L. A. die weltweit innovativsten Architekten damit beauftragten, Bauwerke jenseits aller Konventionen zu errichten. Die Innenstadt mit ihrer wachsenden multikulturellen Bevölkerung bekam ein großstädtisches Flair, das von der neuen City Hall – mit 32 Stockwerken das höchste Gebäude der Stadt – gekrönt wurde. Die Vororte explodierten förmlich, füllten die leere Landschaft mit Reihen von Bungalows, Villen im Tudorstil und Miniatur-Ranchos und dehnten die Stadt ins Unendliche aus. Das Automobil war nun König und machte L. A. zur ersten Metropole, in der Autos das vorrangige Transportmittel waren.

Die Wirtschaftskrise von 1929 markierte für die USA insgesamt und auch für Los Angeles einen tiefen Einschnitt. Dahin war der Optimismus, der die Region durch drei Jahrzehnte ungebremsten Wachstums begleitet hatte. Nur die Olympischen Sommerspiele 1932, zu der die Stadt die Welt einlud, brachten für kurze Zeit ein wenig Aufmunterung.

Zu allem wirtschaftlichen Übel kam im März 1933 noch ein Erdbeben der Stärke 6,4. Später in den 30er-Jahren führten sintflutartige Regenfälle zur Einführung eines Flutkontrollsystems, das die Wassermassen durch ein Kanalsystem direkt in den Ozean leitet. Die Stadt wurde in dieser Zeit auch von einem Korruptionsskandal erschüttert, in den Stadtverwaltung und Polizei verstrickt waren – die Schattenseite einer Stadt im Wandel. Schriftsteller und Filmemacher ließen sich vom kriminellen Milieu inspirieren, dem Gegenstück zum Image von Orangen, Sonne und schneebedeckten Berggipfeln, das die Handelskammer propagierte.

Ungeachtet der ökonomischen Probleme, die den Rest des Landes plagten, florierte die Filmindustrie, die den Menschen eine Flucht vor den Alltagssorgen ermöglichte und zudem eine nicht unbeträchtliche Zahl von Arbeitsplätzen schuf. Die Architektur des expandierenden Los Angeles zeigte sich zukunftsgewandt, vor allem in Form der Streamline-Moderne, die sich in die polyglotte Ansammlung architektonischer Stile der Stadt einreihte. Das Pan-Pacific Auditorium, ein Paradebeispiel für diesen Stil, drückte die Bereitschaft von L.A. aus, alles Neue mit offenen Armen zu empfangen – darunter auch Religionen, evangelikale Bewegungen und Sekten – und verpasste der Stadt den Ruf, verrückt zu sein.

Zu Beginn der 1940er-Jahre setzten auch in L.A. Kriegsvorbereitungen ein, in Südkalifornien hergestellte Flugzeuge kamen sowohl an der europäischen als auch an der pazifischen Front zum Einsatz. Nach Kriegseintritt produzierte die Stadt Rekordmengen an Flugzeugen, Schiffen und anderem Kriegsgerät. Und mit dem Krieg kam auch ein neuer Zuwandererboom: Tausende von Soldaten, Seeleuten und anderen Durchreisenden entschieden, dass ihre Zukunft in Los Angeles lag.

Nachkriegsparadies 1945–1965

Nach dem Krieg strömten wiederum Tausende von Neuankömmlingen in die Stadt. 15 Jahre nach Kriegsende lebten 2,5 Millionen Menschen in L.A., davon allein 800000 im San Fernando Valley. Dieser Massenzuzug zwang die Stadt zu exponentiellem Wachstum: Autobahnen überzogen die Landschaft, Schulen vervielfachten sich und Einkaufszentren schossen aus dem Boden, um eine Vorstadtutopie der Mittelschicht zu erzeugen. Fabriken, die Luftfahrtindustrie, die Automobilbranche, eine aufkommende Bekleidungsindustrie und, zu einem geringeren Teil, Öl und Landwirtschaft waren die Motoren des explosionsartigen ökonomischen Aufschwungs nach dem Krieg.

Mit diesem blühenden Arkadien kamen aber auch Umweltverschmutzung (vor allem der berüchtigte Smog) und Kriminalität. Die Belastung für die natürlichen Ressourcen hatte unerträgliche Ausmaße erreicht, die Probleme einer wachsenden Stadt wurden offensichtlich. Das von Korruption gebeutelte Los Angeles Police Department wurde zu einer paramilitärischen Organisation umfunktioniert, um der Schwierigkeiten Herr zu werden.

Das Los Angeles der frühen 1960er-Jahre war zum Lieblingsthema globaler Medien geworden, es war ein Ort, der Trends und Moden hervorbrachte und weltweit für einen begehrenswerten Lebensstil stand. Sportarten wie Surfen und Spielzeughersteller wie Mattel vermittelten das Southland-Gefühl der ganzen Welt. Los

→
Allan Grant
Fifteen-year-old Kathy Kohner, known as Gidget, was the rare female surfer on a male-dominated beach, Malibu, c. 1957.

Die 15-jährige Kathy Kohner, bekannt als Gidget, war eine der wenigen Surferinnen am männerdominierten Strand, Malibu, um 1957.

Âgée de 15 ans, Kathy Kohner dite Gidget était une des rares surfeuses sur une plage dominée par les garçons, Malibu, 1957.

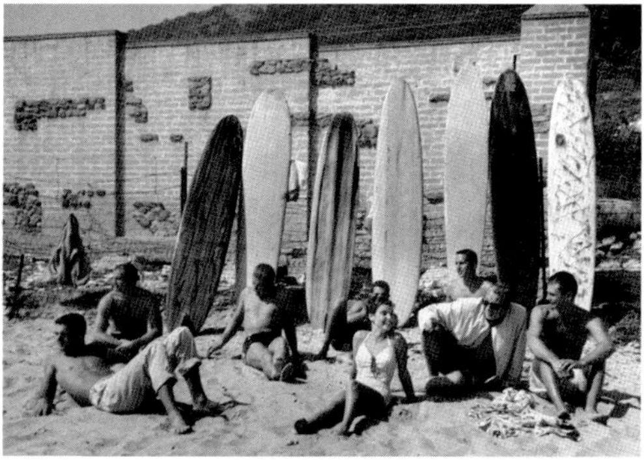

Angeles, die Superstadt, stand an der Schwelle zum globalen Kraftzentrum und die Zukunft verhieß sowohl Gutes als auch Schlechtes.

Lost Angeles – die verlorene Stadt 1965–1980

Das Bild von Los Angeles als urbaner Garten Eden wurde brutal zerstört, als es im Sommer 1965 in dem vorwiegend von Afroamerikanern bewohnten Stadtviertel Watts, südlich von Downtown, zu einem Schlachtfeld der Rassen wurde. Die zunehmende Unzufriedenheit von Minderheiten, die vom Wohlstand der Stadt ausgeschlossen waren, sollte auch die nähere Zukunft von L. A. bestimmen; die turbulenten 60er-Jahre schienen hier ein Epizentrum zu finden. Die Ermordung von Robert F. Kennedy und die von Charles Manson und seinen Anhängern begangenen Morde ließen dunkle Wolken über der Stadt aufziehen.

Scheinbar unberührt davon blieb die aufkeimende Musikszene, die vor allem von den inzwischen zu Teenagern herangewachsenen Babyboomern getragen wurde. Diese Gruppe verbreitete einen regelrechten Jugendwahn und definierte die gesamte Region mit ihrer Besessenheit für Autos, Mode und Sport. Gleichzeitig entstanden in L. A., das bezüglich der bildenden Künste als provinziell galt, kleine Gruppen unabhängiger Künstler, zu denen zum Beispiel Ed Ruscha und Ed Kienholz gehörten, und Galerien wie Ferus. Es entstand ein neues Kunstverständnis, das New York und Paris herausforderte.

In den 60er-Jahren entwickelte sich das Gebilde Los Angeles zu einem lücken- und nahtlosen Netz aus Straßen und Häusern – L. A. war nun mehr eine Idee als

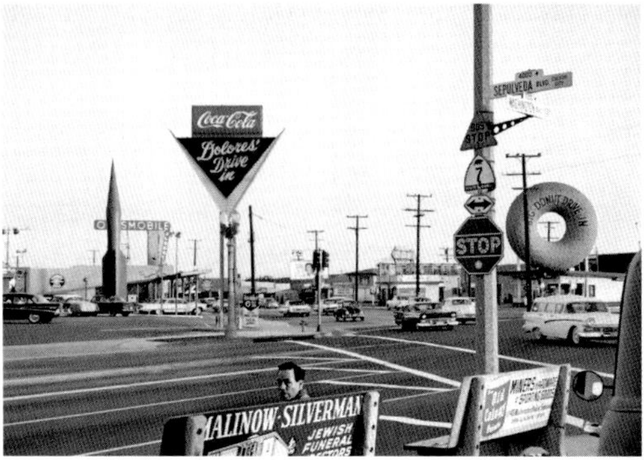

←
Dennis Stock
Pop-culture immersion at the intersection of Washington and Sepulveda boulevards, Culver City, 1960.

Eingetaucht in die Popkultur: die Kreuzung Washington Boulevard und Sepulveda Boulevard in Culver City, 1960.

Immersion dans la Pop Culture *au croisement de Washington Boulevard et Sepulveda Boulevard, Culver City, 1960.*

eine reale Stadt mit physischen Grenzen. Bald breitete sich die urbane Masse über zahlreiche Countys aus und vereinnahmte über 300 km der kalifornischen Küste. Zum ersten Mal seit 100 Jahren wurde die angelsächsische Vorherrschaft zurückgedrängt durch einen multiethnischen Zuzug, angeführt von Migranten aus Mexiko und Lateinamerika.

Auch wirtschaftlich fand ein Umbruch statt: Firmen der Luftfahrtindustrie und anderer Industriezweige, darunter Lockheed, Northrop, Douglas, Goodyear, General Motors und Firestone, fuhren ihre Produktion zurück, fusionierten oder schlossen ganz. Landwirtschaft und Öl wurden größtenteils durch Häuser, Einkaufszentren und Gewerbegebiete ersetzt. Wandel lag in der Luft, doch Veränderung war schon immer das, was Los Angeles antrieb und zu einer Stadt der Zukunft machte.

Apocalypse Now 1980–HEUTE

Hatten sich in den vorherigen Dekaden schon dunkle Wolken über der Stadt zusammengezogen, so verdichteten sich diese nun zu einem gewaltigen Sturm. Die Masseneinwanderung aus Lateinamerika brachte zwar billige Arbeitskräfte, strapazierte die Infrastruktur aber bis aufs Äußerste. Von East L. A. aus breitete sich die Stadt auf das gesamte Becken aus und die Bewohner ärmerer Viertel hielten, im Gegensatz zu früheren Migranten, an den Traditionen ihrer Herkunftsländer fest.

Besonders bedrohlich und zerstörerisch wirkte sich in dieser Periode das Aufkommen von Straßengangs aus, das alle Teile der Bevölkerung in Mitleidenschaft zog. Allein im Jahr 1995 verzeichnete das County L. A. 807 Morde, die mit Gangs in Verbindung standen. Schüsse und der Klang von Polizeihubschraubern gehörten bald zur alltäglichen Geräuschkulisse.

Die schweren Ausschreitungen von 1992, ausgelöst durch den Freispruch von Polizisten, die den schwarzen Autofahrer Rodney King zusammengeschlagen hatten, höhlten das fragile Sozialgefüge weiter aus. Über drei Tage lang wurde gebrandschatzt und geplündert. Der Einsatz der Nationalgarde und die Verhängung des Kriegsrechts machten deutlich, dass dies ein städtisches Kriegsgebiet war. Unter dem auf eine Milliarde US-Dollar bezifferten Schaden litt die gesamte Region. Ein Erdbeben der Stärke 6,7 im Jahr 1994 in Northridge versetzte ihr einen weiteren Schlag und verursachte einen Schaden in Höhe von 20 Milliarden Dollar. Die Bürger von L. A. waren ökonomisch und psychologisch zutiefst erschüttert.

Doch es war nicht alles schlecht in dieser Zeit. Einen Lichtblick bildeten die 23. Olympischen Sommerspiele von 1984. Man hatte mit größten logistischen Problemen gerechnet, doch die Stadt präsentierte sich als effiziente Metropole und zeigte sich auch jenseits von Film und Fernsehen selbstbewusst auf der internationalen Bühne.

Örtliche Architekten wie Frank Gehry führten unter anderem mit der markanten Disney Hall in Downtown die lange Tradition innovativen Bauens fort. Das Getty- und das Hammer-Museum sowie das Museum of Contemporary Art bereicherten die ohnehin schon vielfältige Kunstwelt. Und die kalifornische Küche etablierte sich mit einer Restaurantszene, die Kritiker begeisterte.

Zu Beginn des neuen Jahrtausends hatte Los Angeles alle Erwartungen, die vor 200 Jahren in das staubige Pueblo gesetzt worden waren, bei Weitem überschritten. Diese Stadt ohne vergleichbare Vorgänger setzte neue Maßstäbe. Als Stadt der Zukunft ist sie nicht vollendet und wird es auch niemals sein. Los Angeles ist ein *work in progress*, eine Stadt, die mal geschmäht und mal bewundert wird, aber immer im Zentrum der Weltaufmerksamkeit steht.

p. 22

Ellen von Unwerth

Sunset Boulevard provides the backdrop for model Naomi Campbell on the perpetually "cool" Sunset Strip, 1992.

Der Sunset Boulevard als Kulisse für Naomi Campbell auf dem ewig „coolen" Sunset Strip, 1992.

Sunset Boulevard fournit la toile de fond à cette déambulation du mannequin Naomi Campbell sur le toujours « cool » Sunset Strip, 1992.

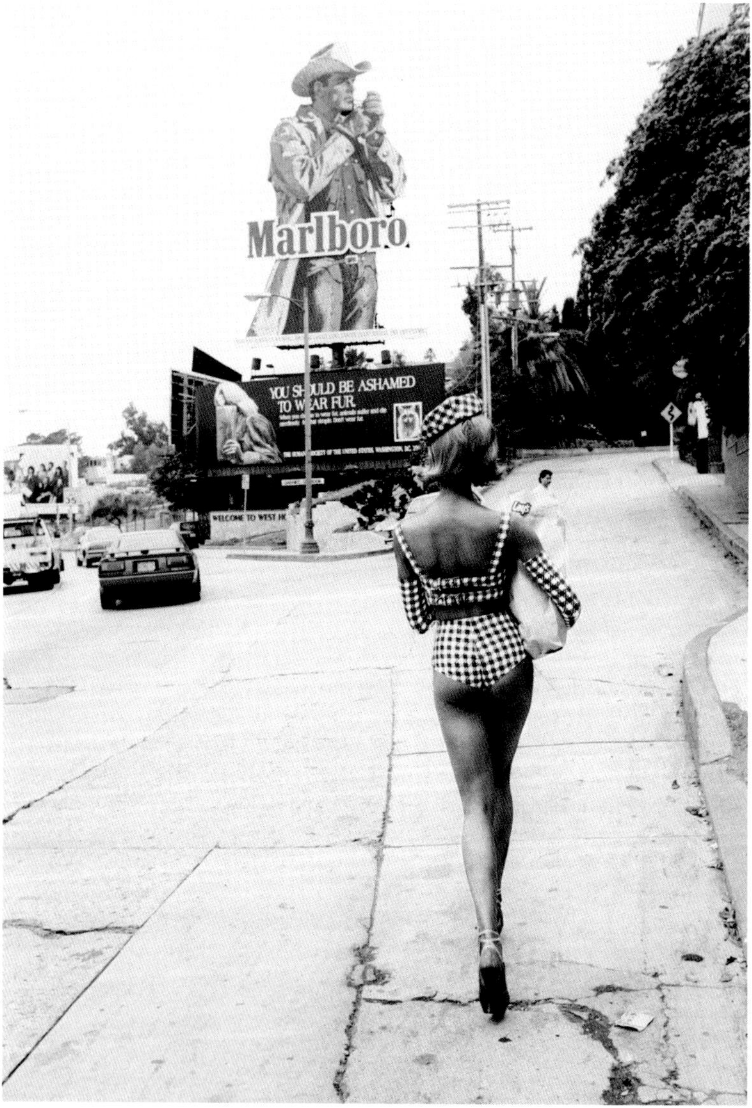
Marlboro
YOU SHOULD BE ASHAMED
TO WEAR FUR.
WELCOME TO WEST H

La Cité des Anges

par Jim Heimann

Orangers en fleurs. Smog. Exotisme. Érotisme. Ghettos déshérités. Hollywood. Paradis. Enfer. Ville des extrêmes, étrange et familière, Los Angeles est depuis le premier jour un paradoxe à elle seule, toujours déconcertant. Naturelle ou factice, sa beauté protéiforme n'en finit pas d'aimanter le regard des voyageurs et des photographes.

Naissance d'une métropole 1862–1900

Longeant les côtes du sud de la Californie en 1542, les explorateurs espagnols distinguèrent au loin la fumée du campement indien qui deviendrait un jour Los Angeles. Les Tongva avaient adossé leur village, Yang-Na, au méandre d'un cours d'eau aujourd'hui mieux connu sous le nom de Los Angeles River. C'est là, face au village indien, qu'un peu plus de deux siècles plus tard, en septembre 1781, les Espagnols planteront leur drapeau, fondant une colonie baptisée *El Pueblo de Nuestra Señora la Reina de Los Angeles del Rio de Porciuncula* : le village de Notre-Dame la Reine des Anges de la Portioncule. À partir du modeste *pueblo*, bientôt capitale de la Californie du Sud, et des missions voisines de San Gabriel et de San Fernando, agriculture et christianisme allaient pouvoir se diffuser dans la région.

Lorsque le Mexique arracha son indépendance à l'Espagne en 1821, Los Angeles se retrouva annexée à la jeune république. Ville frontière, elle se développa progressivement au gré des nouvelles vagues d'immigration d'autres régions des Amériques et d'Europe. Surgirent alors les ranchs immenses et l'industrie bovine et une classe de possédants assez puissante pour résister à tout dirigisme gouvernemental.

En 1846, lors de la guerre opposant le Mexique aux États-Unis, Los Angeles, qui comptait 5 000 habitants, fut envahie par les forces militaires américaines. Quatre ans plus tard, elle intégrait officiellement le nouvel État de Californie, où l'influence anglo-saxonne allait pour un temps prévaloir au détriment des honorables *dons*, témoins d'une époque révolue. L'arrivée en 1876 du chemin de fer qui reliait L.A. à San Francisco encouragea la communauté «anglo», de plus en plus importante, à accélérer le développement de la ville au sud de Sonoratown et de La Plaza. Immeubles de bureaux, transports publics, banlieues: une nouvelle cité s'édifiait peu à peu. La population s'accrut encore, dépassant les 50 000 habitants juste avant le raccordement de la ville au réseau ferroviaire Atchison, Topeka & Santa Fe Railway (1886). La démographie urbaine allait même doubler au tournant du siècle. L.A. s'anglicisait et cependant ses habitants étaient de plus en plus nombreux à se ranger aux influences hispaniques, très puissantes dans la région. Cette toile de fond nourrira l'imagerie romantique dont se serviront les agences de voyage pour «vendre» la Cité des Anges en tant que destination touristique.

L'explosion démographique 1900–1920

Avec ses 102 479 habitants, Los Angeles était en 1900 une cité pleine d'optimisme. En 1905, le promoteur Abbot Kinney fit assécher une zone de marécages en bordure d'océan et creuser un réseau de canaux inspiré de la Venise européenne pour y créer un parc de loisirs et de culture – Venice. Le sud de la Californie se couvrit de vastes plantations d'agrumes, ajoutant encore à sa luxuriance agricole. En 1892, la découverte du pétrole par Edward Doheny suscita instantanément une industrie qui devait dépasser toutes les sources de recettes jamais connues dans la région. En 1913, la ville put bénéficier d'un approvisionnement en eau régulier grâce à l'audace novatrice de l'ingénieur William Mulholland. L.A. doit à cette prouesse sa formidable croissance au XXe siècle.

À la fin des années 1920, Los Angeles était la cinquième agglomération des États-Unis, avec plus d'un demi-million d'habitants. Portée par ses élus et par les promoteurs immobiliers, la ville était parvenue à s'arroger une place de choix à l'échelle nationale. La construction d'un port en eau profonde contribua également à favoriser les échanges internationaux. La chambre de commerce encouragea le développement d'une industrie aéronautique en organisant des meetings aériens, l'hiver, pour valoriser le climat tempéré de la région. Les transports en commun de la Pacific Electric Railway d'Henry Huntington couvraient la région sur plus de 1 500 kilomètres et permettaient de relier efficacement la ville à ses nombreux faubourgs.

De son côté, la toute jeune industrie du film cherchait alors à échapper au cartel qui défendait les brevets cinématographiques de Thomas Edison. Le climat californien, entre autres facteurs, la persuada d'abandonner New York et de migrer vers l'Ouest où allait prospérer, à partir des années 1920, une gigantesque usine à divertissement. Déployés dans les rues et banlieues de la ville, les tournages offriront à Los Angeles une exposition visuelle confortant son statut de métropole émergente.

La ville champignon 1920–1945

Il fallut une dizaine d'années à peine à cette activité naissante pour s'implanter solidement à Los Angeles. Fort de l'essaim de studios qui y avaient élu résidence, Hollywood, municipalité annexée en 1910, s'imposa comme le cœur battant de la nouvelle industrie. Ainsi L.A. commença-t-elle à exercer son emprise sur l'imagination du monde, et la mystique du septième art à attirer à elle des milliers de fans résolus à poursuivre leur rêve, à changer de vie, à repartir à zéro – un attrait qui dure aujourd'hui encore.

La ville, en cet âge dynamique, gagnait en maturité; l'essor démographique et la multiplication des booms immobiliers servaient mécaniquement une croissance tous azimuts. Les arts s'épanouissaient, en particulier l'architecture: des architectes parmi les plus imaginatifs de la planète furent mandatés par des citoyens aisés pour concevoir à leur intention des structures libérées des normes conventionnelles. Le centre-ville, dont la population ne cessait d'augmenter et de se diversifier, assumait chaque jour un peu plus sa dimension métropolitaine, consacrée par l'édification d'un nouveau *City Hall*, le bâtiment le plus élevé de la cité avec ses 31 étages. Les banlieues continuèrent d'enfler, les derniers espaces vacants à se couvrir de bungalows en rangs d'oignons, de manoirs de style Tudor et de ranchs miniatures. L'expansion n'avait plus de limites, l'automobile régnait. L.A. fut la première grande métropole à en faire le moyen de transport prédominant.

Pour Los Angeles et les États-Unis, la Grande Dépression marqua un tournant décisif. L'optimisme qui avait porté la région pendant trois décennies d'expansion continue se figea soudainement, à l'exception d'un répit éphémère lorsque la ville convia le monde entier à lui rendre visite à l'occasion des Jeux olympiques d'été (1932). Une année ne s'était pas écoulée qu'en mars 1933, un séisme de magnitude 6,4 sur l'échelle de Richter frappait la région. Dans les années qui suivirent, des pluies diluviennes provoquèrent de terribles dégâts. Pour prévenir de futures inondations, la ville se dota alors d'un vaste réseau de canaux confinés permettant de détourner vers l'océan les eaux surabondantes. Puis ce fut au tour des scandales et affaires de corruption en tout genre, impliquant édiles et policiers, d'assombrir le ciel d'une ville en plein changement. Romans et scénarios sauront tirer parti de la criminalité ambiante pour explorer la face cachée de l'image de carte postale gorgée de soleil, d'oranges et de sommets neigeux colportée par la chambre de commerce.

L'industrie du cinéma échappa aux difficultés financières qui accablaient le reste du pays. Elle redoubla même de vigueur, offrant à la fois aux Américains une évasion hors du marasme quotidien et une source non négligeable d'emplois pour la région. Vaille que vaille, L.A. continuait à grandir et à épouser ostensiblement l'imagerie futuriste, notamment le style paquebot qui sut harmonieusement s'intégrer à la polyphonie architecturale locale. L'auditorium Pan-Pacific illustra ainsi cette esthétique particulière et témoigna de l'optimisme inné de Los Angeles à chaque fois que l'occasion lui est donnée d'embrasser l'inédit. Mouvements spirituels et cultes divers n'échapperont pas à cette ouverture : la ville imposa très tôt sa nature profondément syncrétique.

À l'aube des années 1940, Los Angeles était parée à fournir un effort de guerre essentiel. Le jour venu, les milliers d'avions construits en Californie servirent sur tous les fronts, en Europe comme dans le Pacifique. La ville produisit également un nombre incalculable de navires et autres matériels militaires. La guerre généra un nouveau boom démographique. Par milliers, soldats, marins ou visiteurs de fortune décidèrent que leur avenir, dorénavant, se jouerait à L.A.

Le paradis de l'après-guerre 1945–1965

Los Angeles accueillit largement ces nouveaux arrivants. Dans les quinze années qui suivront la fin de la guerre, 2,5 millions de personnes feront de L.A. leur cité d'élection, plus de 800 000 d'entre elles choisissant de s'installer dans la vallée de San Fernando. Cette explosion démographique contraignit la ville à une croissance exponentielle et au financement de nouvelles infrastructures. On vit éclore de toutes parts autoroutes, écoles et centres commerciaux, ingrédients d'une utopie nouvelle et suburbaine réservée à la classe moyenne. Par leur dynamisme commun, les industries manufacturière, aérospatiale, automobile ainsi que, dans une moindre mesure, les secteurs pétrolier et agricole, participèrent à l'extraordinaire expansion économique de l'après-guerre. Le développement de cette moderne et florissante Arcadie s'accompagna cependant d'une aggravation de la criminalité et de la pollution, matérialisée par le fameux smog. L'exploitation des ressources naturelles de la région atteignait ses limites. Le chemin de la jeune métropole vers sa maturité se révélait laborieux. La police de Los Angeles, longtemps sujette à la

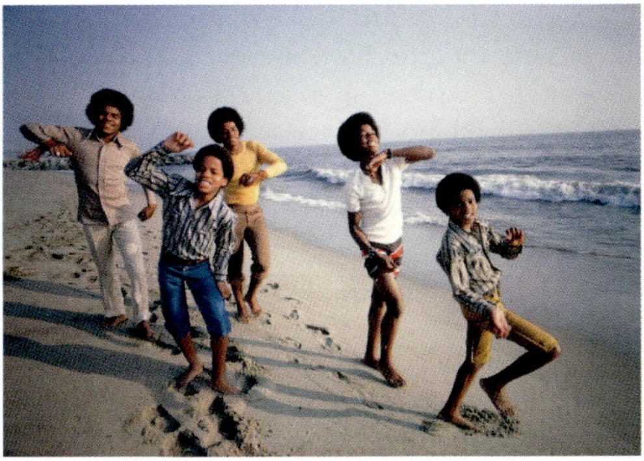

→
Lawrence Schiller
The Jackson 5 in Santa Monica, before the release of their first album, 1970.

Die Jackson 5 in Santa Monica vor der Veröffentlichung ihres ersten Albums, 1970.

Les Jackson Five à Santa Monica, avant la sortie de leur premier album, 1970.

corruption, devint une organisation paramilitaire ayant pour mission d'assurer le calme dans la baie. Au début des années 1960, la ville attirait pourtant l'attention des médias du monde entier, présentée comme le vivier de toutes les tendances en vogue, la prescriptrice d'un style de vie désirable et copié partout. L'impact d'un sport comme le surf et l'efficacité commerciale des géants de l'industrie du jouet, tel Mattel, contribueront à diffuser auprès d'un public toujours plus international, les goûts et les modes inventés dans le *Southland*, ce «grand Los Angeles» étendu sur cinq comtés. L.A. la Superville devenait locomotive planétaire, pour le meilleur et pour le pire.

Un paradis perdu 1965–1980

À l'été 1965, l'aura d'éden urbain qui entourait la Cité des Anges commença à se dissiper lorsque les quartiers afro-américains, situés à Watts dans le sud de la ville, se transformèrent en champ de bataille racial. L'amertume croissante des minorités tenues à l'écart de la prospérité devint une préoccupation de court terme qui affecta la ville de mille façons différentes. L'assassinat de Robert F. Kennedy en 1968 et les meurtres perpétrés par les dévots de Charles Manson un an plus tard viendront encore obscurcir le lourd nuage planant sur la cité.
La scène musicale en revanche, plus effervescente que jamais et stimulée par l'arrivée à l'adolescence des enfants du baby-boom, semblait immunisée contre les désarrois urbains. Les teenagers de L.A., appliqués à propager une inépuisable «culture jeune», s'y entendaient comme personne pour raconter leur région et son

obsession des belles carrosseries, de la mode et des sports de loisir. Longtemps considérée comme un désert en matière d'arts plastiques, la Californie vit également surgir à cette époque des petits groupes d'artistes à l'esprit indépendant tels Ed Ruscha et Ed Kienholz et des galeries comme Ferus, dont l'approche innovante allait permettre à L.A., dans ce domaine aussi, de rivaliser avec New York et Paris.

C'est de ces années 1960 que date le continuum entre rues et bâtiments qui caractérise la géographie urbaine *angelena*. L.A. changeait de nature. Elle ne serait plus une ville contrainte par ses limites physiques, mais un concept. Bientôt la marque «Los Angeles» recouvrirait une mégapole étendue sur de nombreux comtés et plus de 300 kilomètres de côtes. Pour la première fois en plus d'un siècle, la prééminence anglo-saxonne était battue en brèche par un peuplement multiethnique emmené par de nouvelles vagues d'immigrants venus du Mexique et d'Amérique latine.

Sur le plan économique aussi la ville se devait de muter, car l'industrie aérospatiale et de transformation déclinait inexorablement. Lockheed, Northrop, Douglas, Goodyear, General Motors et Firestone s'installèrent ailleurs, réduisirent leurs effectifs ou bien fusionnèrent. À la puissance de l'agriculture et du secteur pétrolier succédèrent la fièvre immobilière, le déploiement massif des centres commerciaux et la multiplication des zones industrielles. Le changement était dans l'air, et c'est sur cette base que Los Angeles sut s'appuyer pour préserver son image de cité d'avenir.

Apocalypse Now DE 1980–À NOS JOURS

L.A., à partir des années 1980, donna l'impression de courir à sa perte. L'immigration latino-américaine massive, si elle procura à l'économie une nouvelle réserve de main d'œuvre à bon marché, mit en effet à rude épreuve les infrastructures locales. Désormais distendus de l'Est de l'agglomération jusqu'à la totalité du bassin urbain, les quartiers les plus populaires changèrent radicalement de physionomie, sans commune mesure avec les transformations antérieures. La ville s'imprégna soudain d'usages et de traditions empruntées à toutes les cultures du monde. Le phénomène le plus ravageur fut sans doute l'apparition d'une *gang culture* qui n'épargna aucune couche de la population. Pour la seule année 1995, on dénombra dans le comté de L.A. 807 homicides liés aux gangs de rue – un record. Armes à feu et hélicoptères de la police composaient désormais la bande-son de la ville. Les émeutes de 1992, consécutives à l'acquittement de quatre policiers coupables de violences sur l'automobiliste Rodney King, fragilisèrent encore le contrat social déjà ténu. La ville s'enflamma, livrée aux pillages pendant plus de trois jours. La garde nationale fut appelée à l'aide, et la loi martiale instaurée: L.A. était devenue une

→
Ed Fox
Apocalyptic Los Angeles was realized in the collapse of a freeway overpass in the 6.7-magnitude Northridge earthquake, January 17, 1994.

Seine apokalyptische Seite zeigte Los Angeles beim Einsturz einer Autobahnbrücke während des Northridge-Erdbebens mit einer Stärke von 6,7 am 17. Januar 1994.

Le tremblement de terre de Northridge, d'une magnitude de 6,7 a transformé Los Angeles en paysage apocalyptique, le 17 janvier 1994.

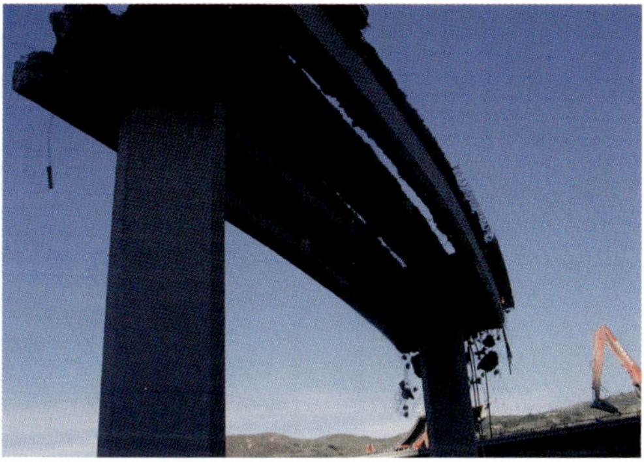

zone de guerre urbaine. Se soldant par un milliard de dollars de dégâts, les violences de ce printemps-là coûtèrent très cher à la région. Deux ans plus tard, le Southland convalescent dut endurer le séisme de Northridge, de magnitude 6,7, qui causa plus de 20 milliards de dollars de dommages matériels et d'incalculables détresses psychologiques.

Tout, pourtant, ne fut pas sombre en cette fin de siècle. Ainsi les XXIIIe Jeux olympiques d'été, organisés à L.A. en 1984. En termes d'embouteillages et de mouvements de foule, les prévisionnistes annonçaient le pire. Or l'événement se déroula au mieux et conforta l'image de capitale internationale à laquelle prétendait Los Angeles. Plus la ville engrangeait de confiance sur la scène mondiale, plus se confirmait son potentiel culturel, au-delà des seules industries télévisuelle et cinématographique. Des architectes locaux comme Frank Gehry poursuivirent la longue tradition d'innovation de L.A., avec l'emblématique Disney Hall, en centre-ville. On vit les musées croître et se multiplier : le Getty, le Hammer et le Musée d'Art contemporain vinrent enrichir un paysage artistique déjà foisonnant. La gastronomie californienne se trouva une identité propre saluée par la critique.

À l'heure du nouveau millénaire, Los Angeles avait dépassé tous les espoirs du *pueblo* poussiéreux des premiers jours. Les mots commençaient à manquer pour définir une ville sans tradition. Mais le temps de son accomplissement n'était pas encore venu, et ne viendra jamais. Décriée aussi fort qu'elle est admirée, Los Angeles est un projet en devenir continuel, une ville qui ne cesse d'en appeler à l'attention du monde – et la reçoit chaque jour.

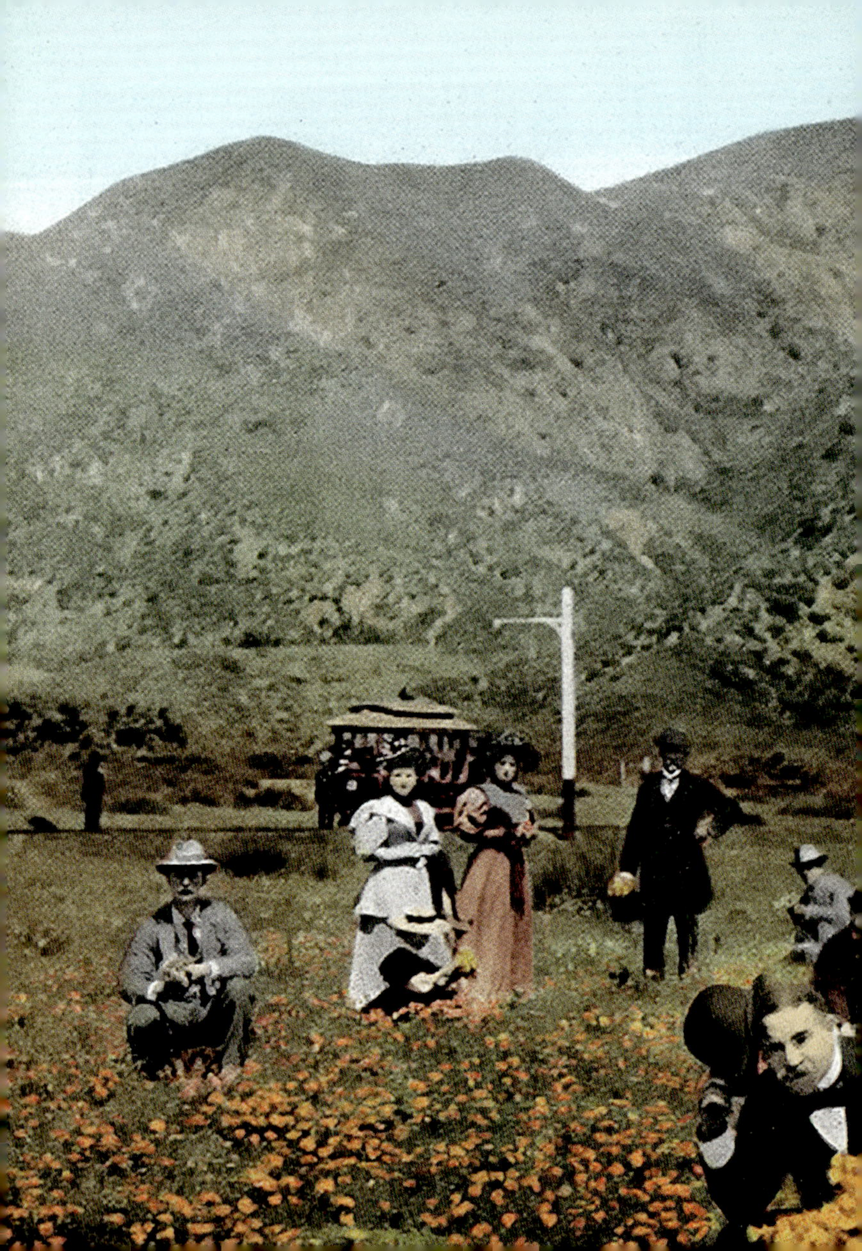

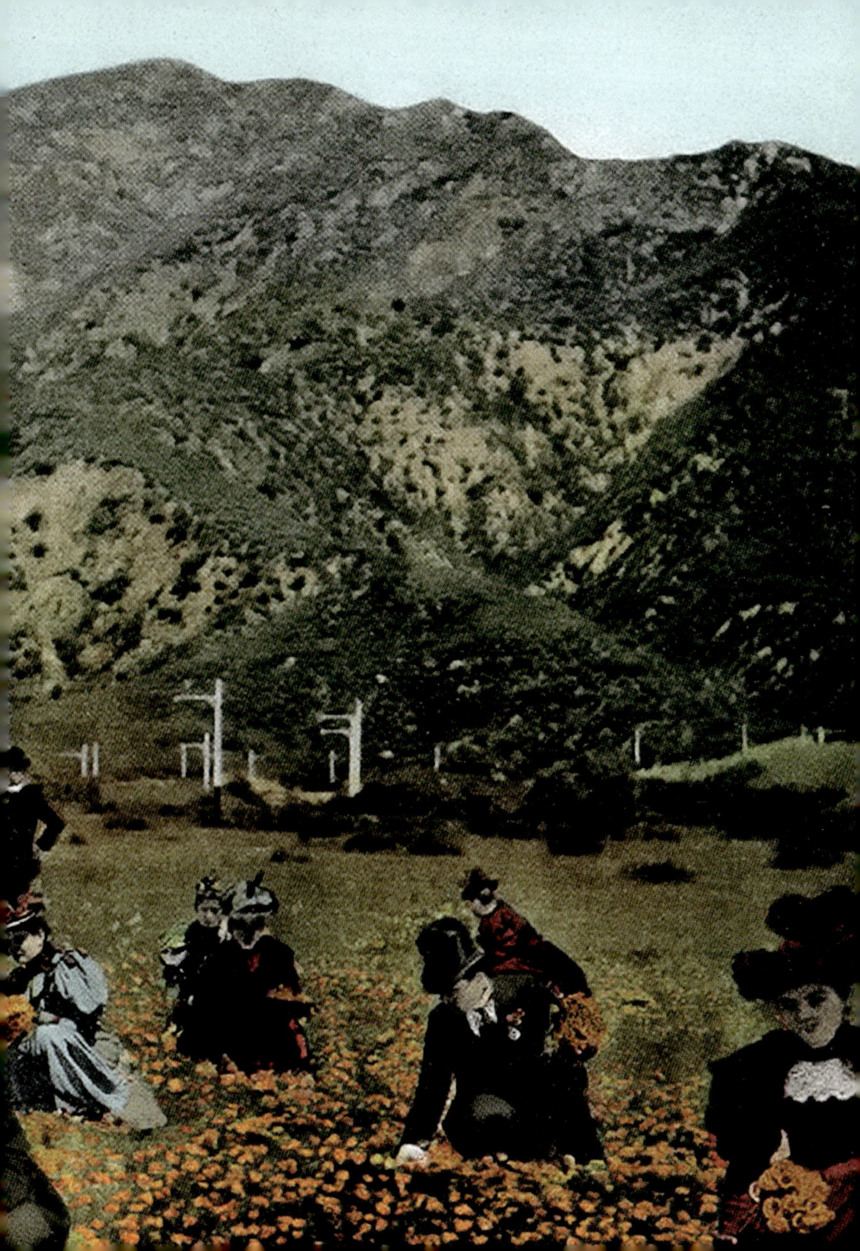

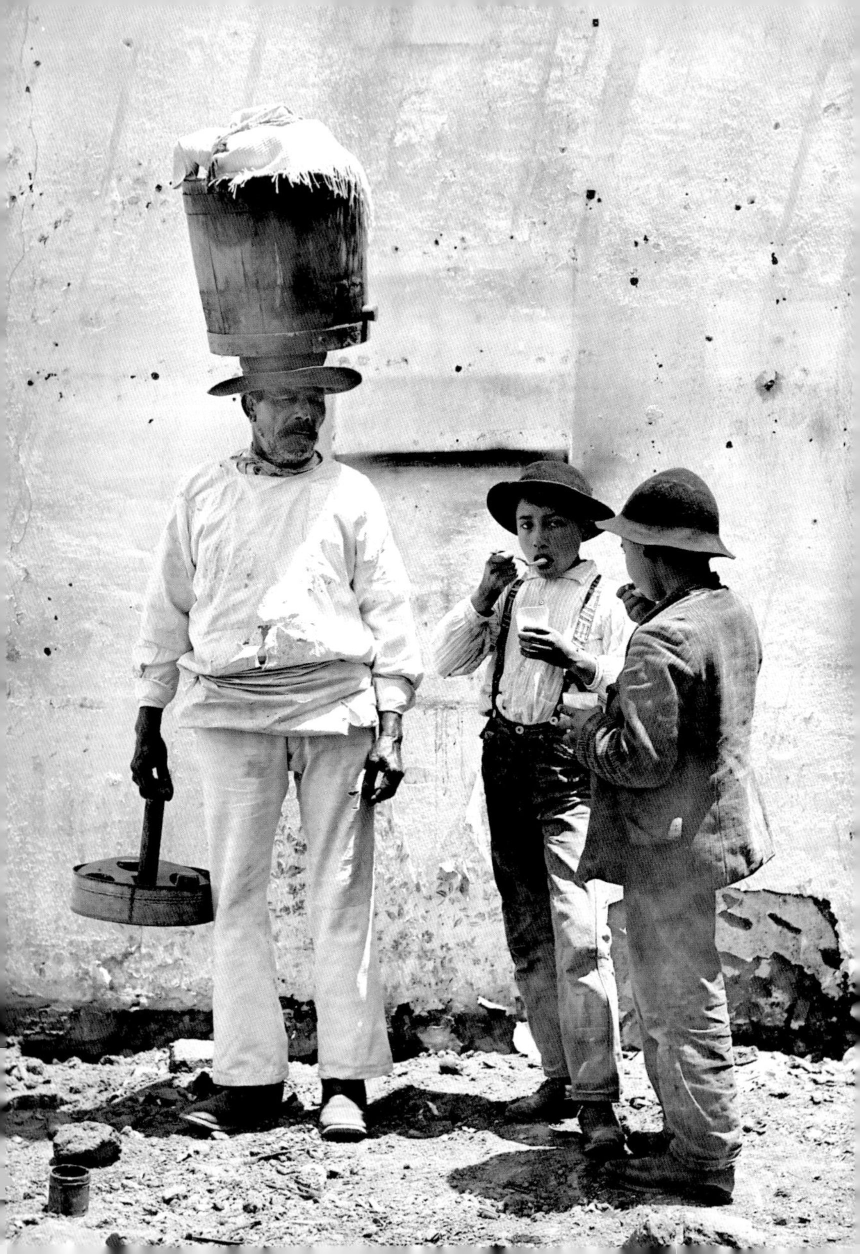

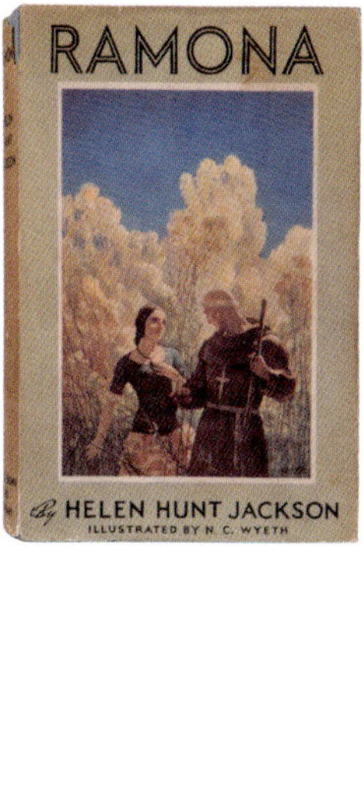

"The Americans would not let an Indian do anything but plough and sow and herd.... But his labors did not receive the reward that they deserved... he saw the whites gaining, his people surely losing ground, and his anxieties deepened."

„Die Amerikaner ließen einen Indianer nichts anderes tun als pflügen, säen und das Vieh hüten ... Doch all seine Bemühungen blieben ohne den gebührenden Erfolg. Er sah, wie die Weißen weiter vordrangen und sein Volk zurückweichen musste, und seine Unruhe wuchs."

« Les Américains ne laissaient faire aucune autre activité à un Indien que labourer, semer et garder les troupeaux... Mais son travail ne recevait pas la récompense méritée... Il voyait les Blancs progresser, ses compatriotes perdre irrésistiblement du terrain et ses angoisses s'aggraver. »

Helen Hunt Jackson, *Ramona*, 1884

p. 30/31

Anonymous

Gathering poppies in Altadena, c. 1896. A popular tourist image, it advertised the mild midwinter climate.

Mohnpflücken in Altadena, um 1896. Das bei Touristen populäre Motiv warb für das milde Winterklima.

Cueillette des coquelicots à Altadena, vers 1896. Cette image touristique populaire faisait la promotion du climat hivernal tempéré.

←

C. C. Pierce

Nicolas Martinez, tamale and ice cream salesman, Olvera Street, 1890.

Nicolas Martinez, Eis- und Tamalesverkäufer auf der Olvera Street, 1890.

Nicolas Martinez, marchand de tamales *et de glaces, Olvera Street, 1890.*

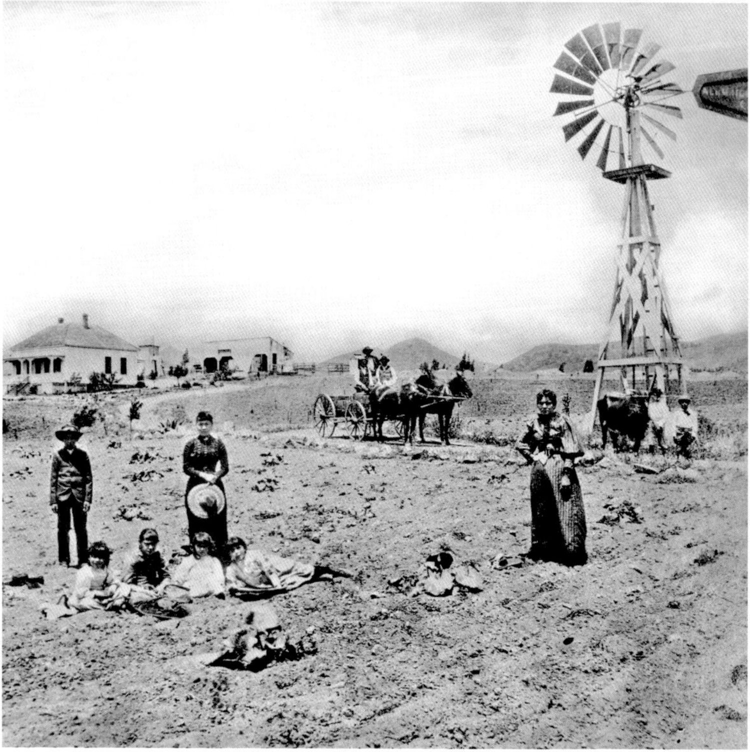

↑
C. C. Pierce
The José Mascarel Ranch, in what is now Hollywood, c. 1896. Mascarel, a sea captain from France, came to L. A. and sold his ship to purchase 40 acres of land on which to start his farm.

Die Ranch von José Mascarel, gelegen im heutigen Hollywood, um 1896. Mascarel, ein französischer Kapitän, war nach Los Angeles gekommen, wo er sein Schiff verkaufte, um rund 16 Hektar Land zu erwerben und eine Ranch zu errichten.

Le ranch José Mascarel, sur le site de l'actuel Hollywood vers 1896. Mascarel, Français et capitaine au long cours, est venu à L. A. et a vendu son bateau pour acquérir 16 ha de terre sur lesquels il a démarré son exploitation agricole.

→
Anonymous
Los Angeles firefighters and their horse-drawn fire engine at the corner of First and Main streets, c. 1885.

Feuerwehrmänner in Los Angeles mit ihrem von Pferden gezogenen Löschwagen an der Ecke First Street und Main Street, um 1885.

Les pompiers de Los Angeles, et leur voiture tirée par des chevaux, à l'angle de First Street et de Main Street, vers 1885.

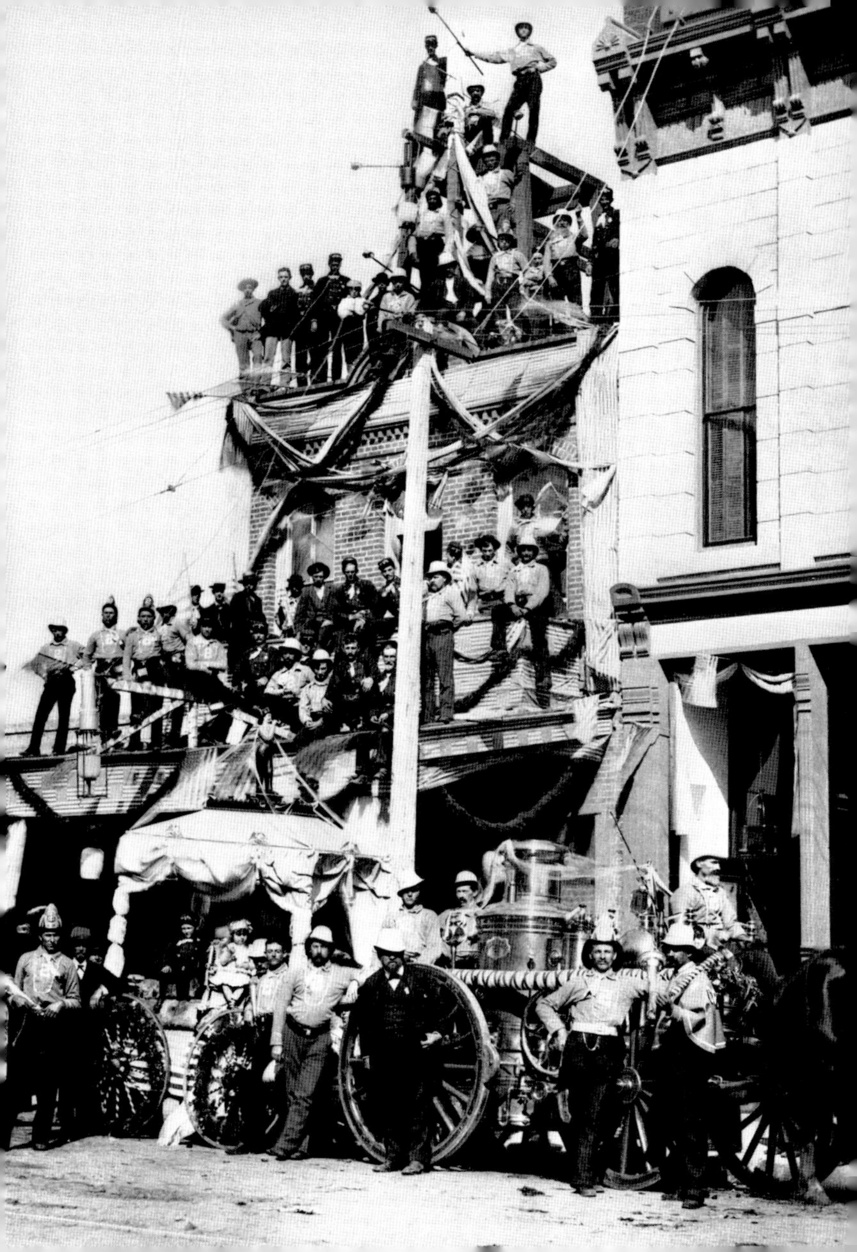

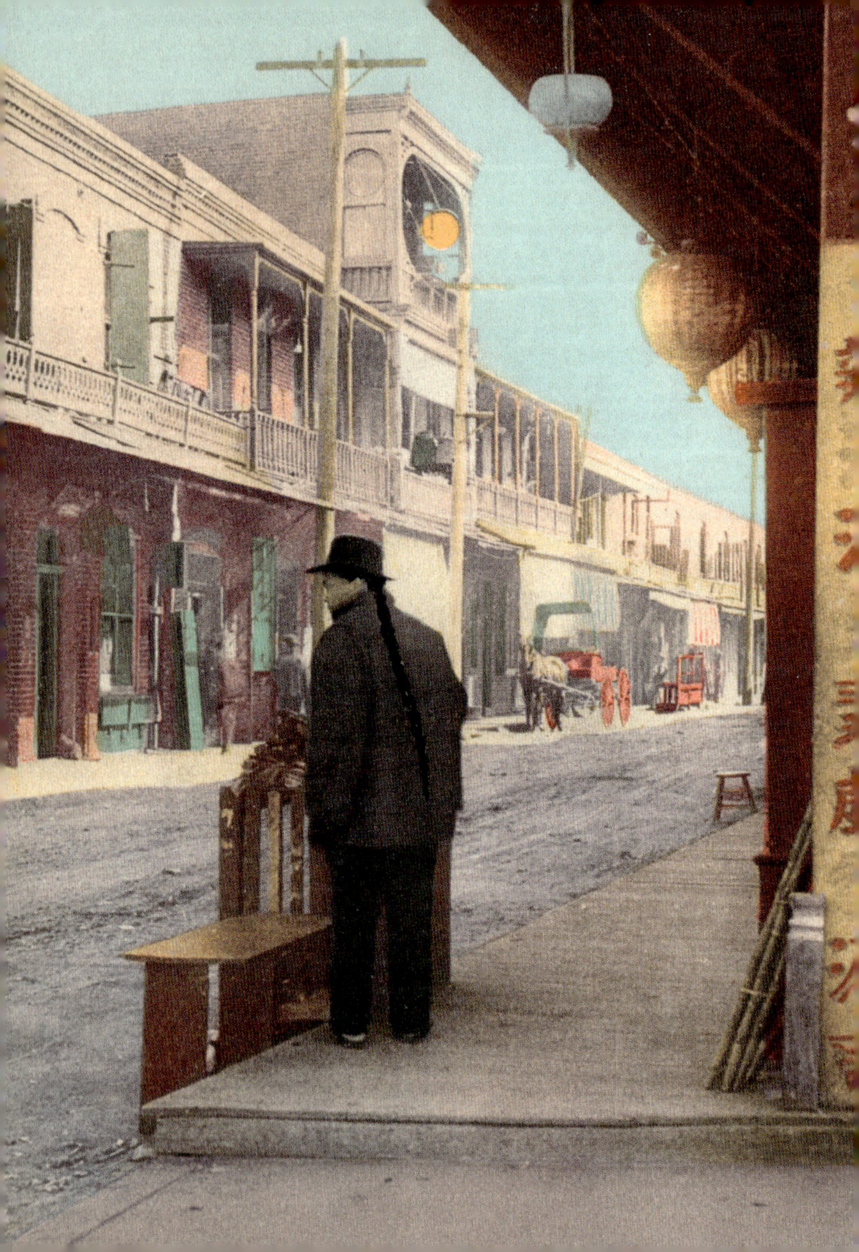

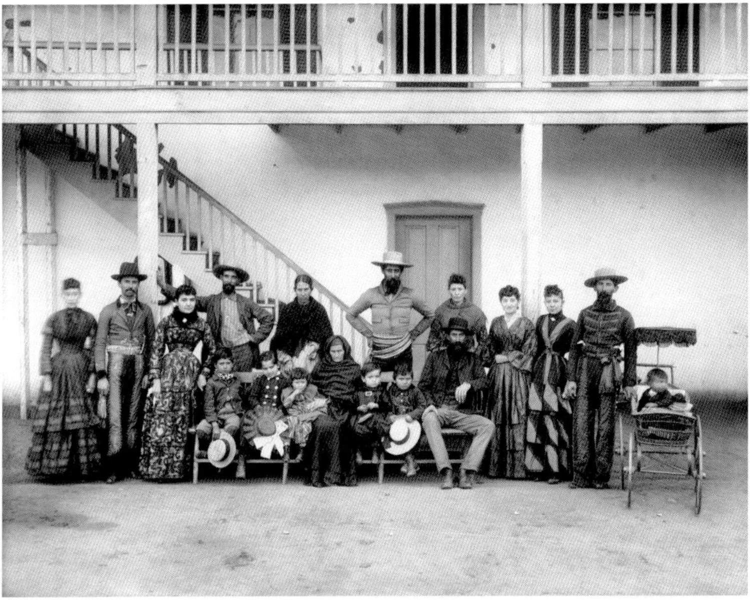

←

William Henry Jackson

A street in Chinatown, c. 1900.

Eine Straße in Chinatown, um 1900.

Une rue de Chinatown, vers 1900.

↑

Anonymous

The wealthy and influential Lugo family of rancheros at home, c. 1888. In 1851, two members of the clan were acquitted of murder in a famous trial that prefigured the racial tensions that have persisted throughout L.A.'s history.

Die wohlhabende und einflussreiche Rancherfamilie Lugo auf ihrem Anwesen, um 1888. Zwei Familienmitglieder wurden 1851 wegen Mordes angeklagt, jedoch freigesprochen. Der berühmte Prozess ließ die Rassenkonflikte ahnen, die sich durch die Geschichte von L.A. ziehen sollten.

L'influente et privilégiée famille Lugo dans son ranch, vers 1888. En 1851, deux d'entre eux furent jugés pour meurtre et acquittés, dans un célèbre procès préfigurant les tensions raciales qui ont persisté tout au long de l'histoire de Los Angeles.

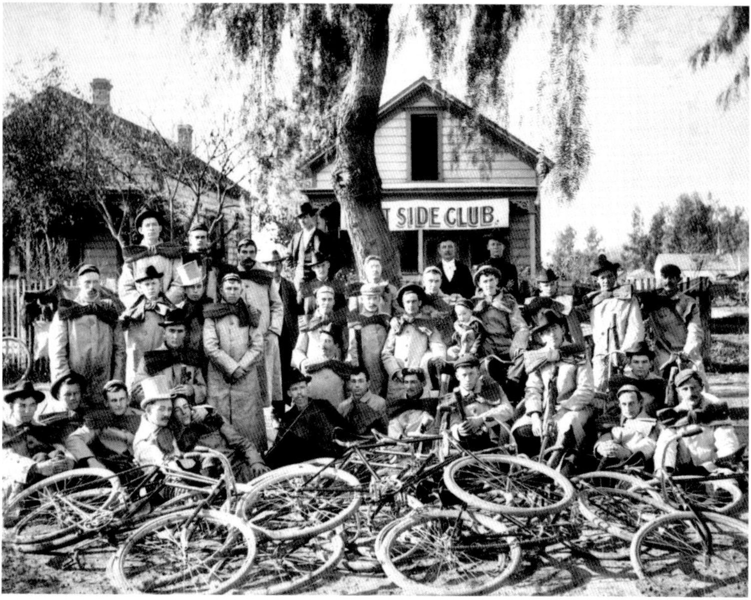

↑
Anonymous
Members of the East Side Bicycling Club, c. 1896. The cyclists were photographed at Agricultural Park, later to become Exposition Park.

Mitglieder des East-Side-Fahrradklubs, um 1896. Fotografiert wurden die Fahrradfahrer im Agricultural Park, dem späteren Exposition Park.

Des membres de l'East Side Bicycling Club, vers 1896. Les cyclistes ont été photographiés dans l'Agricultural Park qui allait devenir par la suite l'Exposition Park.

→
Anonymous
The North Beach Bath House and Eckert & Hoff's Restaurant, Santa Monica, c. 1898.

Das Badehaus am Nordstrand und das Restaurant Eckert & Hoff, Santa Monica, um 1898.

L'établissement de bains de North Beach et le restaurant Eckert & Hoff, *Santa Monica, vers 1898.*

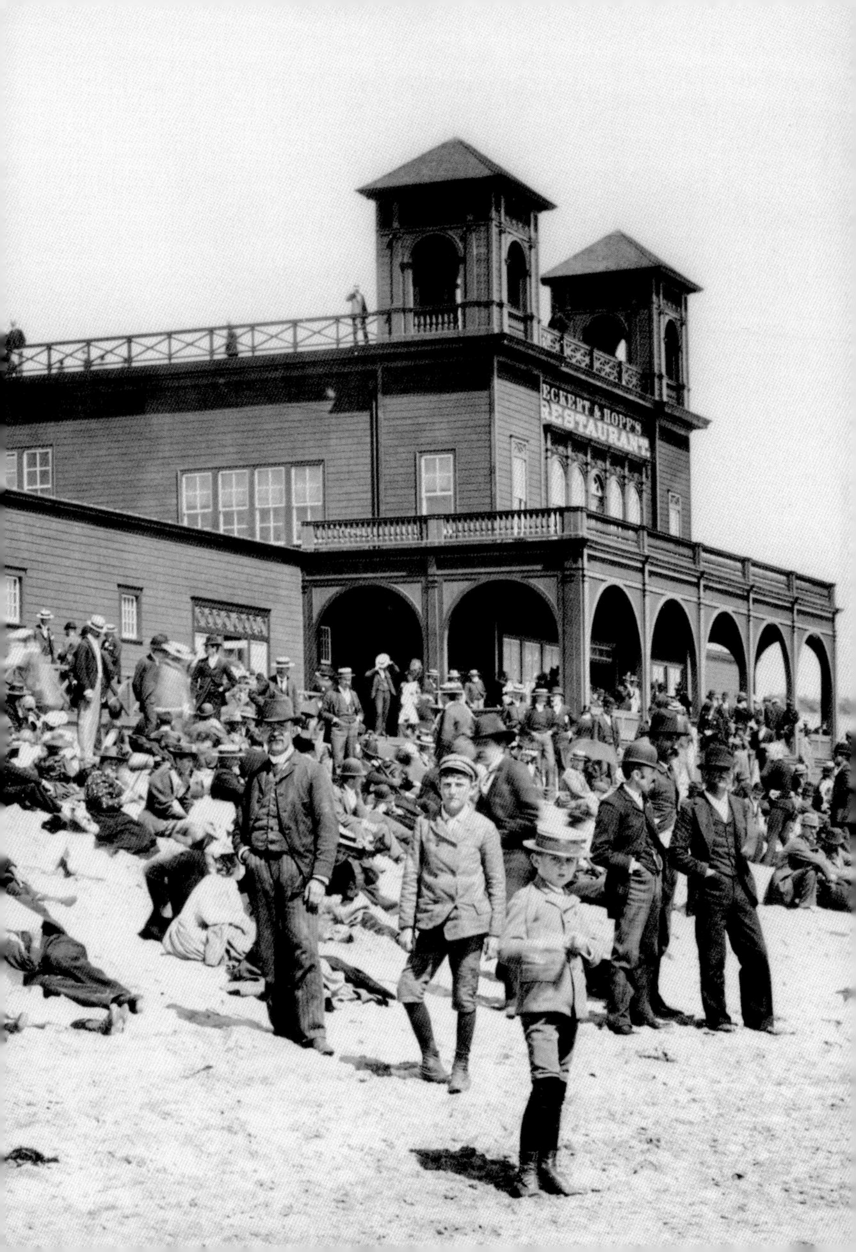
ECKERT & HOPP'S
RESTAURANT

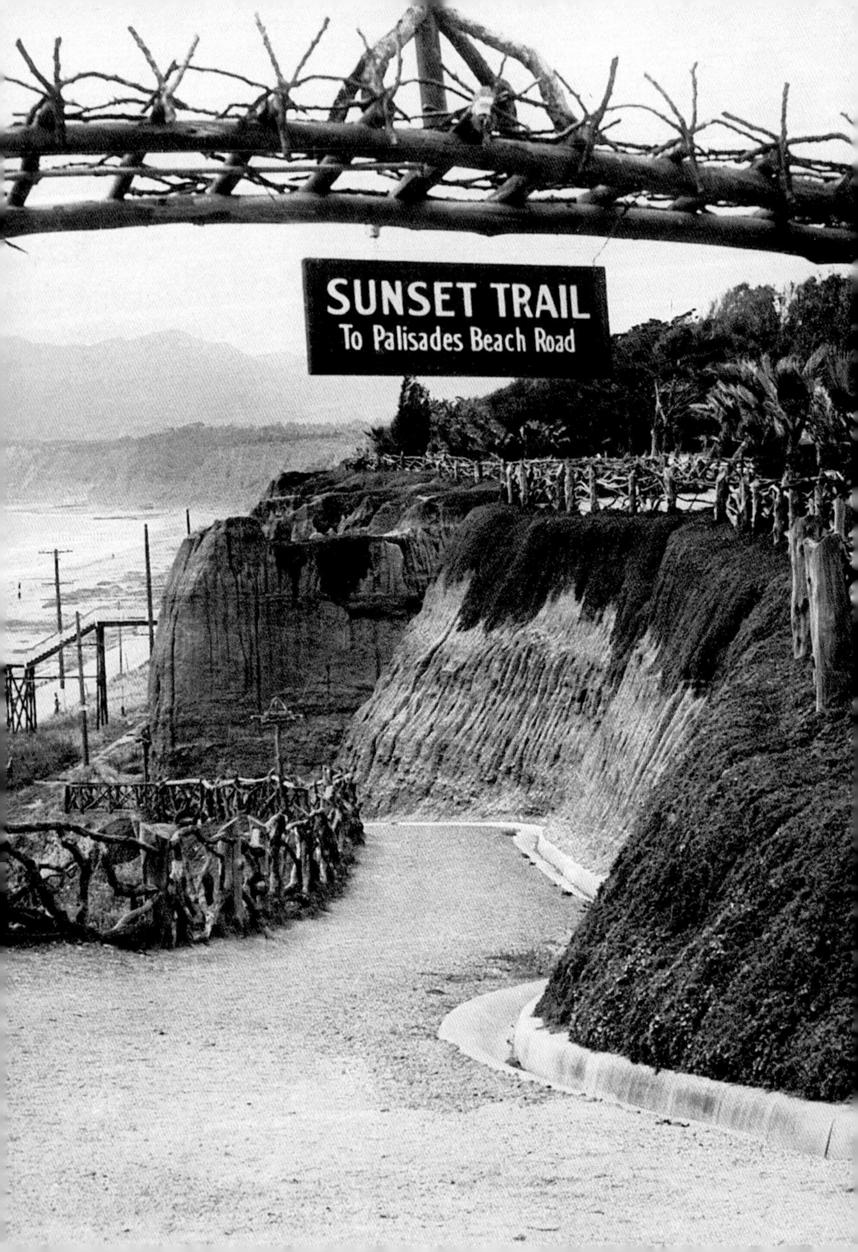
SUNSET TRAIL
To Palisades Beach Road

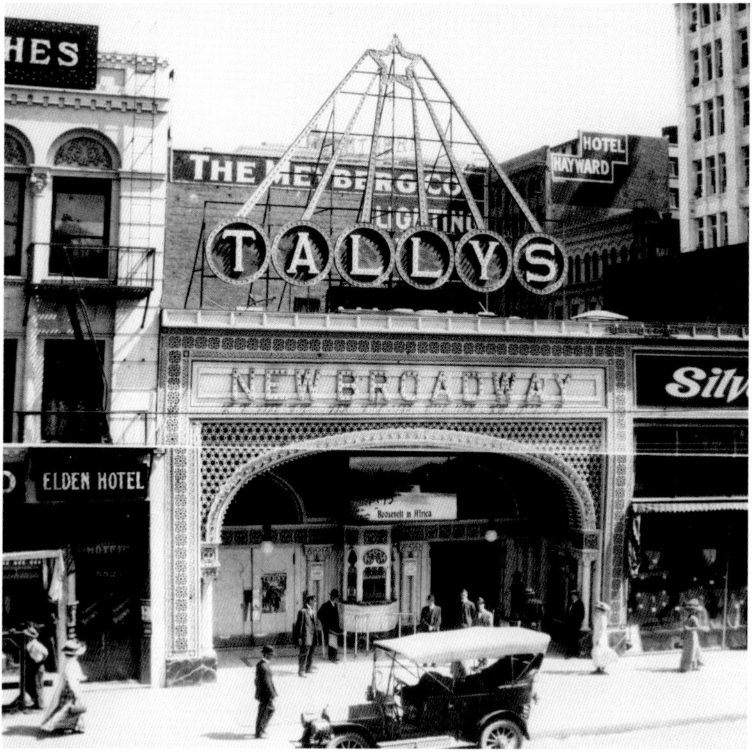

←
Taylor Studio
Sunset Trail, Santa Monica Palisades, c. 1907. This path down to Palisades Beach Road would later be called the California Incline.

Sunset Trail, Santa Monica Palisades, um 1907. Dieser Weg hinunter zur Palisades Beach Road wurde später in California Incline umbenannt.

Sunset Trail (« chemin du soleil couchant »), Santa Monica Palisades, vers 1907. Ce chemin menant à la route de Palisades Beach fut rebaptisé ensuite California Incline (le « coteau californien »).

↑
Anonymous
Tallys Theater, corner of Sixth Street and Broadway, 1910.

Das Tallys Theater, Ecke Sixth Street und Broadway, 1910.

Le Tallys Theater, un cinéma à l'angle de la 6ᵉ Rue et de Broadway, 1910.

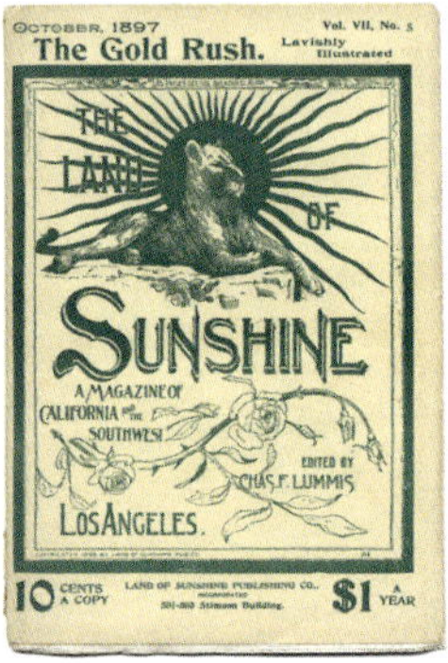

"In ten years from now — unless our intelligence shall awaken at once — there will remain of these noble piles nothing but a few indeterminable heaps of adobe."

„In nur zehn Jahren werden von diesen erhabenen Bauten – falls wir nicht schnellstens zu Sinnen kommen – nichts als einige armselige Haufen ungebrannter Lehmziegel bleiben."

« D'ici dix ans, à moins que notre intelligence ne s'éveille subitement, il ne restera de ces nobles constructions en adobe que quelques tas informes et méconnaissables. »

Charles F. Lummis,
***Land of Sunshine* magazine, 1895**

→

Anonymous

Passengers ride the Mount Lowe Railway on the attraction's opening day, July 4, 1893. Here, the train passes over a curving trestle bridge offering a panoramic view from the San Gabriel Mountains out to the sea.

Fahrgäste der Mount Lowe Railway bei der Eröffnung dieser neuen Attraktion am 4. Juli 1893. Hier passiert die Bahn eine geschwungene Bockbrücke mit weitem Blick von den San Gabriel Mountains auf das Meer.

Des passagers sur le petit train du Mount Lowe, le jour de l'ouverture de l'attraction au public, le 4 juillet 1893. On peut voir passer le train sur un pont en courbe sur chevalet offrant une vue panoramique, des montagnes de San Gabriel jusqu'à la mer.

p. 44/45

Anonymous

The intersection of Spring and First streets looking south, c. 1902.

Blick nach Süden über die Kreuzung Spring Street und First Street, um 1902.

Le croisement de Spring Street et de First Street dans la direction du sud, vers 1902.

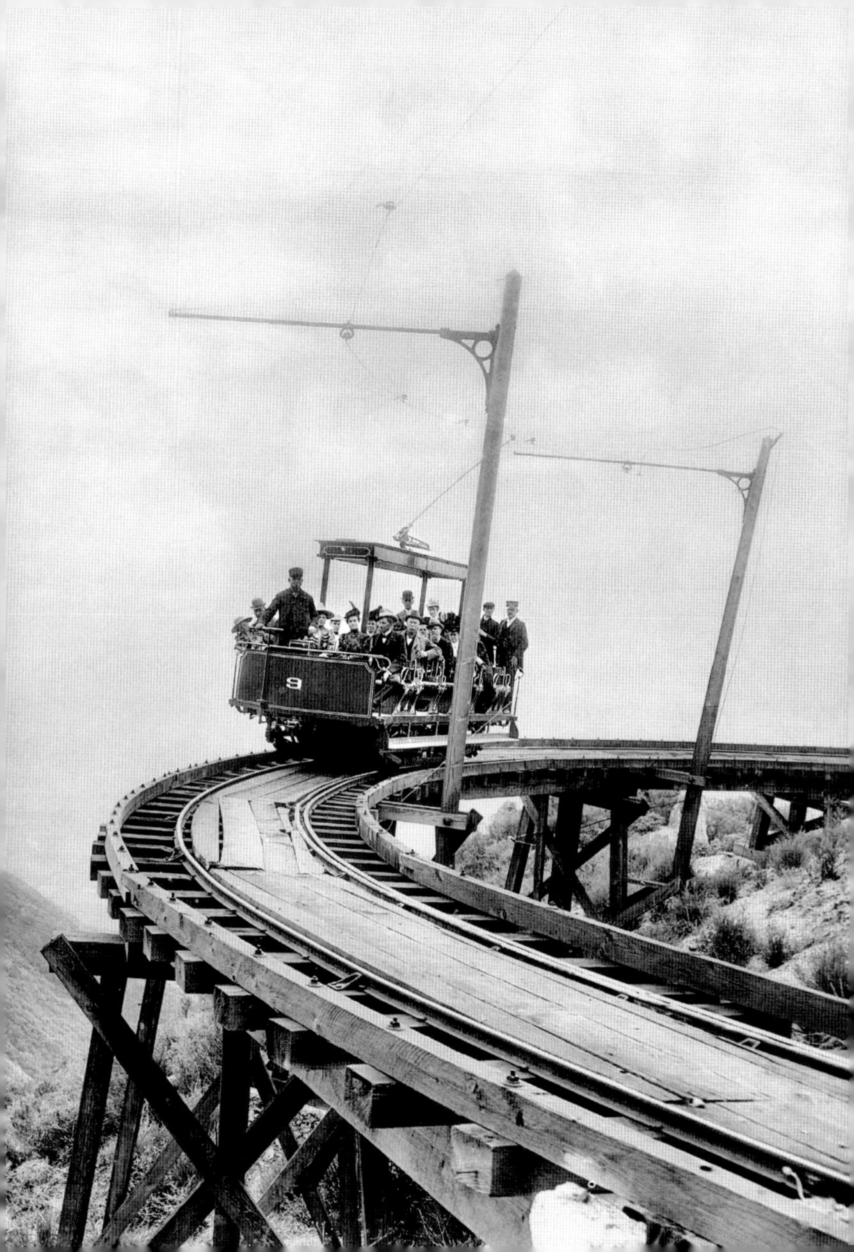

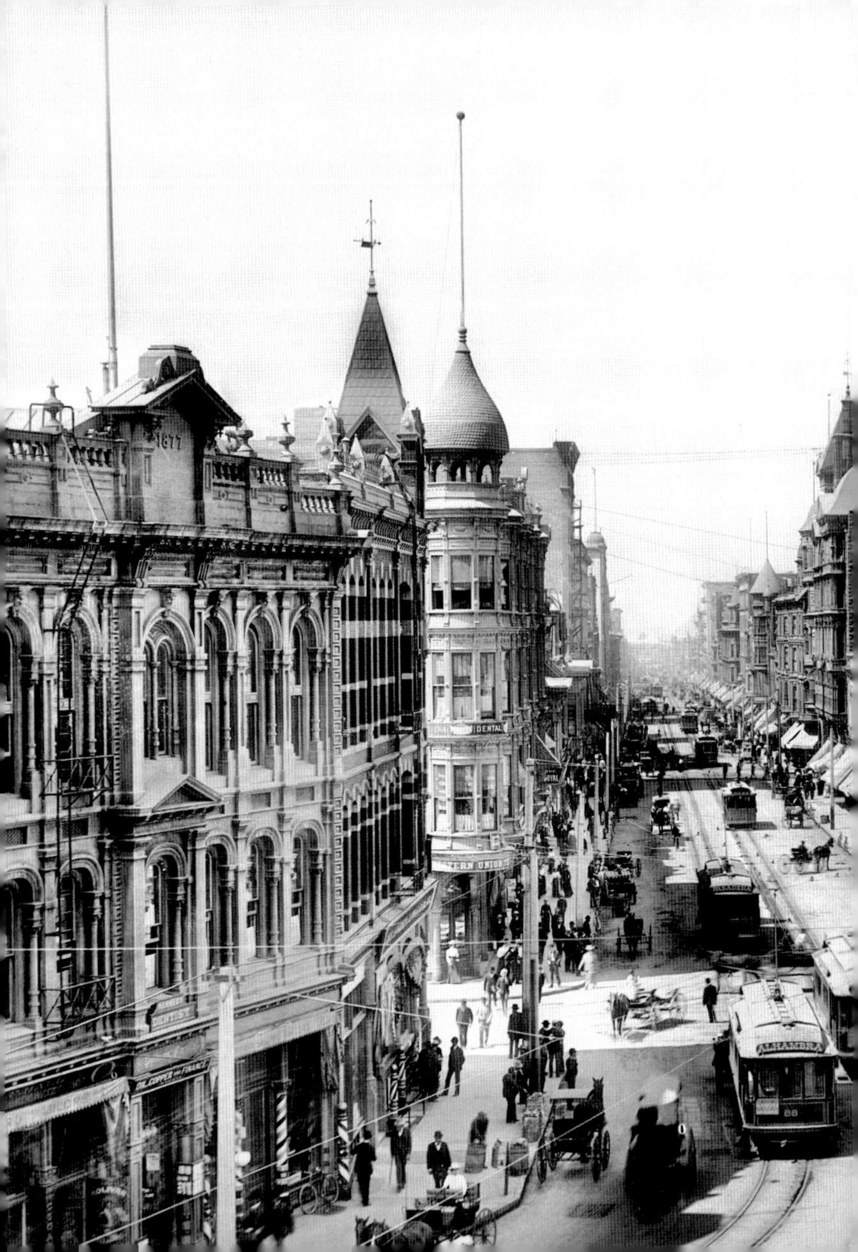
1877
DENTAL
DENTIST
ALHAMBRA

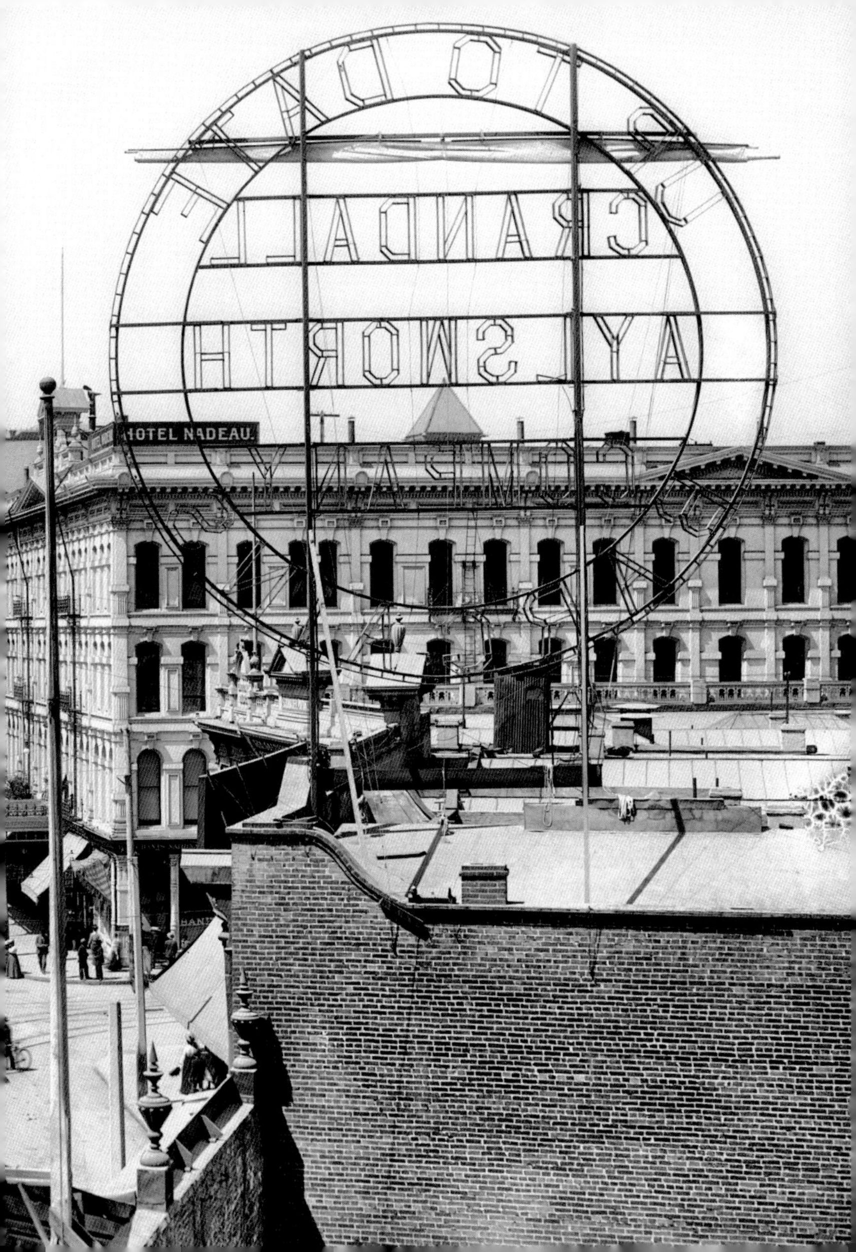
HOTEL NADEAU.

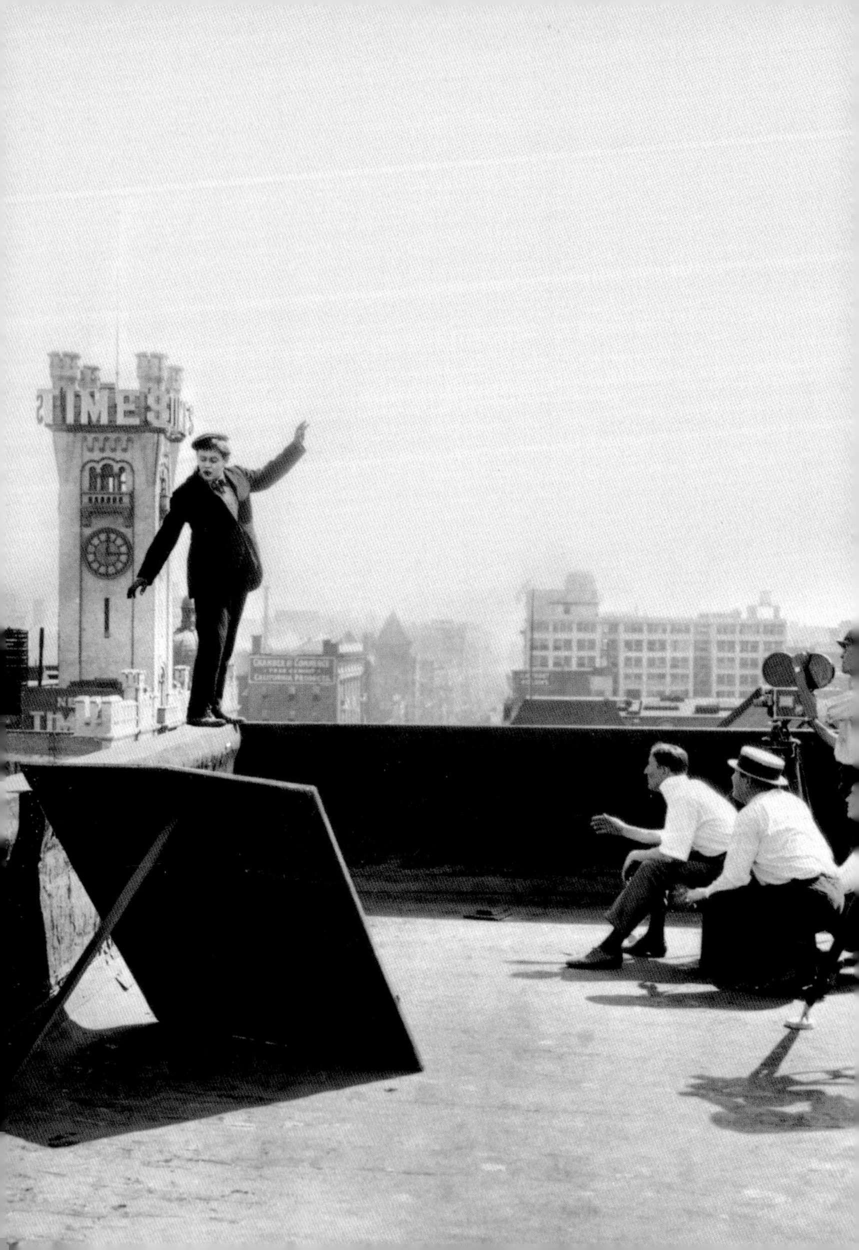

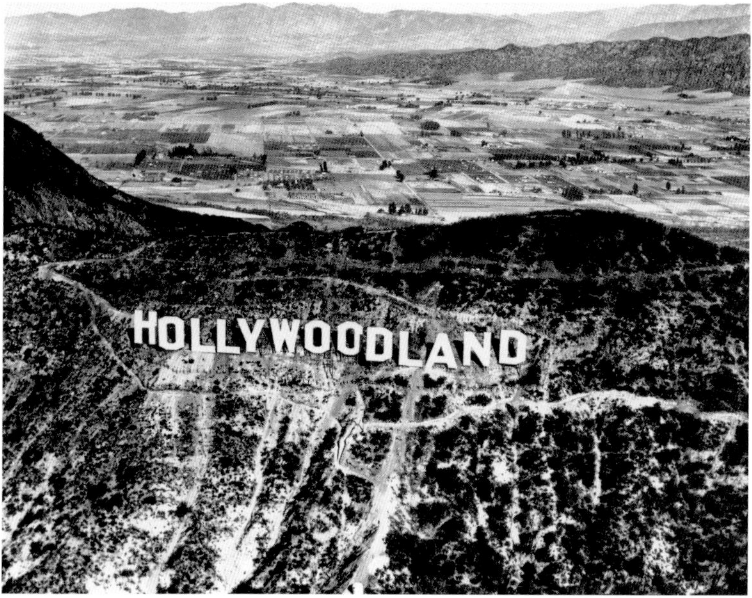

←

Anonymous

Rooftop location shoot, downtown Los Angeles, 1922.

Dreharbeiten auf einem Dach in Downtown Los Angeles, 1922.

Tournage sur un toit d'immeuble au centre de Los Angeles, 1922.

↑

Anonymous

The Hollywood sign was built in 1923 as an advertisement for Los Angeles Times *scion Harry Chandler's "Hollywoodland" real estate development. In the background, the San Fernando Valley remains largely rural and undeveloped.*

Der Hollywoodschriftzug war 1923 als Werbung für „Hollywoodland" errichtet worden, ein Immobilienprojekt von Harry Chandler, dem Erben der Los Angeles Times*. Im Hintergrund das San Fernando Valley, noch überwiegend ländlich und unerschlossen.*

Le panneau Hollywood a été érigé en 1923 pour promouvoir « Hollywoodland », le projet immobilier de Harry Chandler, propriétaire du Los Angeles Times*. À l'arrière-plan, la vallée de San Fernando reste largement rurale et inhabitée.*

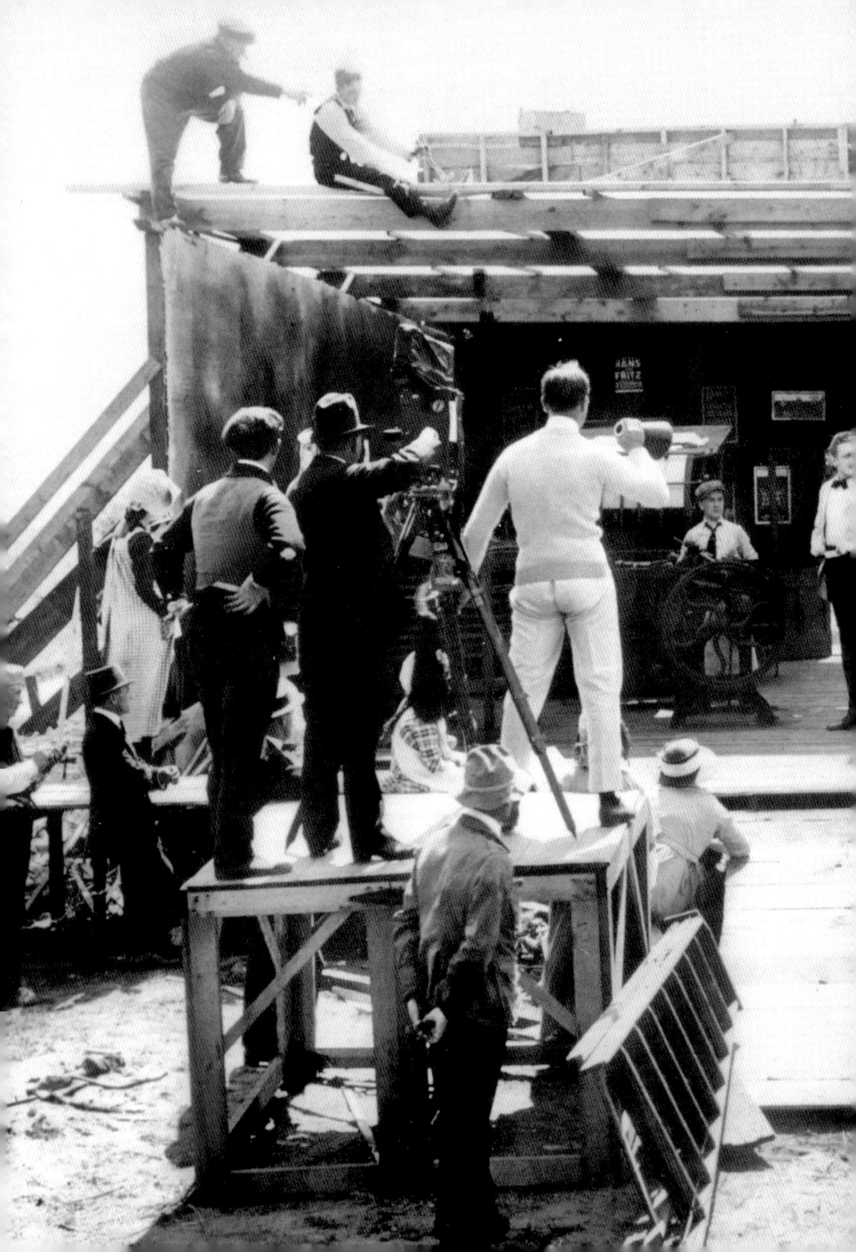
HANS
FRITZ

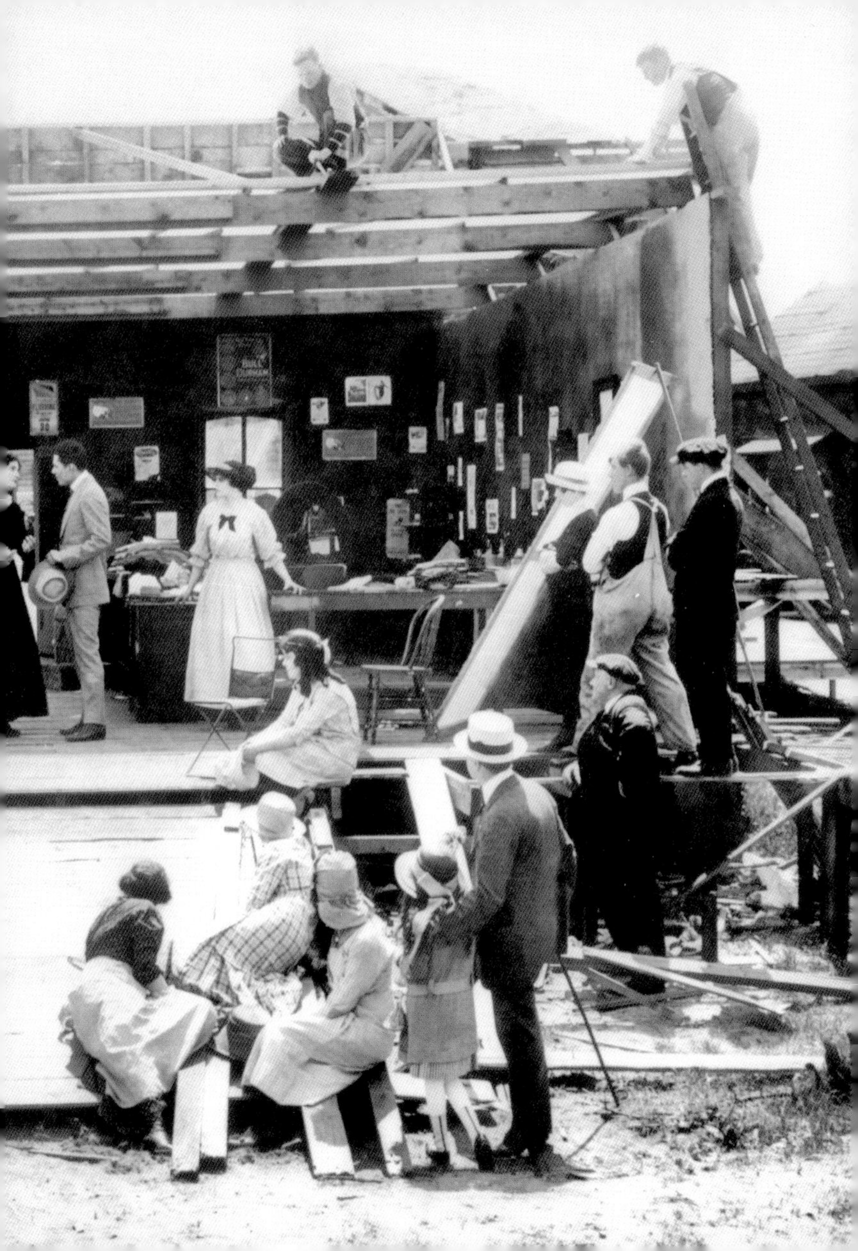

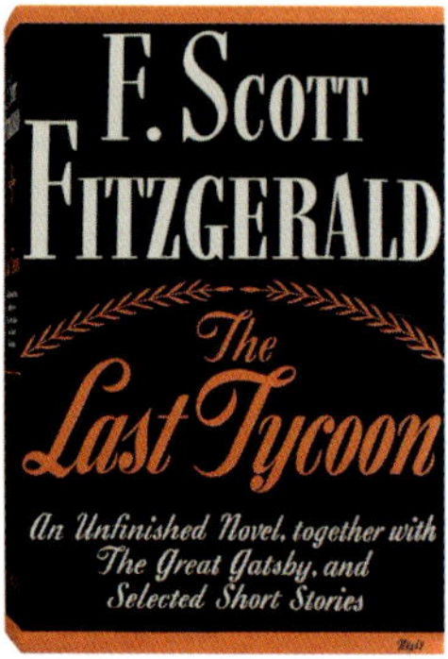

"Though I haven't ever been on the screen, I was brought up in pictures. Rudolph Valentino came to my fifth birthday party—or so I was told."

„Obwohl ich nie selbst auf der Leinwand zu sehen war, bin ich mit dem Kino aufgewachsen. Rudolph Valentino war Gast auf der Feier zu meinem fünften Geburtstag – das hat man mir zumindest erzählt."

«Je n'ai jamais paru à l'écran, mais j'ai été élevé dans le cinéma. Rudolph Valentino vint célébrer l'anniversaire de mes cinq ans – en tout cas, c'est ce qu'on m'a raconté.»

F. Scott Fitzgerald, *The Last Tycoon*, 1941

p. 48/49
Anonymous
Filming outdoors at Vitagraph Studios, Hollywood, 1917.

Außenaufnahmen in den Vitagraph Studios, Hollywood, 1917.

Tournage en extérieur aux studios Vitagraph, Hollywood, 1917.

→
Anonymous
The Ennis House, a Frank Lloyd Wright textile block house, Hollywood Hills, 1924.

Das Ennis House, eines von Frank Lloyd Wrights Betonblock-Häusern, Hollywood Hills, 1924.

La Ennis House, autre résidence en blocs de ciment moulés bâtie par Frank Lloyd Wright, Hollywood Hills, 1924.

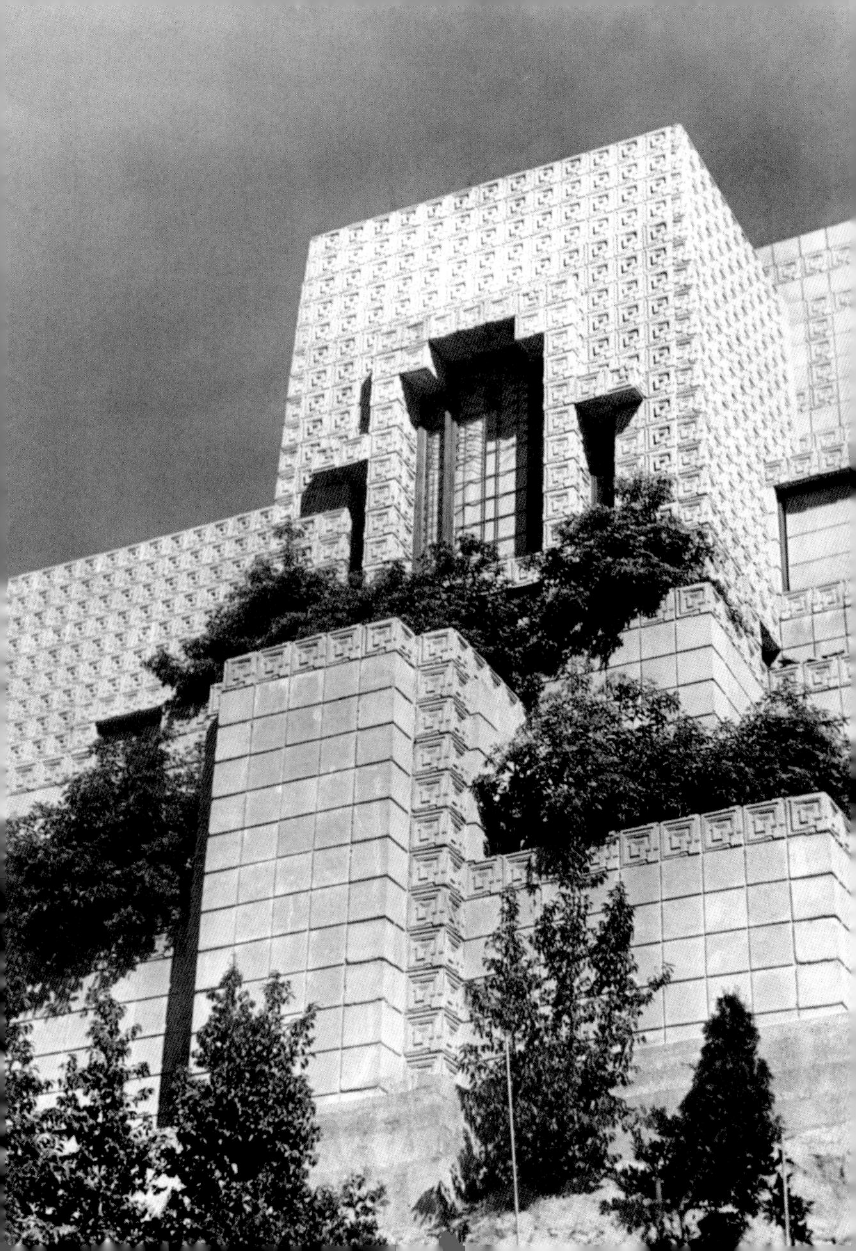

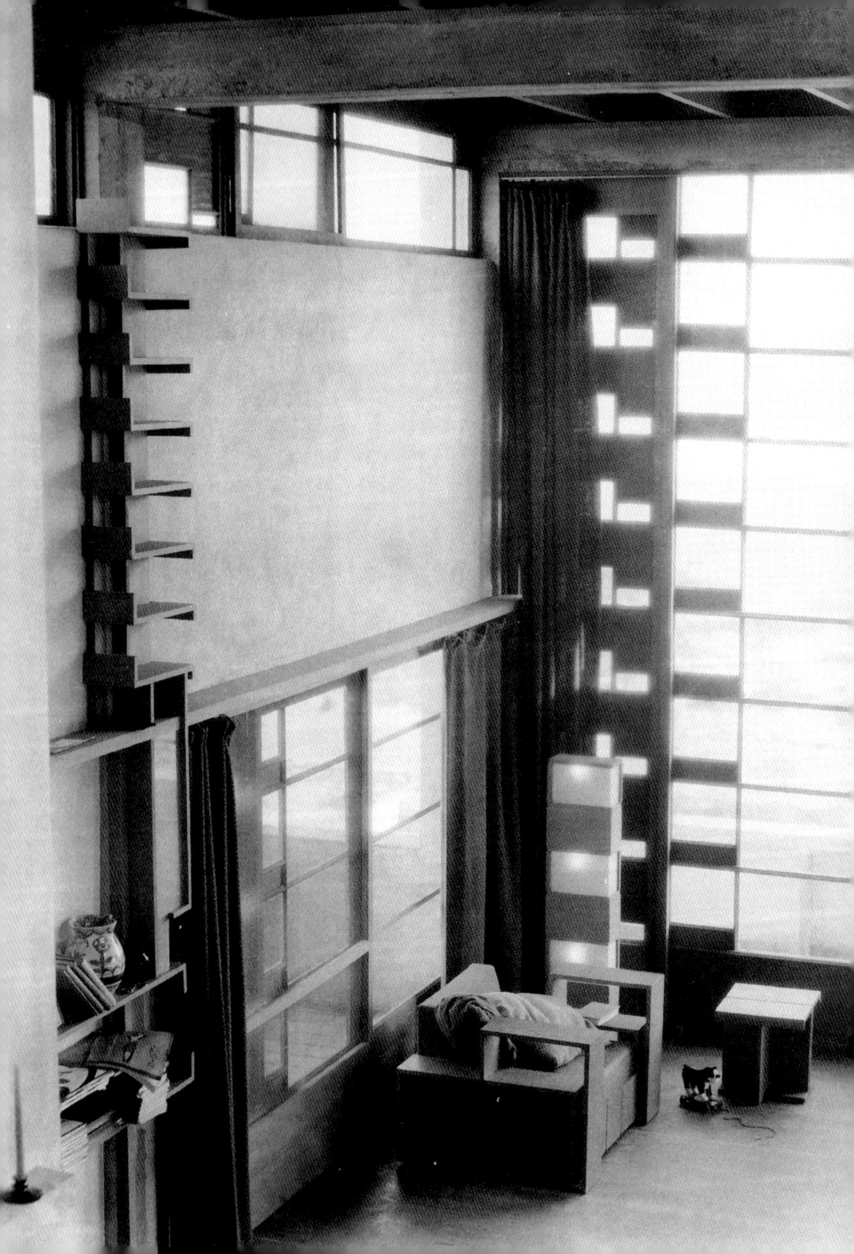

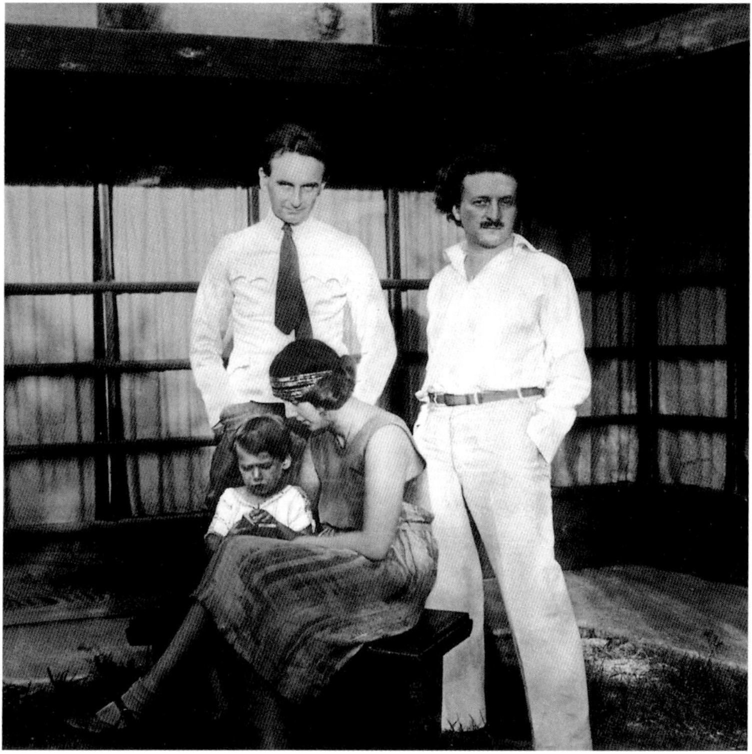

←
Anonymous
Rudolf Schindler's Lovell Beach House interior, Newport Beach, c. 1926.

Interieur von Rudolf Schindlers Lovell Beach House, Newport Beach, um 1926.

L'intérieur de la Lovell Beach House, résidence de Rudolf Schindler, Newport Beach, vers 1926.

↑
Julius Shulman
Richard Neutra and his family pose with fellow architect Rudolf Schindler in the courtyard of the Schindler Studio House in West Hollywood, 1928.

Der Architekt Richard Neutra posiert mit seiner Familie und dem Berufskollegen Rudolf Schindler im Innenhof des Schindler Studio House in West-Hollywood, 1928.

Richard Neutra et sa famille posent avec leur ami architecte Rudolf Schindler dans le jardin de la Schindler Studio House, réalisée à West Hollywood, 1928.

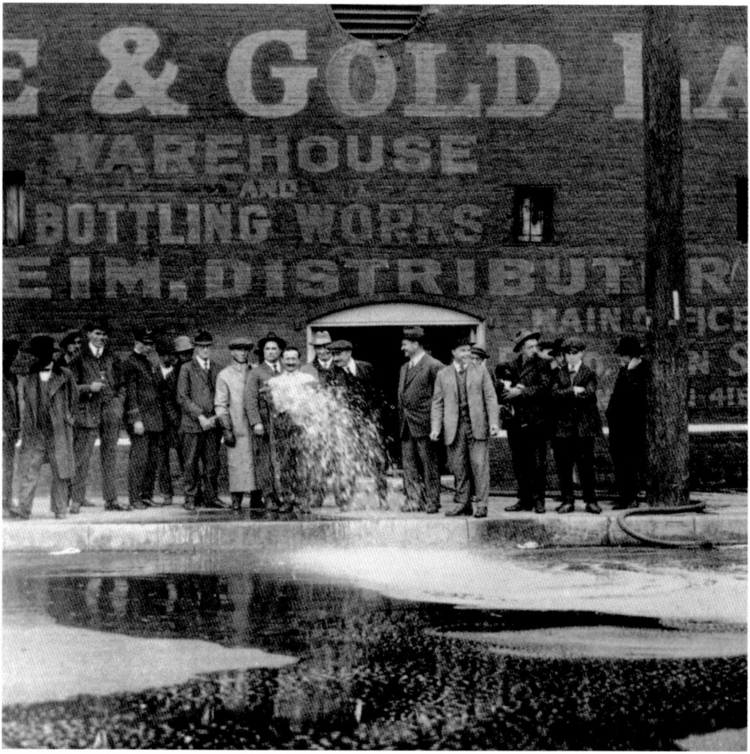

↑
Anonymous
Prohibition begins, February 1920, North Cucamonga Winery.

Beginn der Prohibition im Februar 1920, North-Cucamonga-Weingut.

Les débuts de la prohibition en février 1920, devant les entrepôts de l'entreprise vinicole North Cucamonga.

→
Cliff Wesselmann
In 1927, James "Two-Gun" Davis inherited and perpetuated a department that was notoriously corrupt. He wanted gunmen "brought in dead, not alive, and will reprimand any officer who shows the least mercy to a criminal."

1927 übernahm James „Two-Gun" Davis die für ihre Korruption berüchtigte Polizei und führte sie in demselben Stil weiter. Davis proklamierte, er wolle „Gangster tot, nicht lebendig, und werde jeden Beamten scharf verweisen, der auch nur die geringste Nachsicht gegenüber einem Kriminellen zeigt".

James « Two-Gun » (« Deux-Flingues ») Davis, en 1927. Il hérite alors d'un service notoirement corrompu qu'il prolongera. « Je veux qu'on m'amène les gangsters morts, pas vifs, et je sanctionnerai tout agent qui montrera la moindre pitié envers un criminel. »

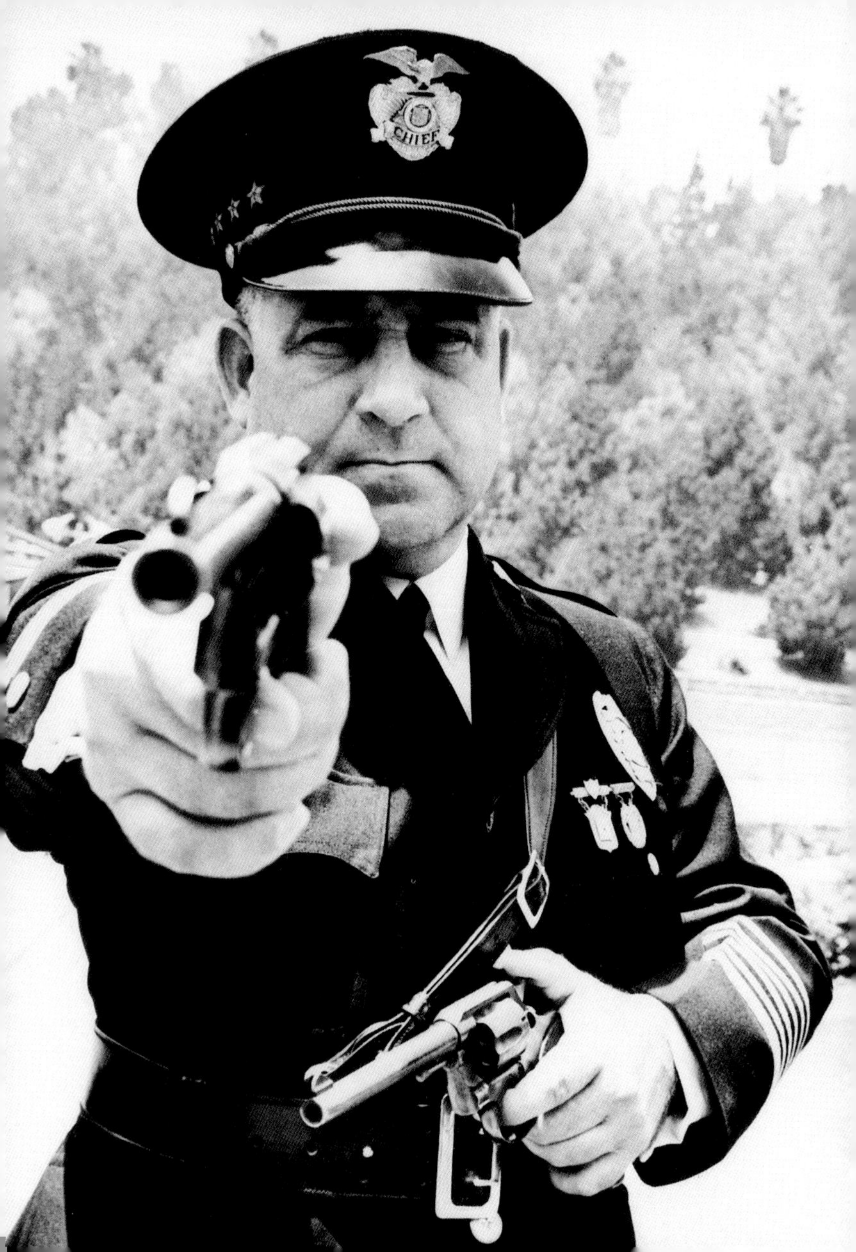
CHIEF

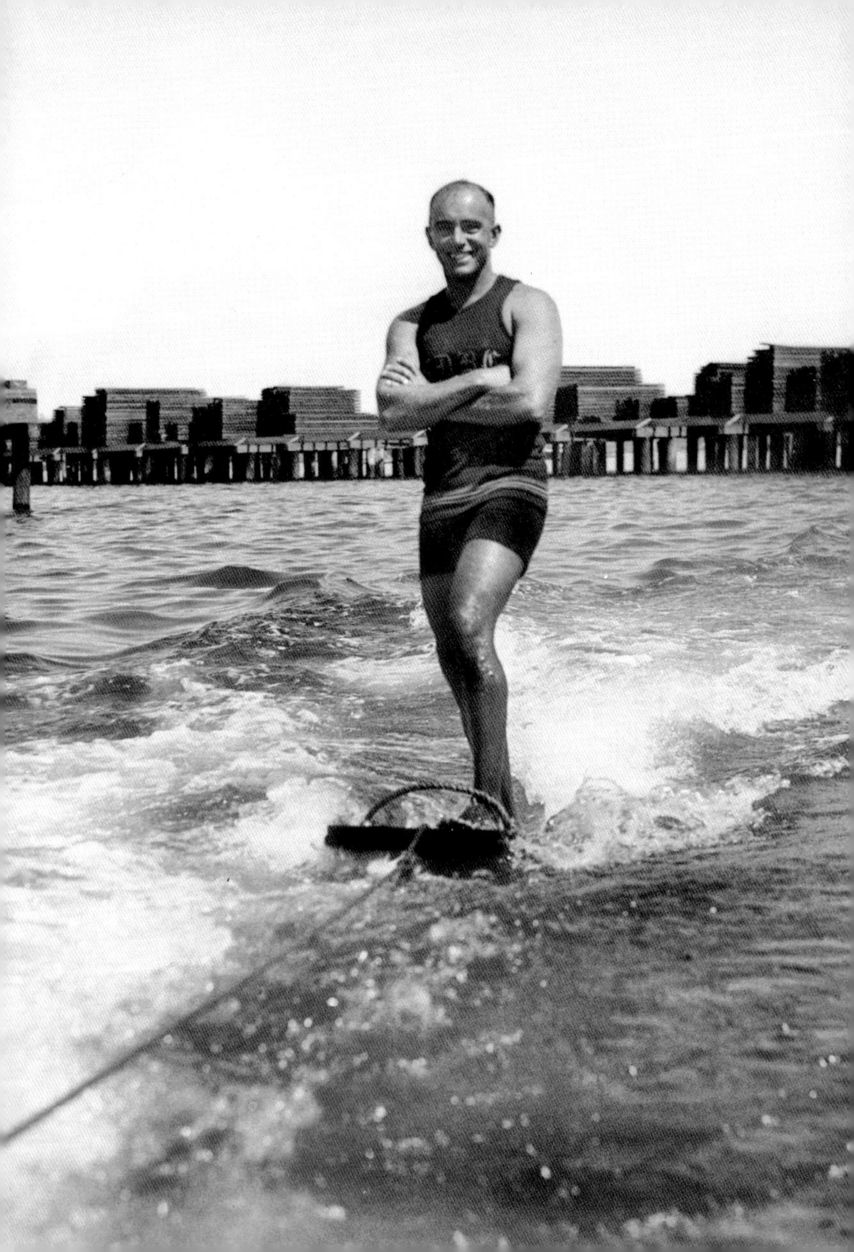

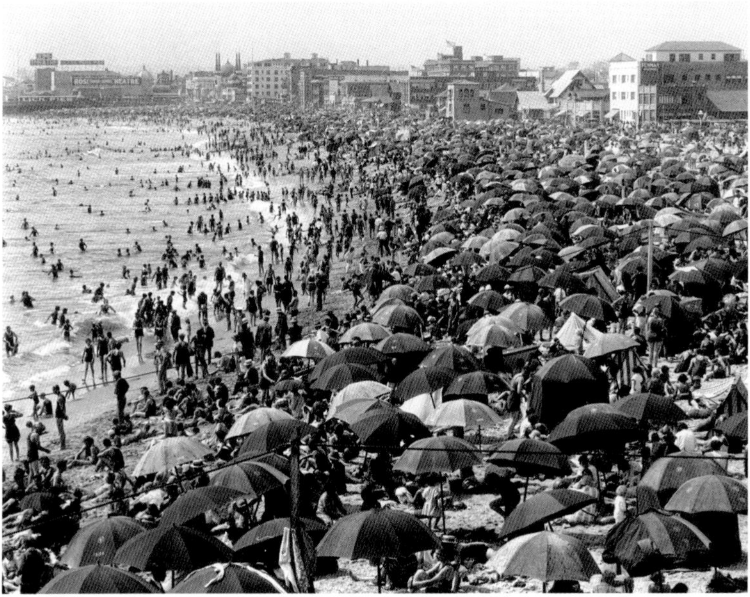

←

Anonymous

George Freeth, commonly regarded as the first Southern California surfer, c. 1919.

George Freeth gilt als erster südkalifornischer Surfer, um 1919.

George Freeth, généralement considéré comme le premier surfeur de Californie du Sud, vers 1919.

↑

Anonymous

Crowds cover the sand and spill into the water in Santa Monica, c. 1922.

Menschenmengen in Santa Monica drängen sich am Strand und strömen ins Wasser, um 1922.

Une foule de baigneurs a envahi la plage et s'ébroue dans l'eau à Santa Monica, vers 1922.

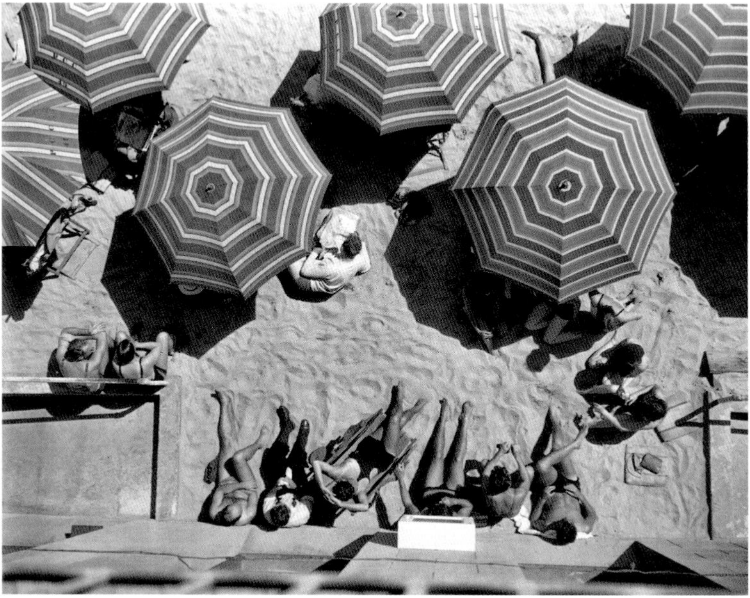

↑
Will Connell
Beachgoers relax under the sun and shade at Santa Monica, 1927.

Strandbesucher in Santa Monica entspannen sich in der Sonne oder im Schatten, 1927.

Des estivants se détendent sur la plage ensoleillée de Santa Monica, 1927.

→
Will Connell
Cars line Pacific Coast Highway in Santa Monica, 1927. The styles may have changed but this remains a perennial Southern California scene.

Wagen säumen den Pacific Coast Highway in Santa Monica, 1927. Abgesehen von den sich ändernden Modellen ist dies nach wie vor eine typisch südkalifornische Szenerie.

Procession de véhicules sur la voie rapide qui longe le Pacifique à Santa Monica, 1927. Le design automobile a peut-être changé, mais cette scène reste un classique de la Californie du Sud.

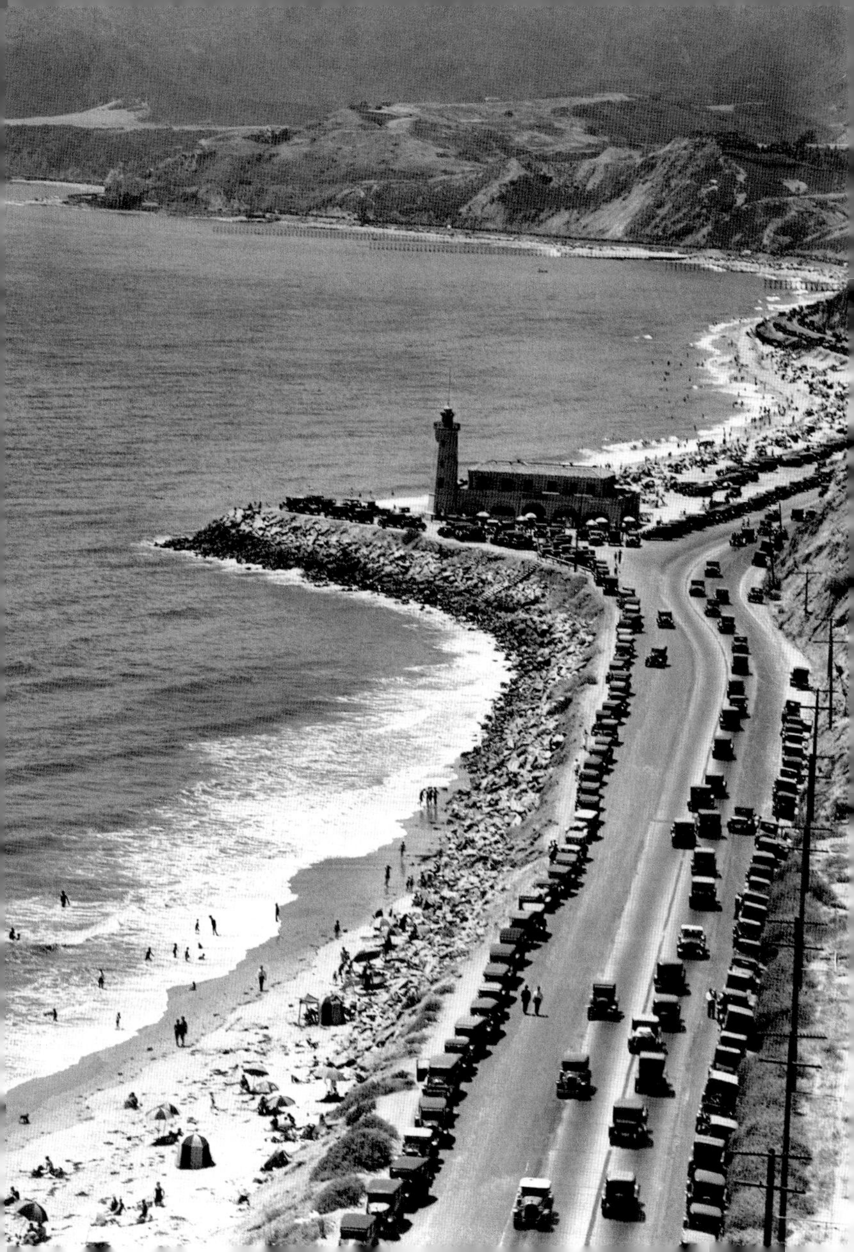

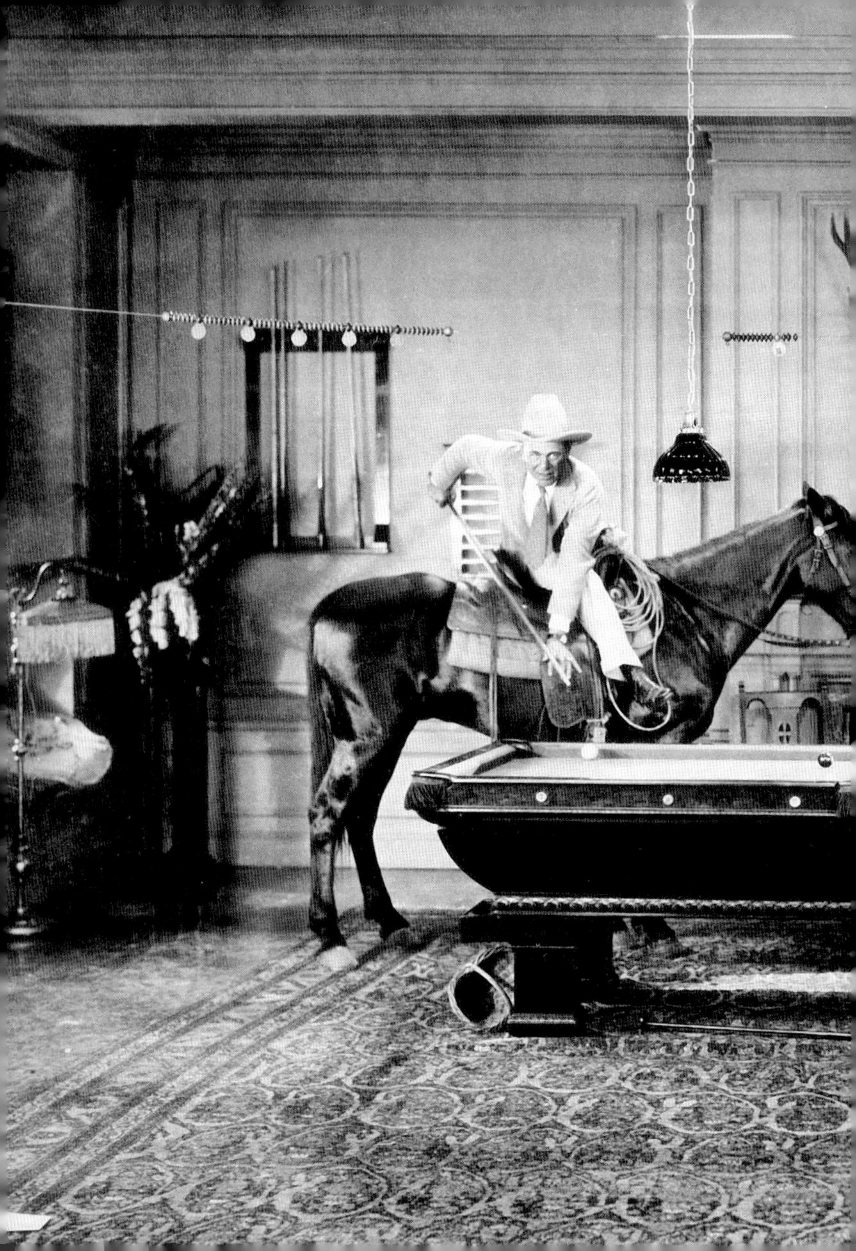

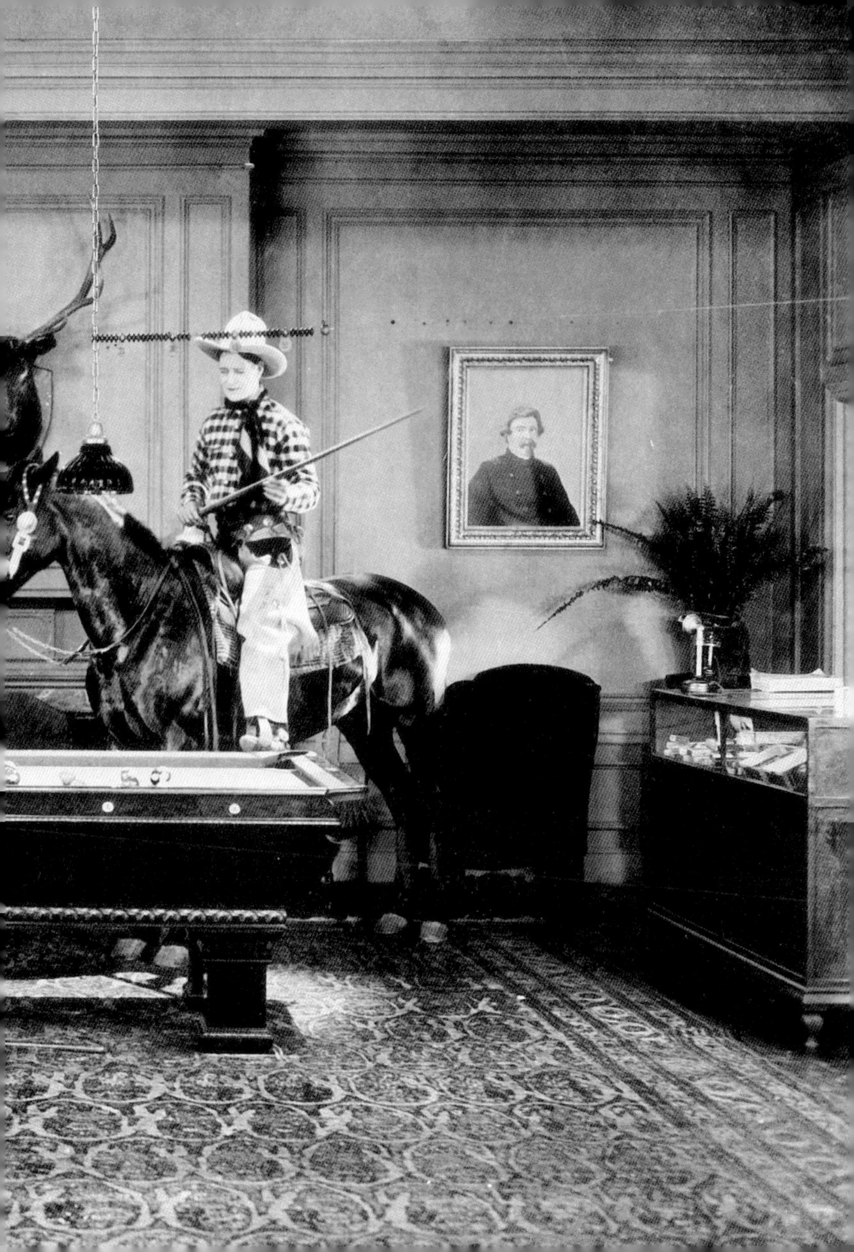

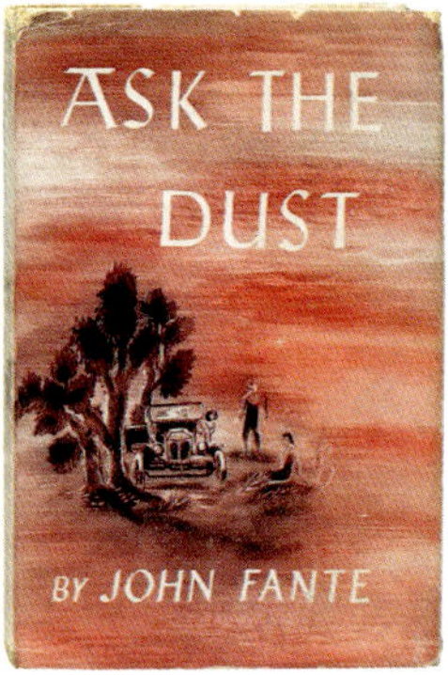

"The lean days…a sea of blue day after day, the sun floating through it. The days of plenty—plenty of worries, plenty of oranges. Eat them in bed, eat them for lunch, push them down for dinner. Oranges, five cents a dozen."

„Die mageren Tage … ein Meer von Blau, Tag für Tag, vom Sonnenlicht durchflutet. Die üppigen Tage – Sorgen im Überfluss, Orangen im Überfluss. Im Bett gegessen, zum Lunch gegessen, runtergewürgt zum Dinner. Orangen, fünf Cent das Dutzend."

« Des jours… sans jamais un nuage, un océan de bleu jour après jour, et le soleil qui flotte dedans. Des jours d'abondance aussi avec plein de soucis, plein d'oranges. On les mange au lit, on les mange au déjeuner, on se force à les avaler au souper. Cinq cents la douzaine, les oranges. »

John Fante, *Ask the Dust,* 1939

p. 60/61
C. C. Pierce
In a publicity shot two "cowboys" play a game of billiards on horseback, c. 1927.

Zwei „Cowboys" spielen für eine Werbeaufnahme zu Pferd Billard, um 1927.

Une photo publicitaire montre deux « cow-boys » à cheval jouant au billard, vers 1927.

→
Anonymous
Broadway, lit for the holidays, looking north from Tenth Street, c. 1928.

Der weihnachtlich geschmückte Broadway, Blick von der Tenth Street nach Norden, um 1928.

Broadway avec ses décorations de Noël, vue en direction du nord depuis la 10e Rue, vers 1928.

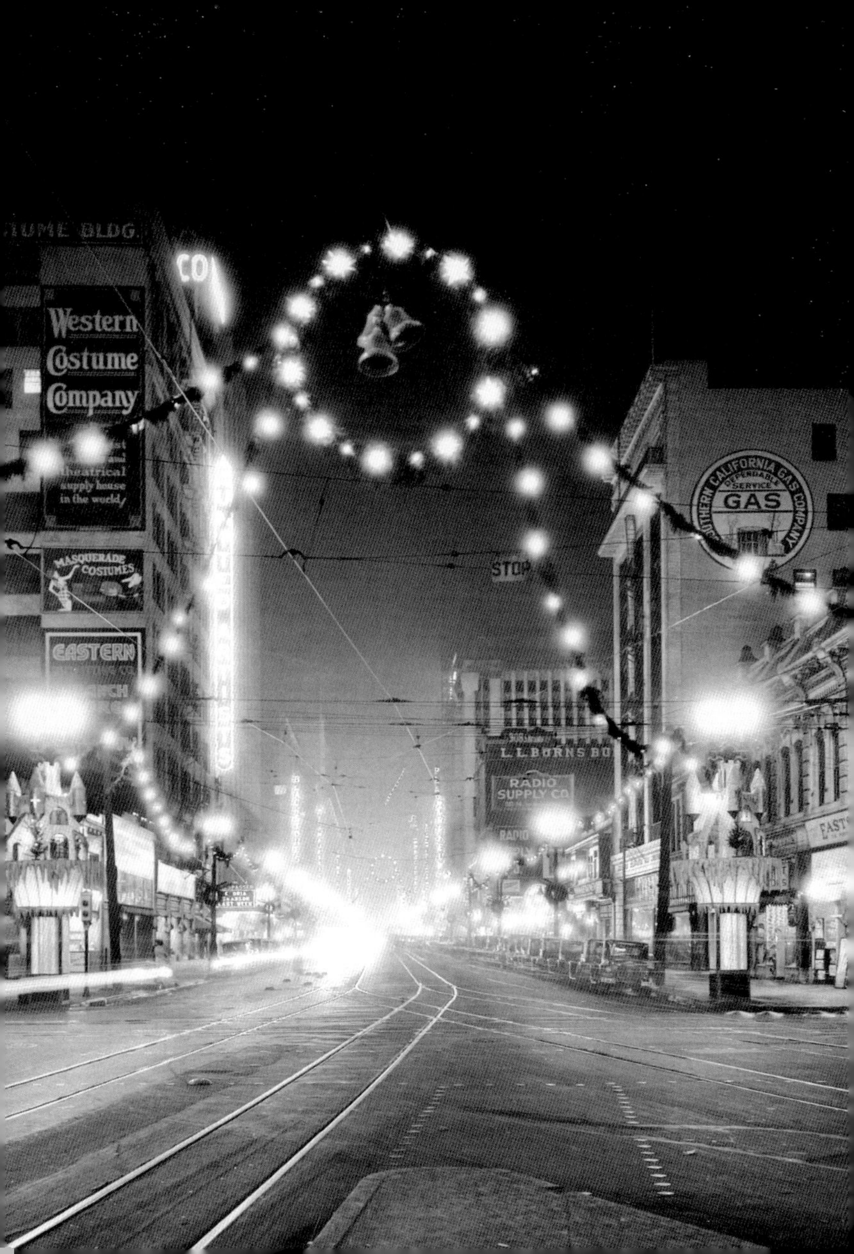

Western Costume Company
theatrical supply house in the world
MASQUERADE COSTUMES
EASTERN
SOUTHERN CALIFORNIA GAS COMPANY
DEPENDABLE SERVICE
GAS
RADIO SUPPLY CO.

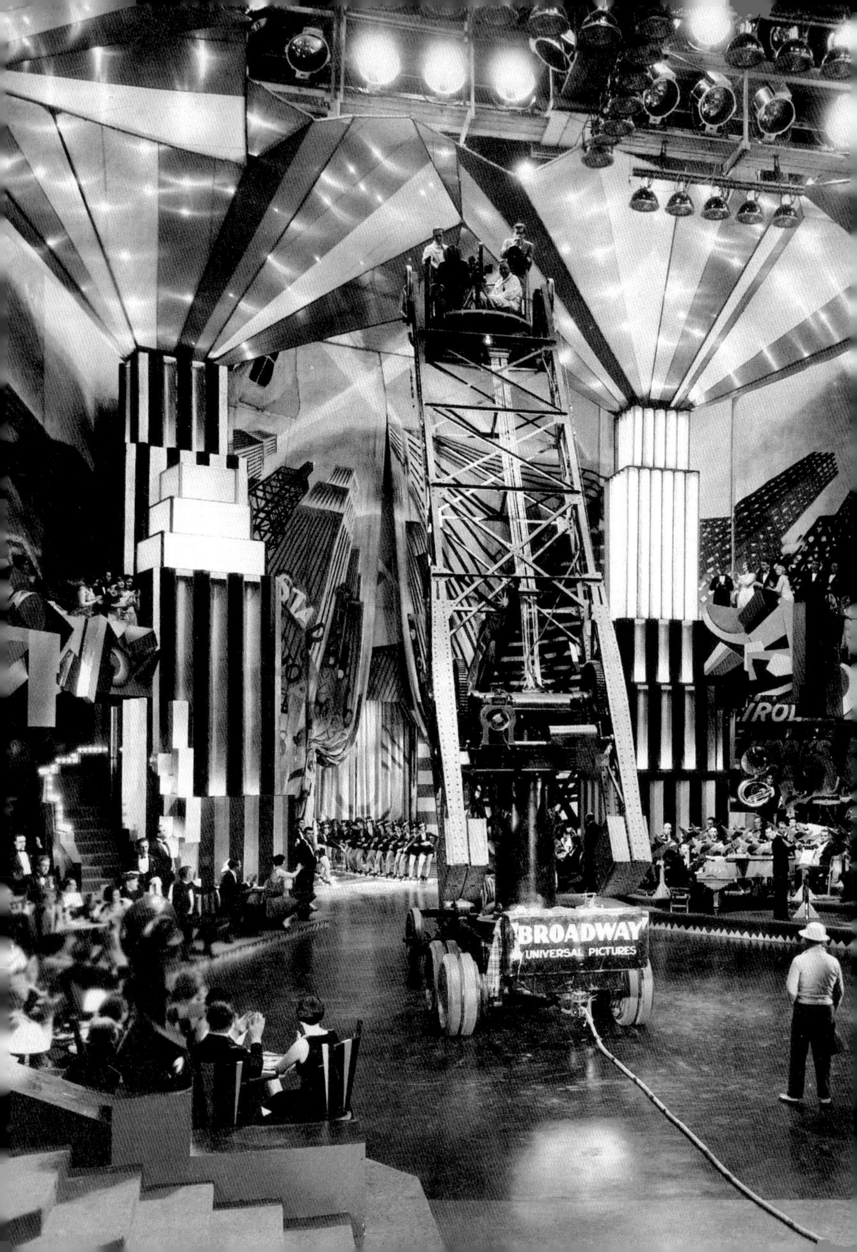
BROADWAY
UNIVERSAL PICTURES

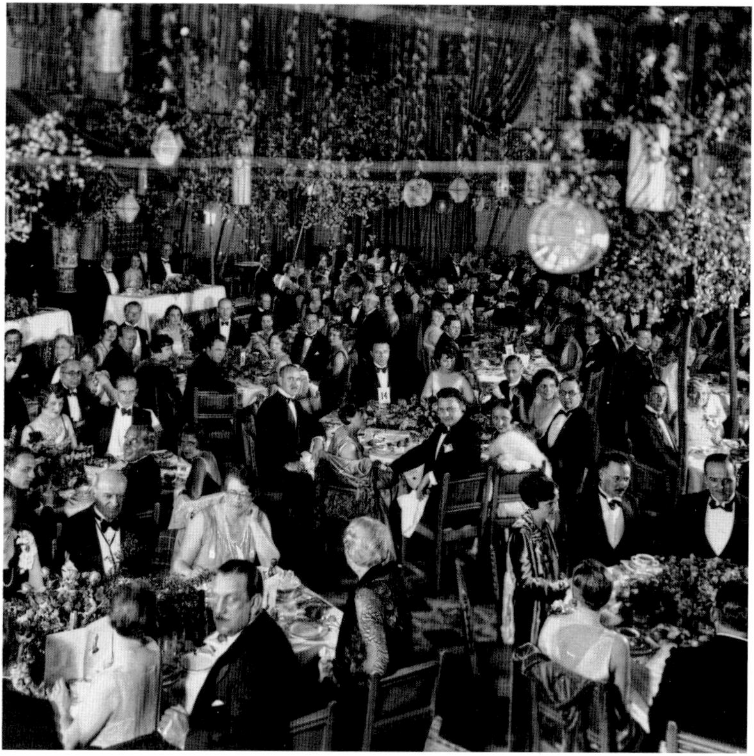

←
Anonymous
A lavish nightclub set, for Broadway Melody, *Universal Studios, c. 1929.*

Ein aufwendiges Filmset für die Nachtklubszenen in Broadway Melody, *Universal Studios, um 1929.*

Un élégant décor de night-club pour le film Broadway Melody, *Universal Studios, vers 1929.*

↑
Anonymous
The Academy Awards were first presented on May 16, 1929, at a dinner for 250 people in the Blossom Room of the Roosevelt Hotel.

Die Oscars wurden erstmals am 16. Mai 1929 bei einem Bankett für 250 geladene Gäste im Blossom Room des Roosevelt Hotel verliehen.

Les oscars ont été décernés pour la première fois, le 16 mai 1929, lors d'un dîner de gala de 250 couverts dans la Blossom Room de l'hôtel Roosevelt.

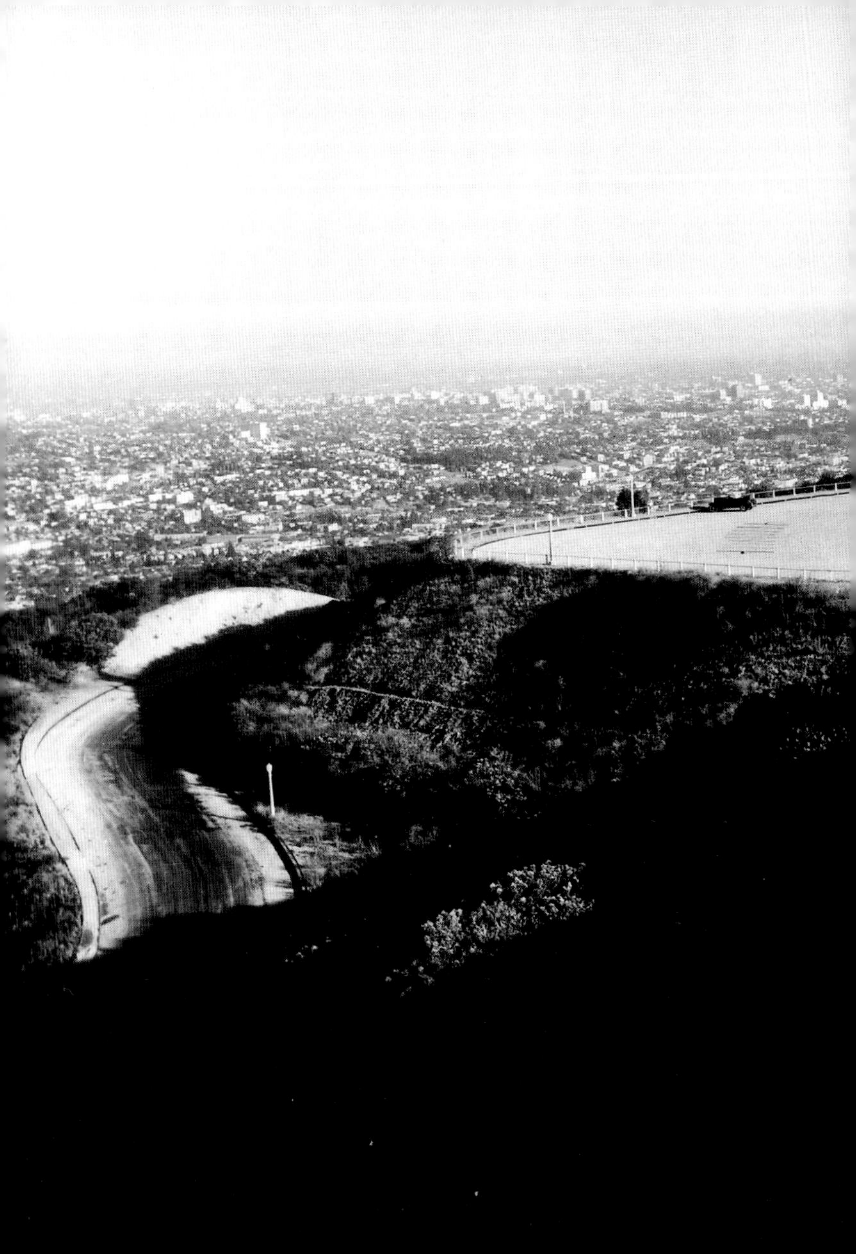

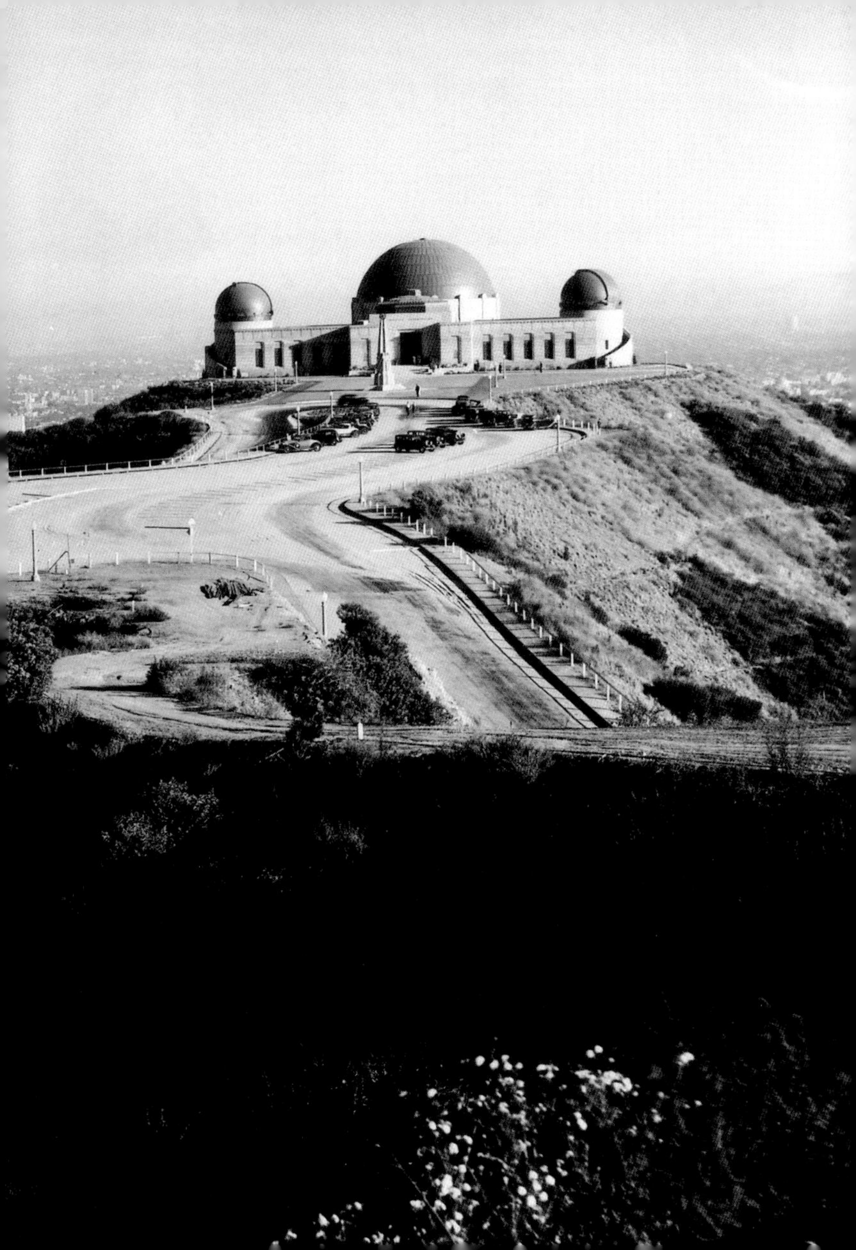

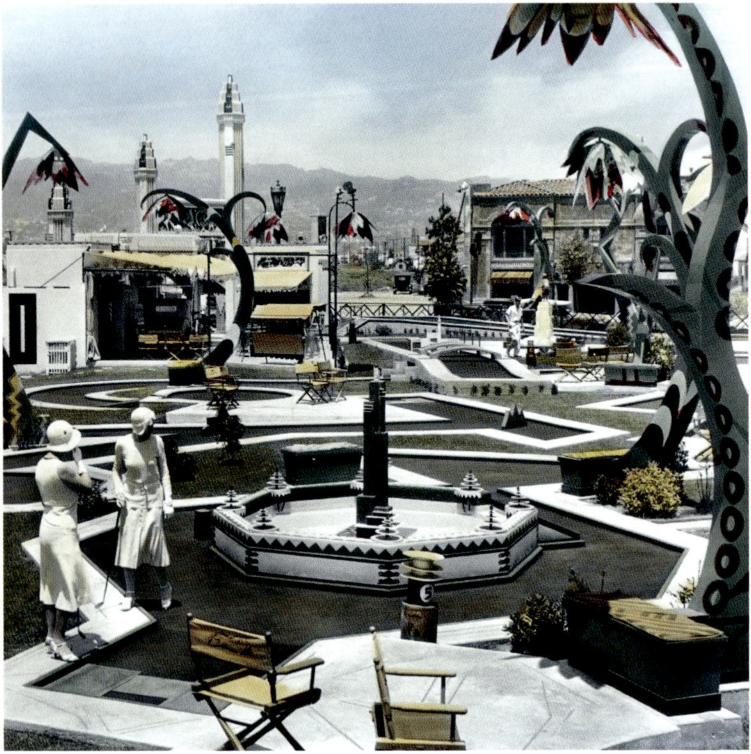

p. 66/67
Mott Merge
Griffith Observatory, shortly after construction in the early 1930s.

Das Griffith-Observatorium kurz nach seiner Fertigstellung Anfang der 1930er-Jahre.

L'observatoire de Griffith, peu après sa construction au début des années 1930.

↑
Burton Holmes
Built by Mary Pickford, Wilshire Links miniature golf course at Wilshire and La Cienega boulevards, c. 1930.

Der von Mary Pickford angelegte Minigolfparcours Wilshire Links, Ecke Wilshire und La Cienega Boulevard, um 1930.

Édifié par Mary Pickford, le parcours de golf miniature de Wilshire Links au coin des Wilshire Boulevard et La Cienega Boulevard, vers 1930.

→
Mott Merge
McDonnell's Drive-In restaurant at Beverly Boulevard and La Brea Avenue epitomizes the spirit of car culture, c. 1930.

Das Drive-in-Restaurant McDonnell's, Ecke Beverly Boulevard und La Brea Avenue, verkörperte die Automobilkultur, um 1930.

Le restaurant drive-in McDonnell, *au coin de Beverly Boulevard et de La Brea Avenue, illustre l'esprit de la culture automobile, vers 1930.*

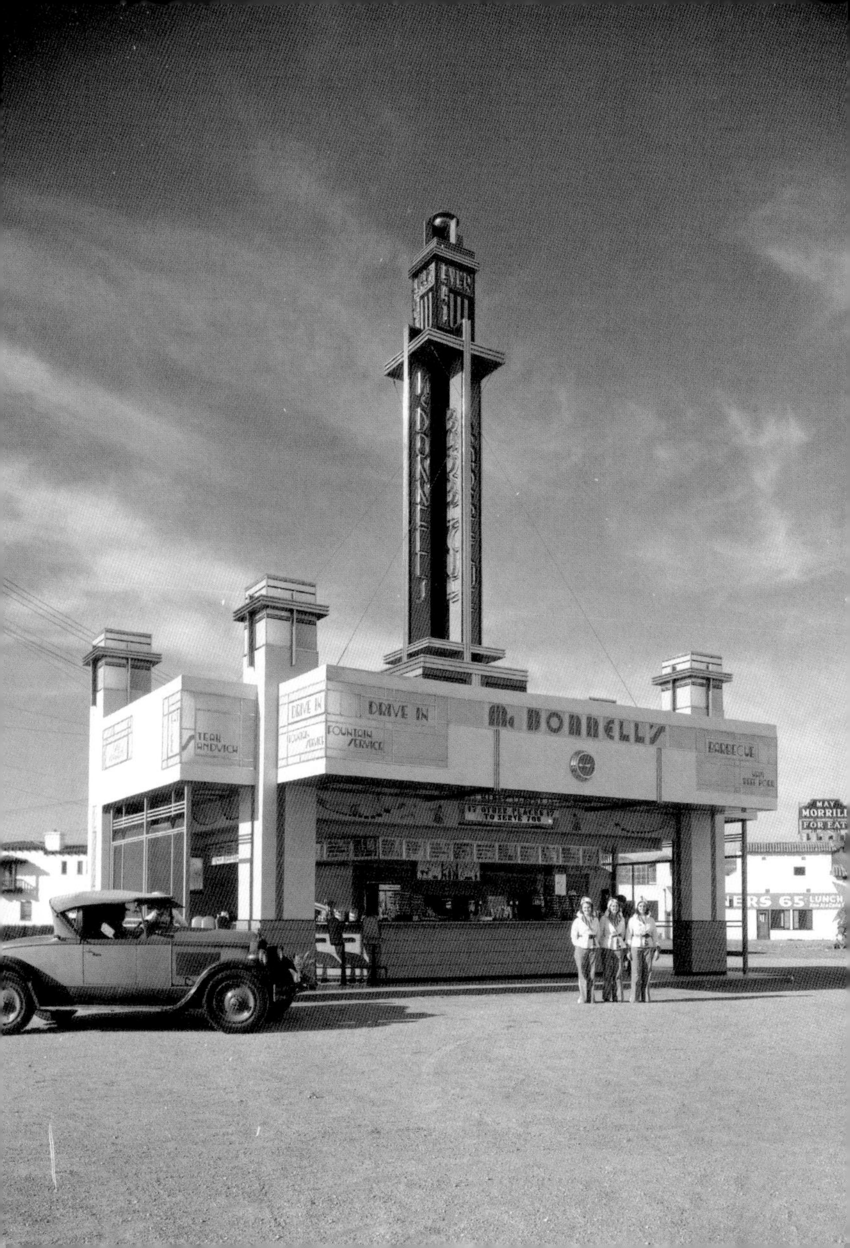
DRIVE IN
DRIVE IN
FOUNTAIN SERVICE
Mc DONNELL'S
BARBECUE

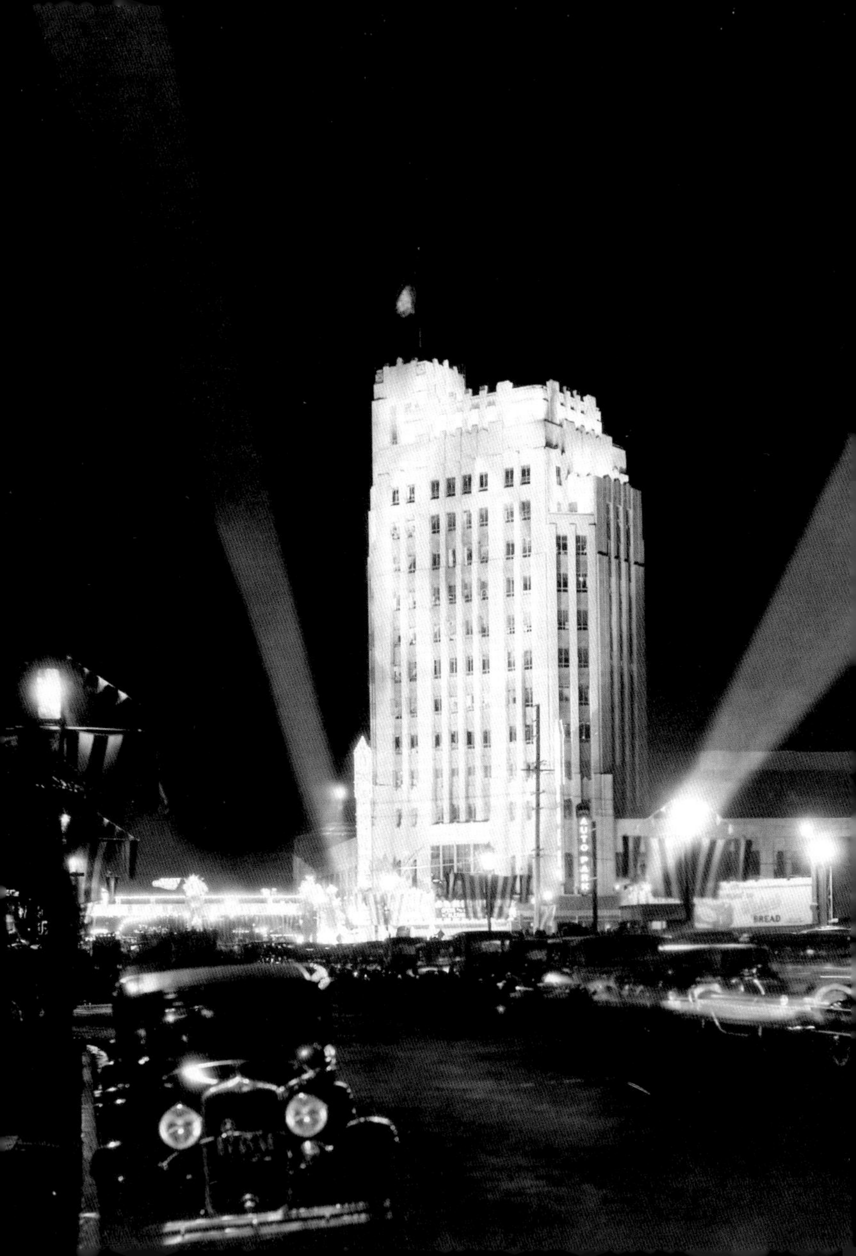
AUTO PARK
BREAD

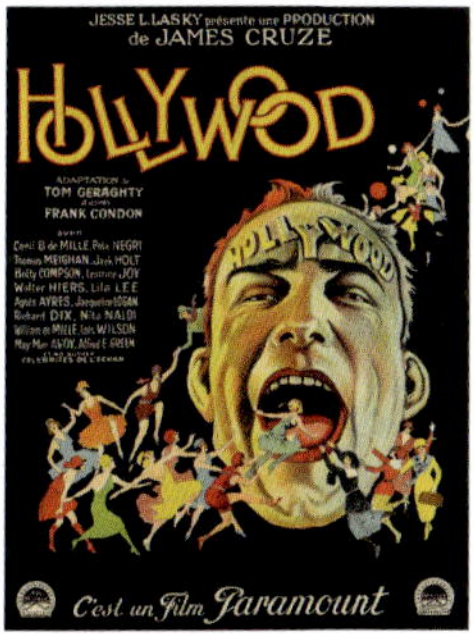

"The usual tale of a pretty girl from the sticks trying to break into movies...just about every star in Hollywood—not just those at Paramount—has a cameo at one point or another..."

„Die übliche Geschichte von einem hübschen Mädchen aus der Provinz, das versucht, im Filmgeschäft Fuß zu fassen ... so gut wie jeder Hollywoodstar – und zwar nicht nur die Paramount-Stars – hat irgendwann einen Gastauftritt ..."

« L'histoire habituelle de la jolie fille de la cambrousse essayant de percer au cinéma... presque toutes les stars d'Hollywood – pas seulement celles de la Paramount – ont un petit rôle à un moment ou un autre... »

Hollywood*, 1923; no print extant, reviewed by Janet Garza, *All Movie Guide

←
Mott Studios
Opening of the Warner Theater, later the Wiltern, Wilshire Boulevard and Western Avenue, October 7, 1931.

Eröffnung des Warner Theater, des späteren Wiltern, Ecke Wilshire Boulevard und Western Avenue, 7. Oktober 1931.

Inauguration du Warner Theater, qui deviendra le Wiltern, Wilshire Boulevard et Western Avenue, 7 octobre 1931.

p. 72/73
Anonymous
Amusement-park piers like Santa Monica's, pictured here c. 1930, were big business in Southern California from the 1880s to the 1940s, but they began to disappear after World War II.

Piers mit ihren Vergnügungsangeboten, wie dieser in der Santa Monica Bay, um 1930, waren von den 1880er- bis in die 1940er-Jahre ein lukratives Geschäft in Südkalifornien, verschwanden nach dem Zweiten Weltkrieg aber allmählich.

Les embarcadères-parcs d'attractions, comme celui-ci dans la baie de Santa Monica, vers 1930, ont prospéré en Californie du Sud des années 1880 aux années 1940, mais ils ont peu à peu disparu après la Seconde Guerre mondiale.

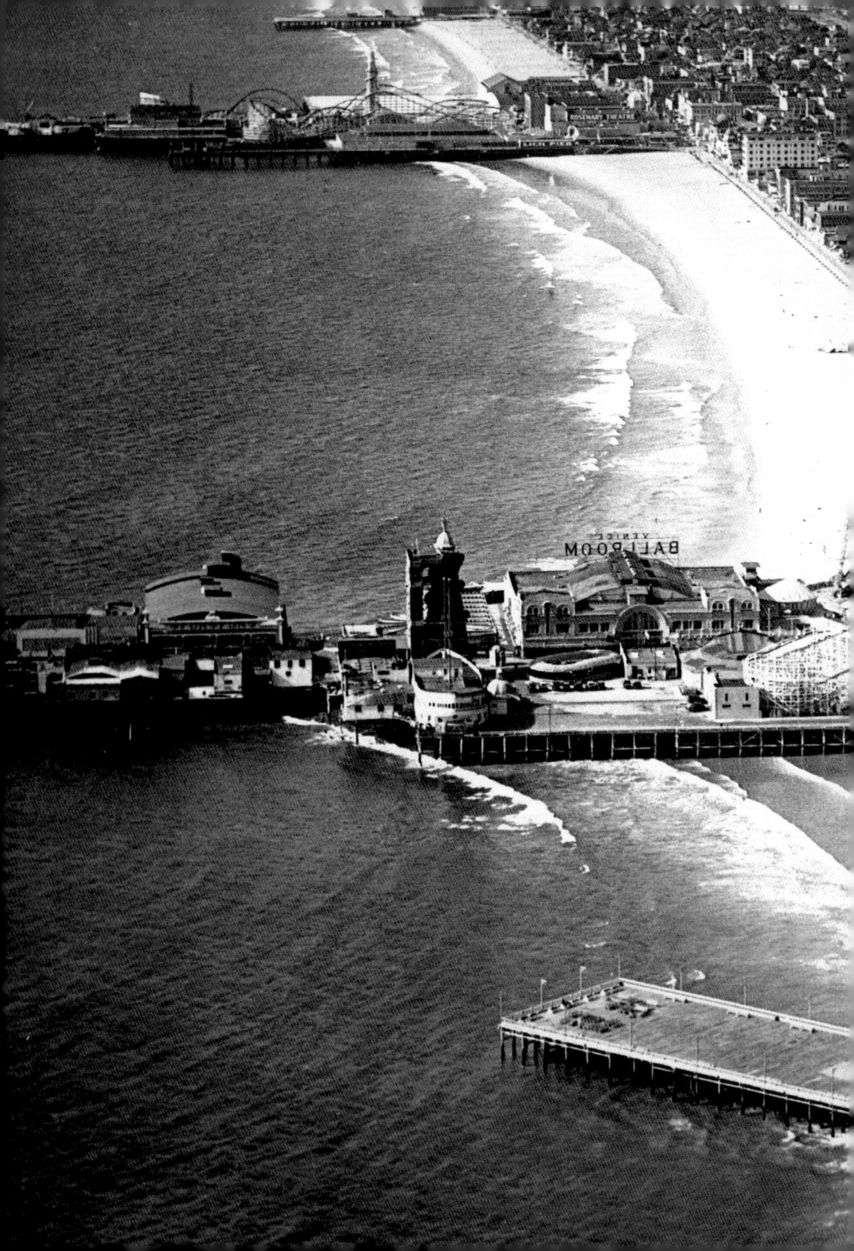

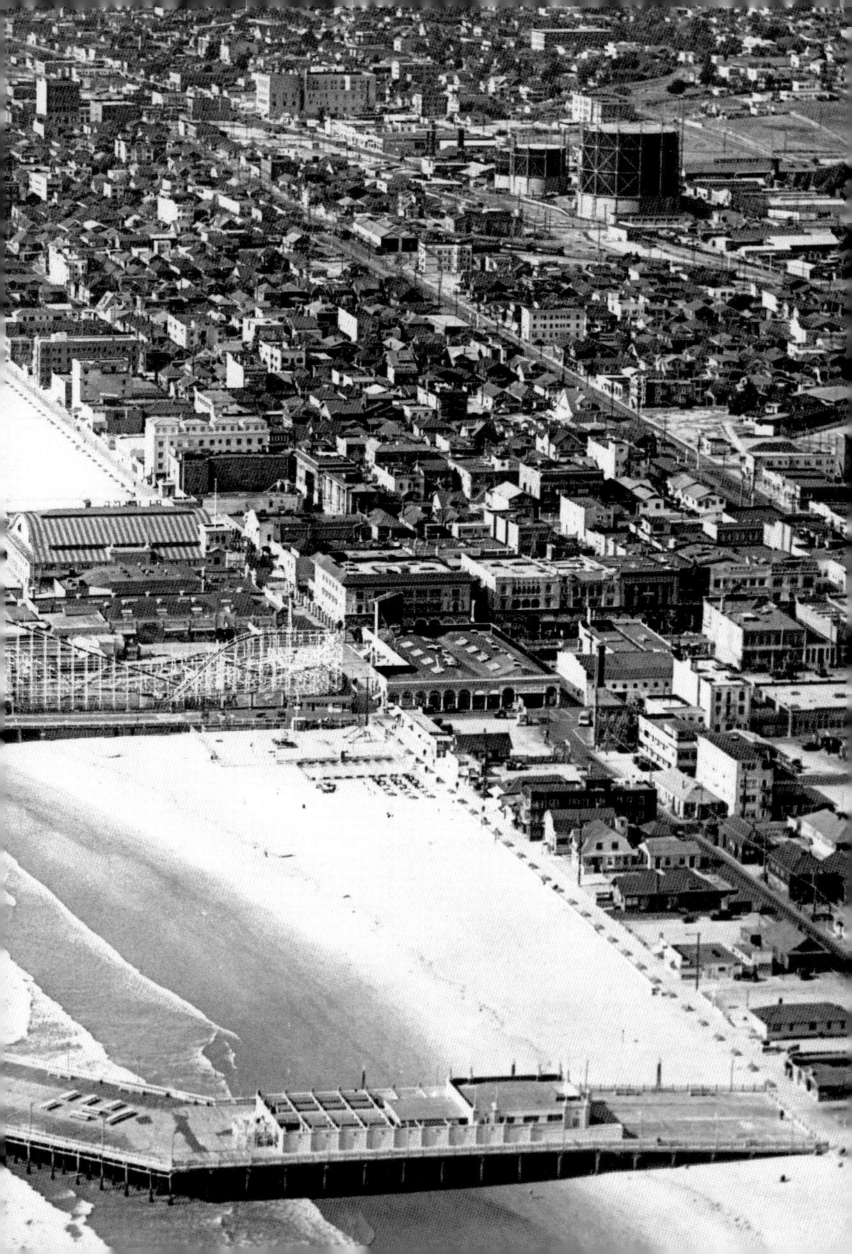

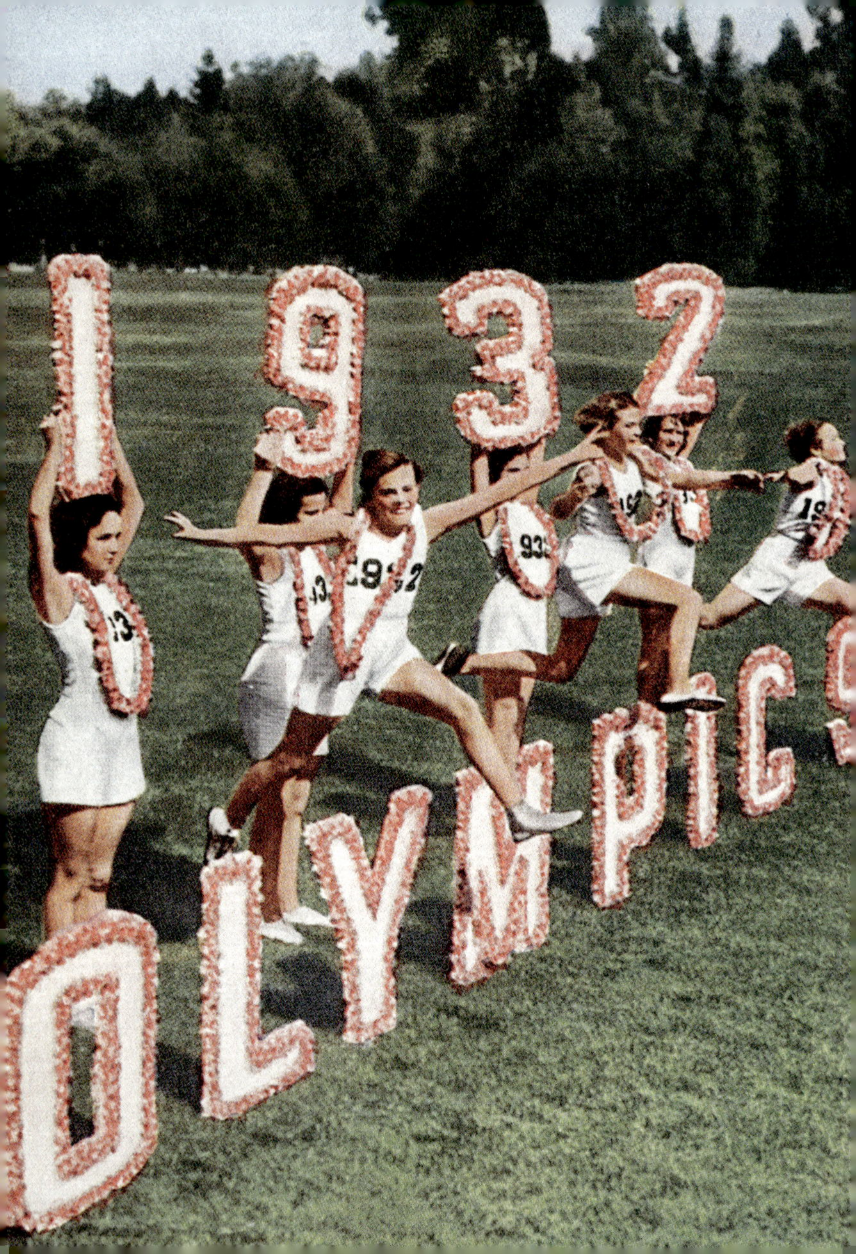
1932
OLYMPIC

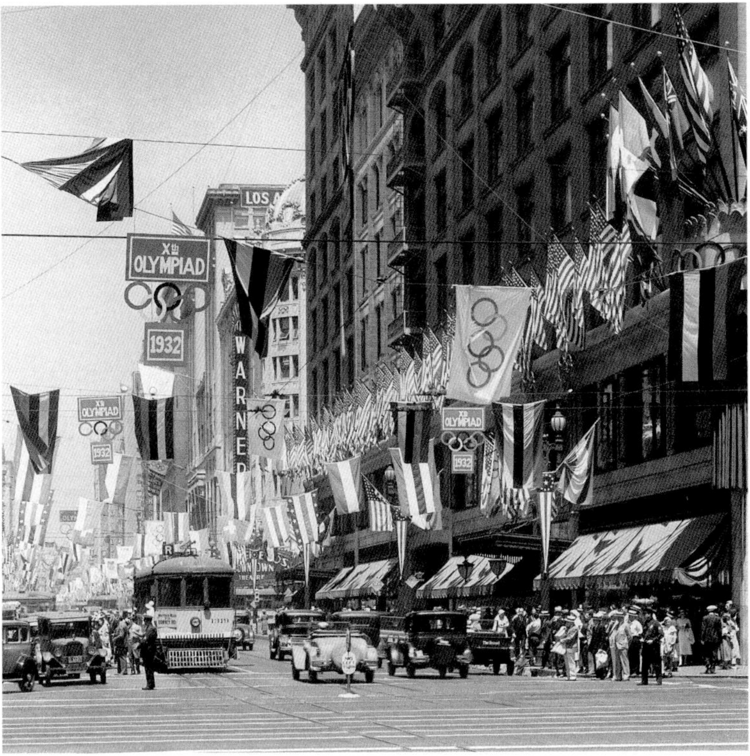

←

Anonymous

A living advertisement for the Los Angeles Olympics, 1932.

Lebende Werbung für die Olympischen Spiele in Los Angeles, 1932.

Publicité vivante pour les Jeux olympiques de Los Angeles, 1932.

↑

Anonymous

Seventh Street, decorated for the Olympic Games, 1932.

Seventh Street, geschmückt für die Olympischen Spiele, 1932.

La 7e Rue décorée pour les Jeux olympiques, 1932.

p. 76/77

Dick Whittington

Exercise guru Paul Bragg and his adherents display one aspect of Los Angeles's early health movement, 1929.

Fitnessguru Paul Bragg und seine Anhänger führen eine Erscheinungsform der frühen Gesundheitsbewegung in Los Angeles vor, 1929.

Le gourou de la gym, Paul Bragg, et ses adeptes présentent un aspect du premier mouvement pour la santé à Los Angeles, 1929.

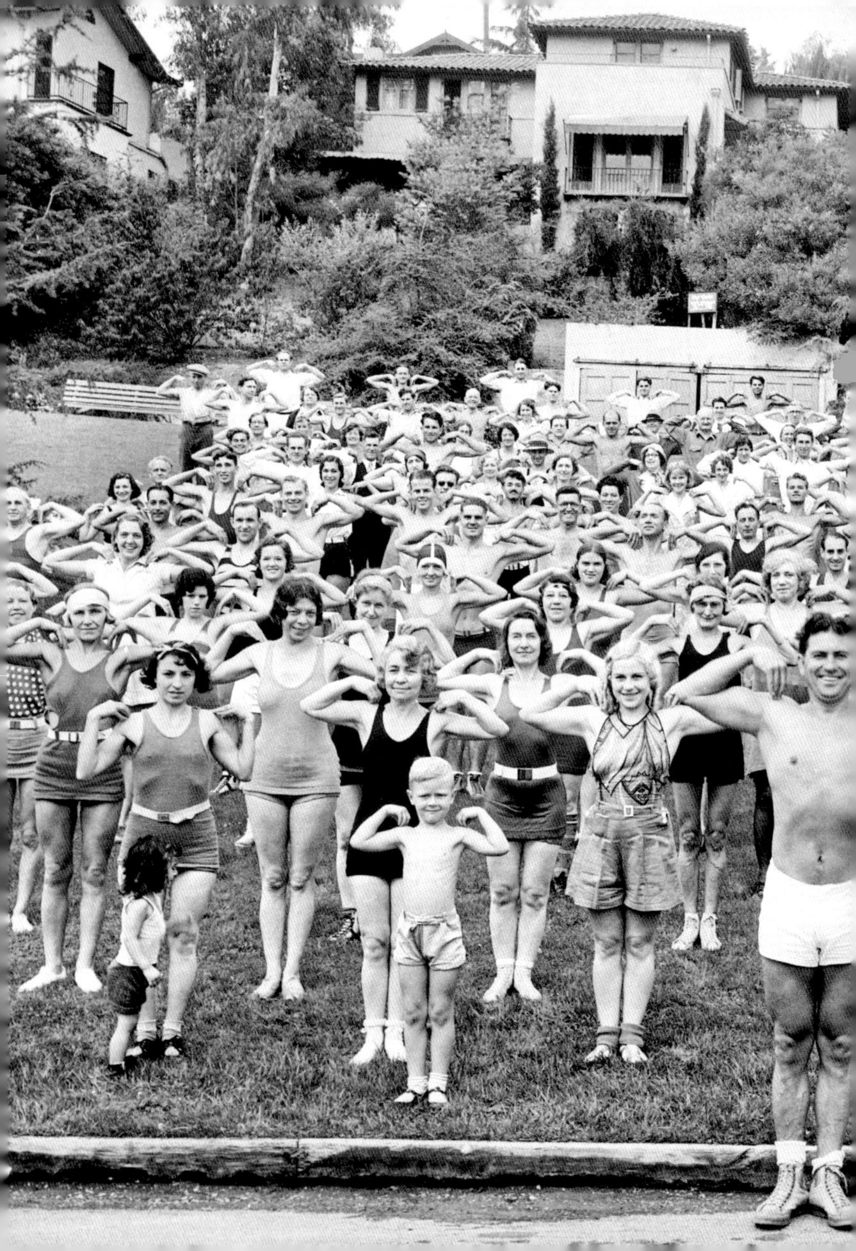

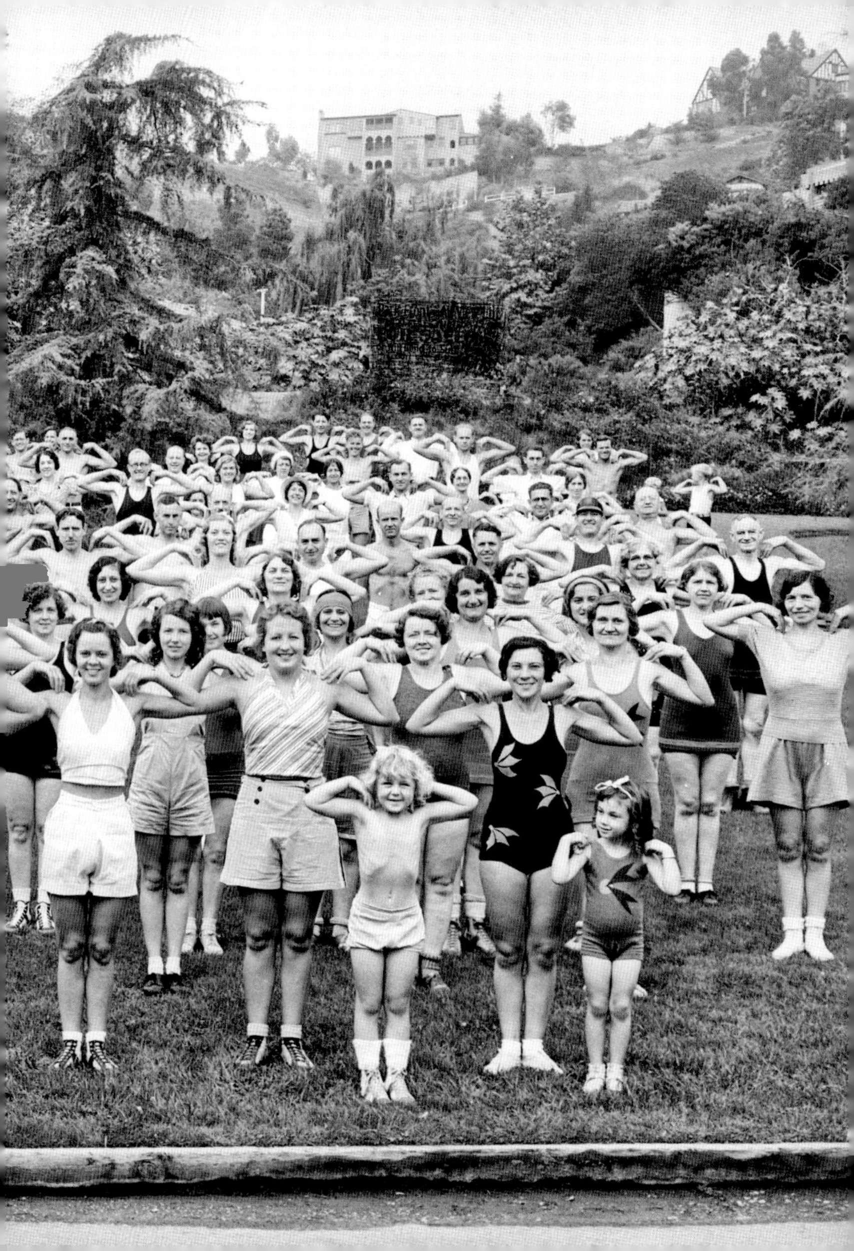

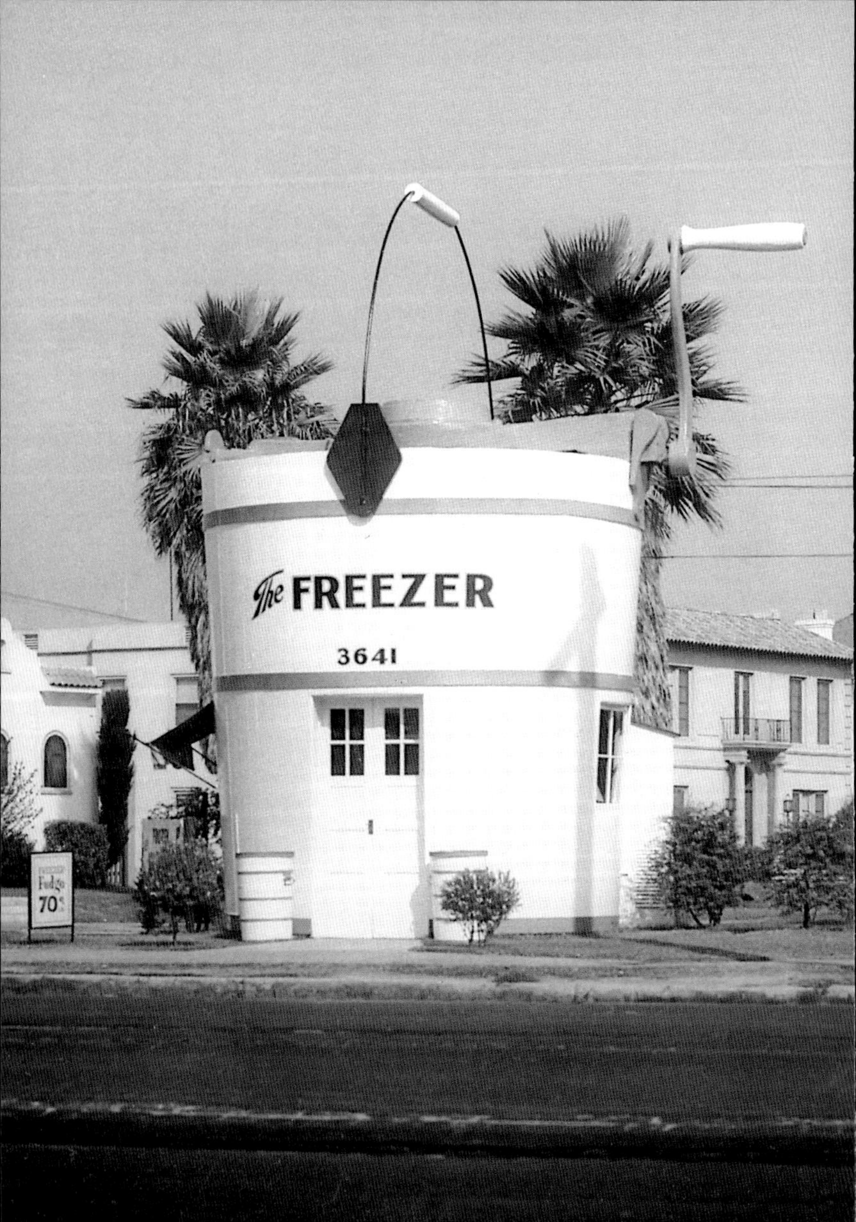
The FREEZER
3641
70

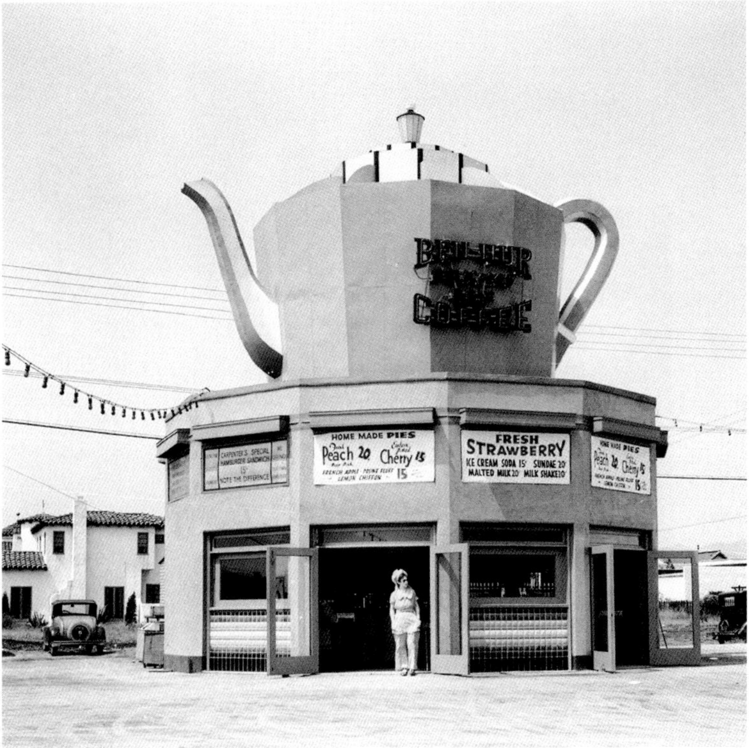

←
Cliff Wesselmann
The Freezer ice cream stand featured kinetic parts and neon, c. 1934.

Die Eisdiele Freezer war mit Neonlicht und beweglichen Elementen ausgestattet, um 1934.

Le glacier Freezer était équipé de néons et d'éléments mobiles, vers 1934.

↑
Burton Holmes
Part of a chain of drive-ins, Sanderson's Coffee Pot poured steam from its spout, Beverly Boulevard, c. 1931.

Sanderson's Coffee Pot gehörte zu einer Kette von Drive-in-Restaurants und stieß Dampfwölkchen aus seiner Tülle, Beverly Boulevard, um 1931.

La cafetière Sanderson's, qui faisait partie d'une chaîne de drive-in, laissait échapper de la vapeur par son bec verseur, Beverly Boulevard, vers 1931.

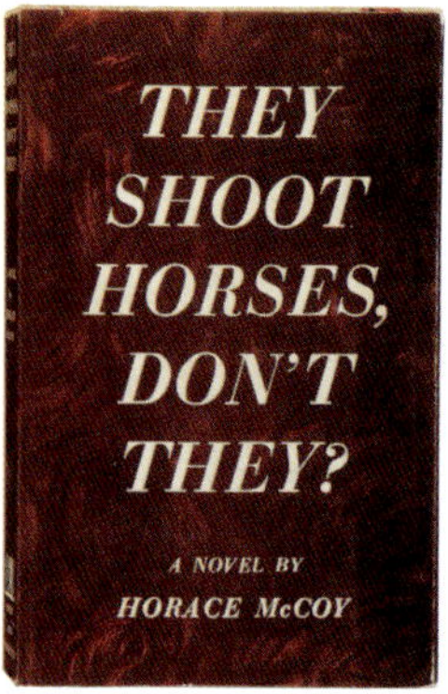

"Everybody's feet and legs swelled and down beneath the ocean kept pounding, pounding against the pilings all the time. Before I went into this marathon dance, I used to love the Pacific Ocean.... But not anymore."

„Jeder hatte geschwollene Füße und Beine, und unter ihnen dröhnte der Ozean in einem fort, schlug unermüdlich gegen die Pfähle des Piers. Ehe ich an diesem Tanzmarathon teilnahm, hatte ich den Pazifik geliebt … Doch nun nicht mehr."

« Les pieds et les jambes de tout le monde enflaient, et, en bas, sous le plancher, l'océan ne cessait de battre, de battre, de battre sans cesse contre les piliers. Avant de me lancer dans ce marathon de danse, j'aimais l'océan Pacifique… Mais plus maintenant. »

Horace McCoy,
***They Shoot Horses, Don't They?,* 1935**

→
Cliff Wesselmann

The Depression hits at Hollywood and Vine, c. 1932.

Die Wirtschaftskrise kommt an der Ecke Hollywood Boulevard und Vine Street an, um 1932.

Un visage de la crise au coin de Hollywood Boulevard et Vine Street, vers 1932.

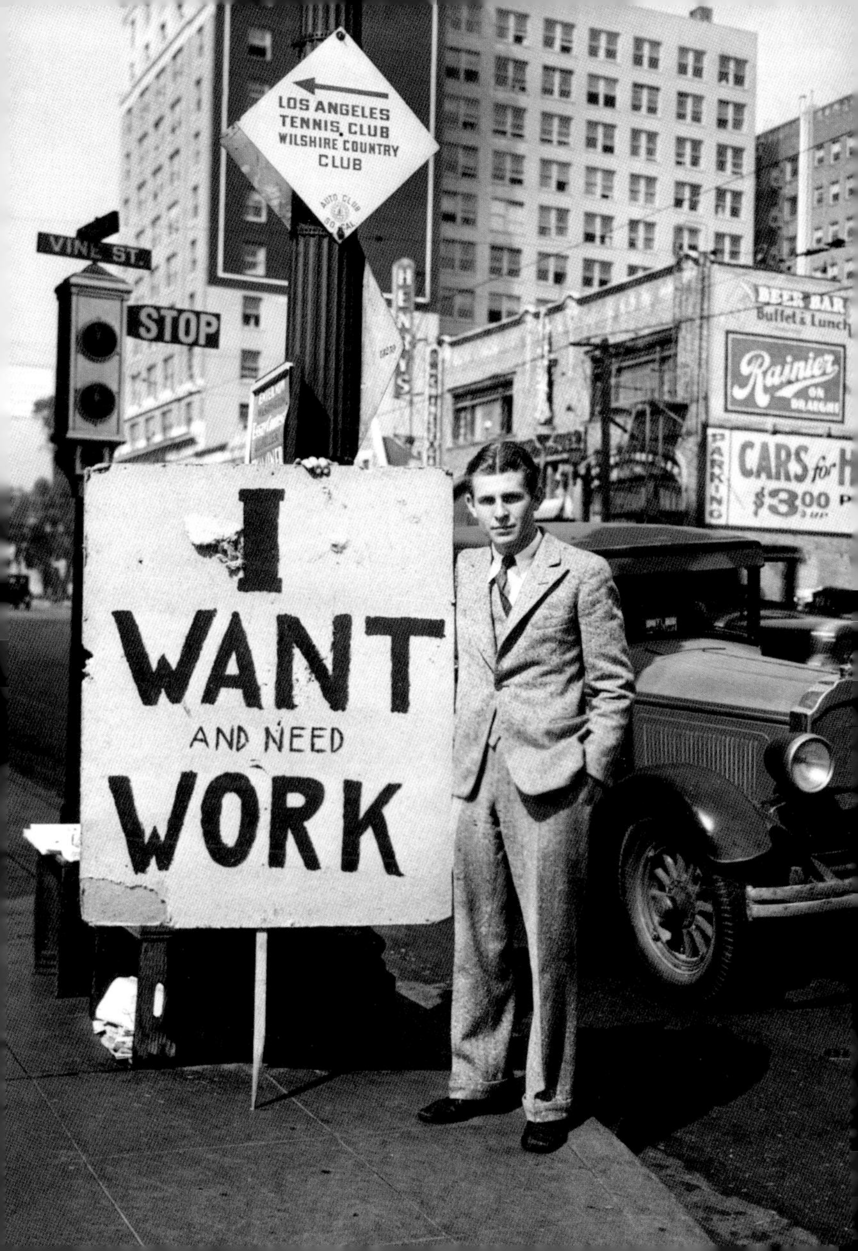
LOS ANGELES
TENNIS CLUB
WILSHIRE COUNTRY
CLUB
VINE ST.
STOP
I
WANT
AND NEED
WORK
BEER BAR
Buffet & Lunch
Rainier
PARKING
CARS for
$3.00

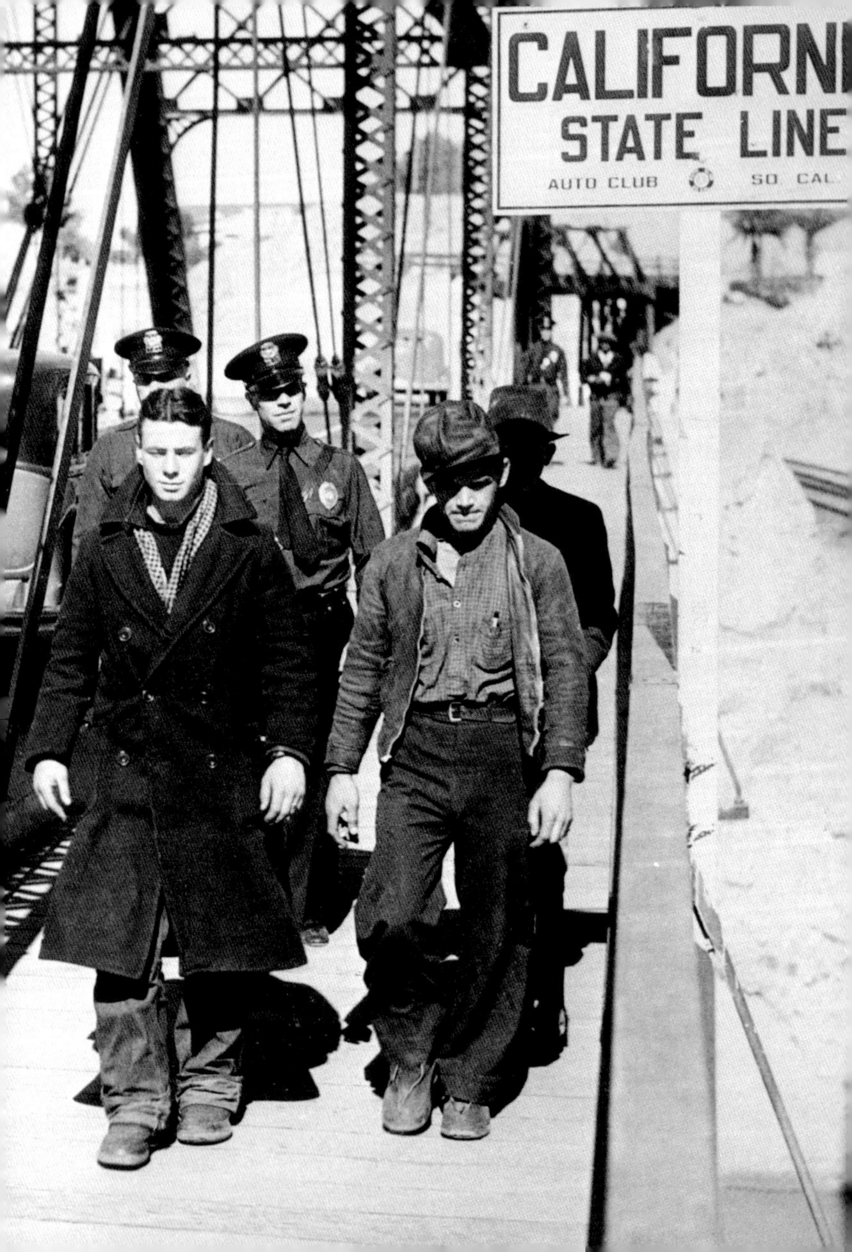
CALIFORN
STATE LINE
AUTO CLUB
SO. CAL

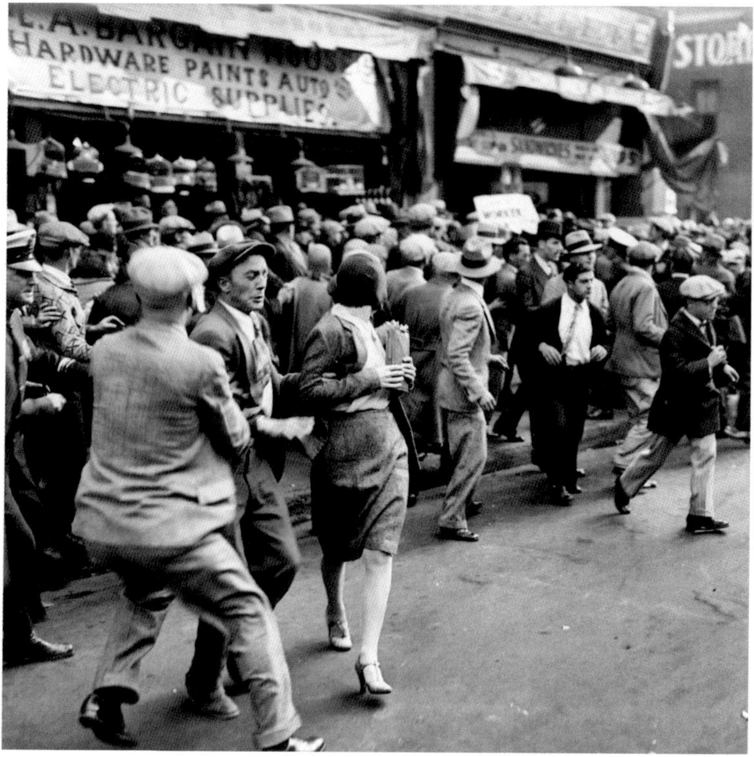

←

Anonymous

Officers of the Los Angeles Police Department, acting illegally as border-patrol agents to prevent undesirable and out-of-work migrants from entering the city, turn away men at the California border, 1936.

Beamte des Los Angeles Police Department im illegalen Einsatz als Grenzschützer. Um unerwünschte und arbeitslose Wanderarbeiter daran zu hindern, in die Stadt zu kommen, weisen die Polizisten Männer an der kalifornischen Grenze ab, 1936.

À la frontière de l'État californien, des agents du Los Angeles Police Department jouant illégalement le rôle de douaniers pour empêcher des immigrants indésirables et sans emploi de pénétrer dans la ville, font rebrousser chemin à des inconnus, 1936.

↑

Anonymous

Demonstrators downtown participate in the so-called "Red Riot," a protest led by communists against unemployment, 1930.

Demonstranten in Downtown bei der sogenannten Red Riot, einer von Kommunisten geführten Protestveranstaltung gegen Arbeitslosigkeit, 1930.

Manifestants dans le centre de Los Angeles lors de la « Red Riot », manifestation antichômage déclenchée par les communistes, 1930.

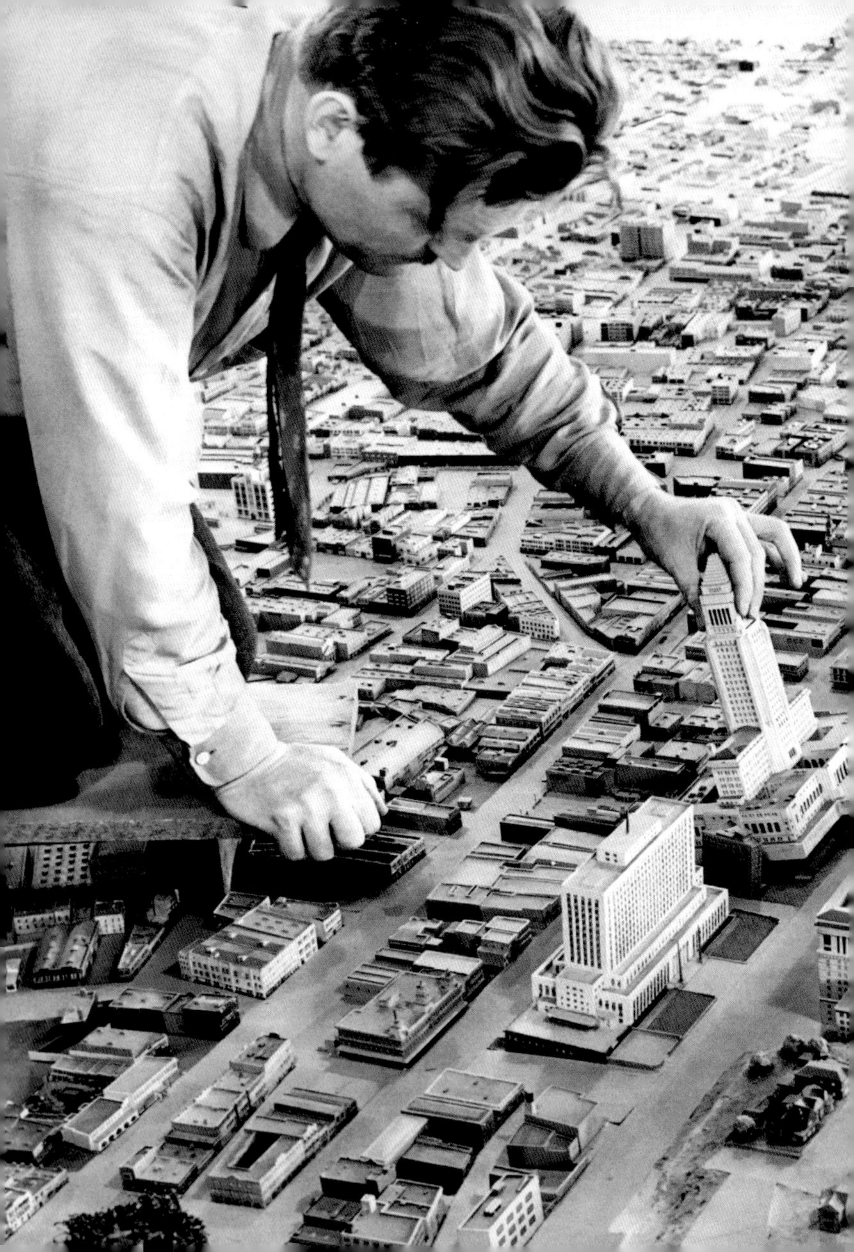

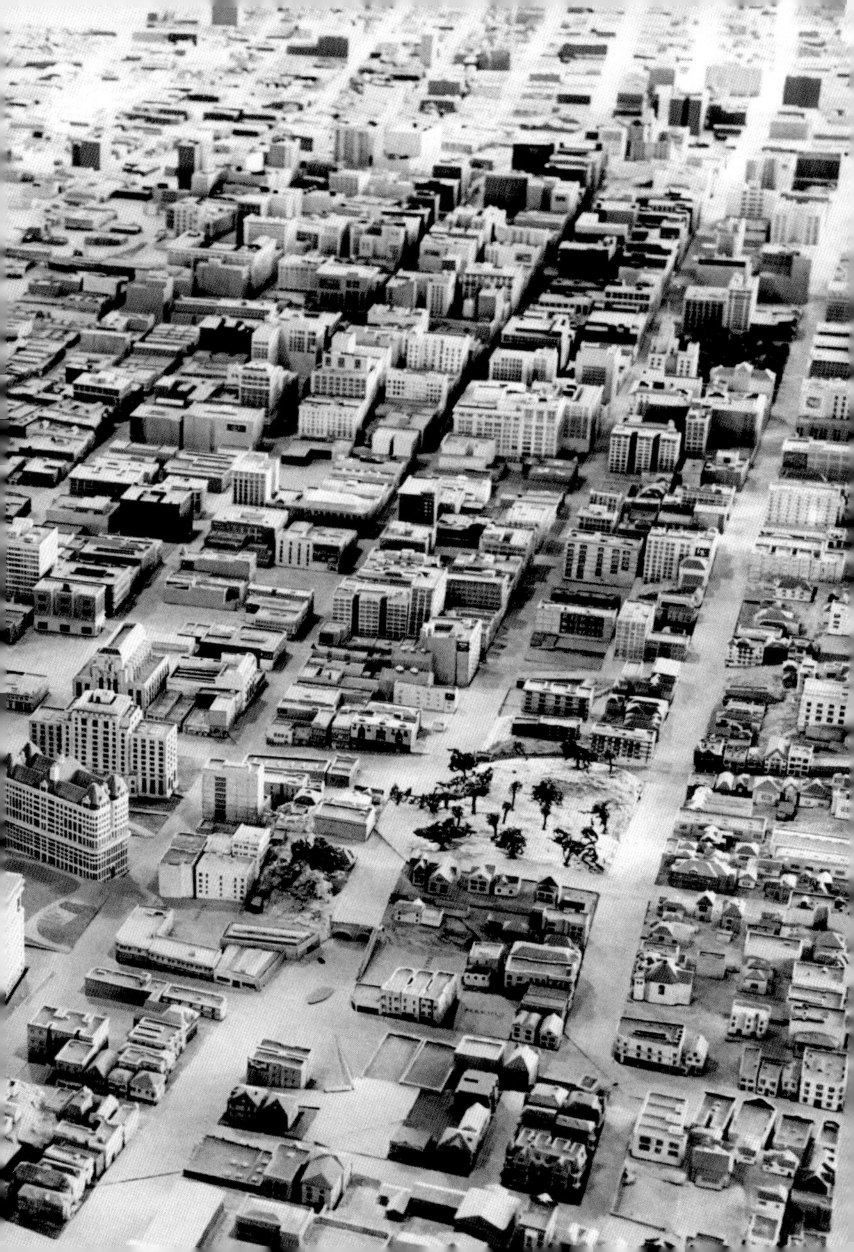

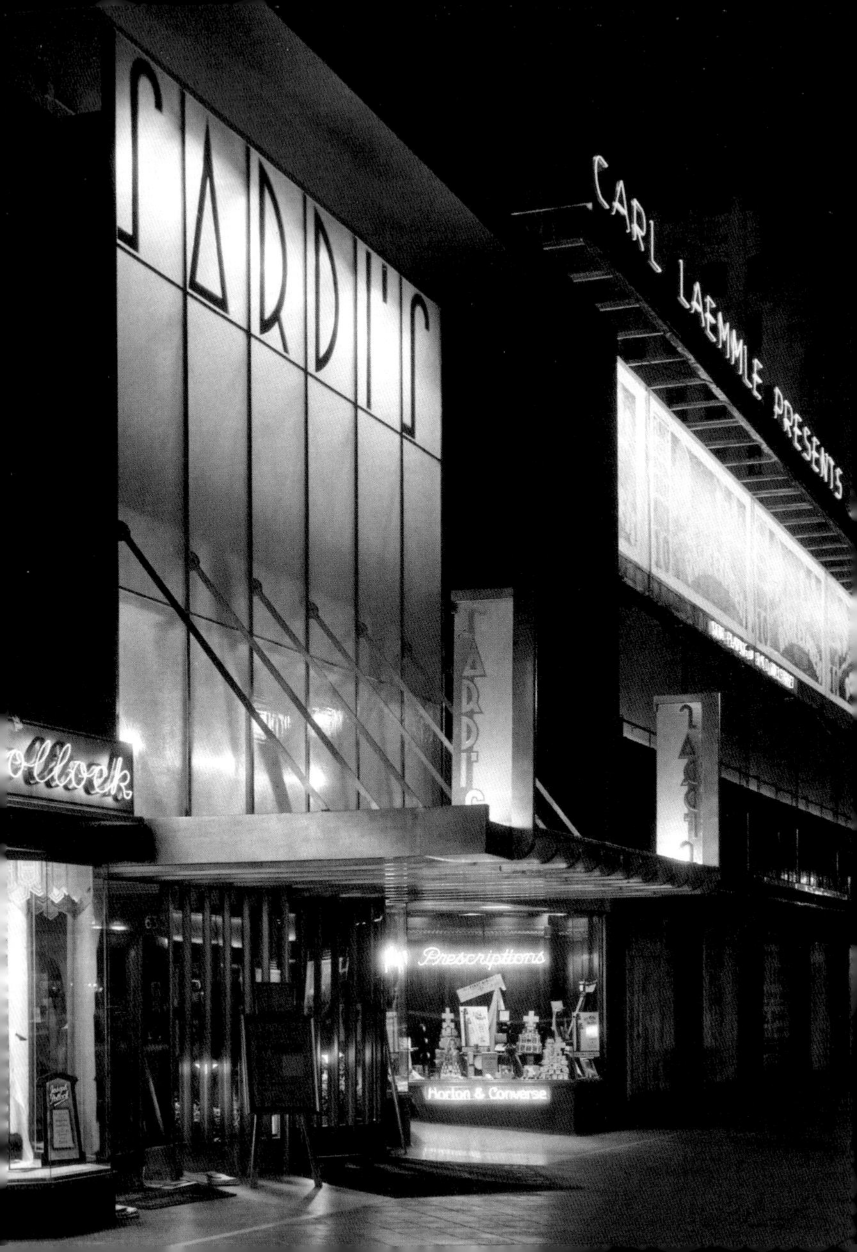
CARL LAEMMLE PRESENTS
Prescriptions
Horton & Converse

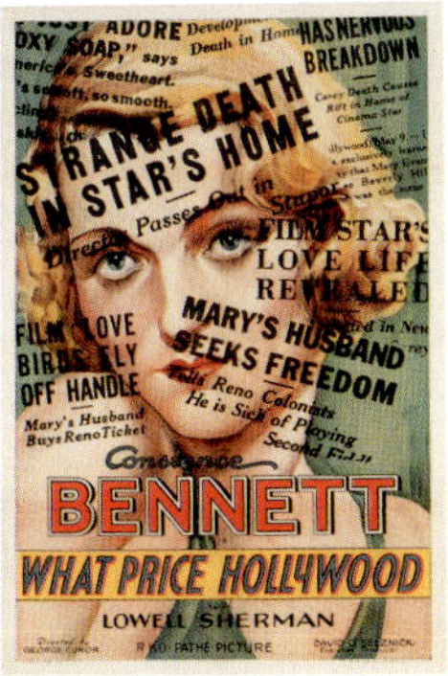

"Let me give you a tip about Hollywood. Always keep your sense of humor, then you can't miss."

„Lassen Sie mich Ihnen einen Rat für Hollywood geben. Bewahren Sie sich stets Ihren Sinn für Humor, dann können Sie nichts falsch machen."

« Laissez-moi vous donner un conseil à propos d'Hollywood. Gardez toujours votre sens de l'humour, ainsi vous ne pourrez pas vous tromper. »

***What Price Hollywood,* 1932**

p. 84/85

Anonymous

A minutely detailed model of downtown Los Angeles was a WPA project displayed at the Museum of Natural History, 1940.

Das bis ins Detail ausgearbeitete Modell von Downtown Los Angeles war ein Arbeitsbeschaffungsprojekt der WPA (Works Progress Administration) und wurde im Museum of Natural History ausgestellt, 1940.

Cette maquette minutieusement détaillée du centre-ville de Los Angeles, commanditée par la WPA (Works Progress Administration), fut exposée au Muséum d'histoire naturelle, 1940.

←

Mott Studios

Hollywood Boulevard, home to Sardi's, designed by Richard Neutra, and the neighboring Coco Tree Café, by Rudolf Schindler, c. 1936.

Das Café Sardi's von Richard Neutra am Hollywood Boulevard, unmittelbar neben Rudolph Schindlers Coco Tree Café, um 1936.

Conçu par Richard Neutra, le café Sardi, sur Hollywood Boulevard, était voisin du Coco Tree Café, dessiné par Rudolph Schindler, vers 1936.

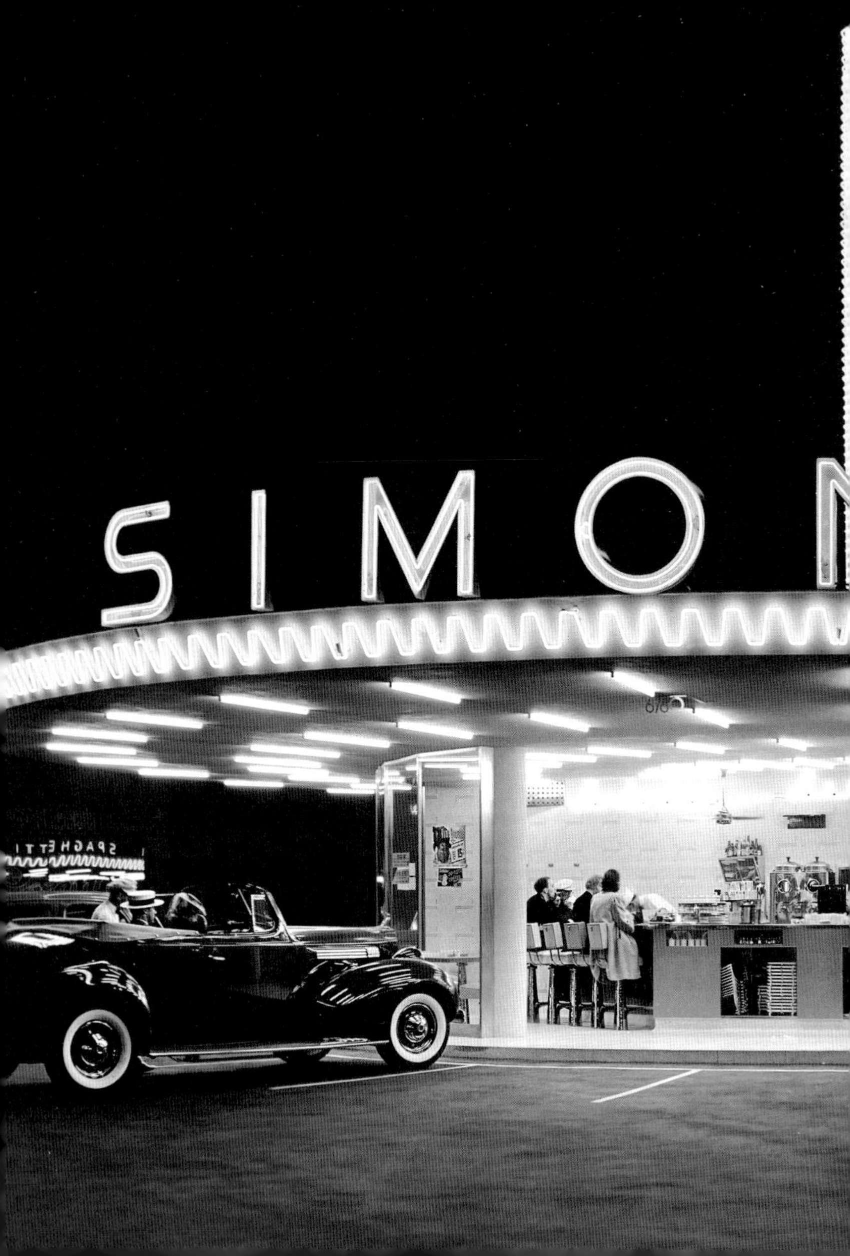
SIMON

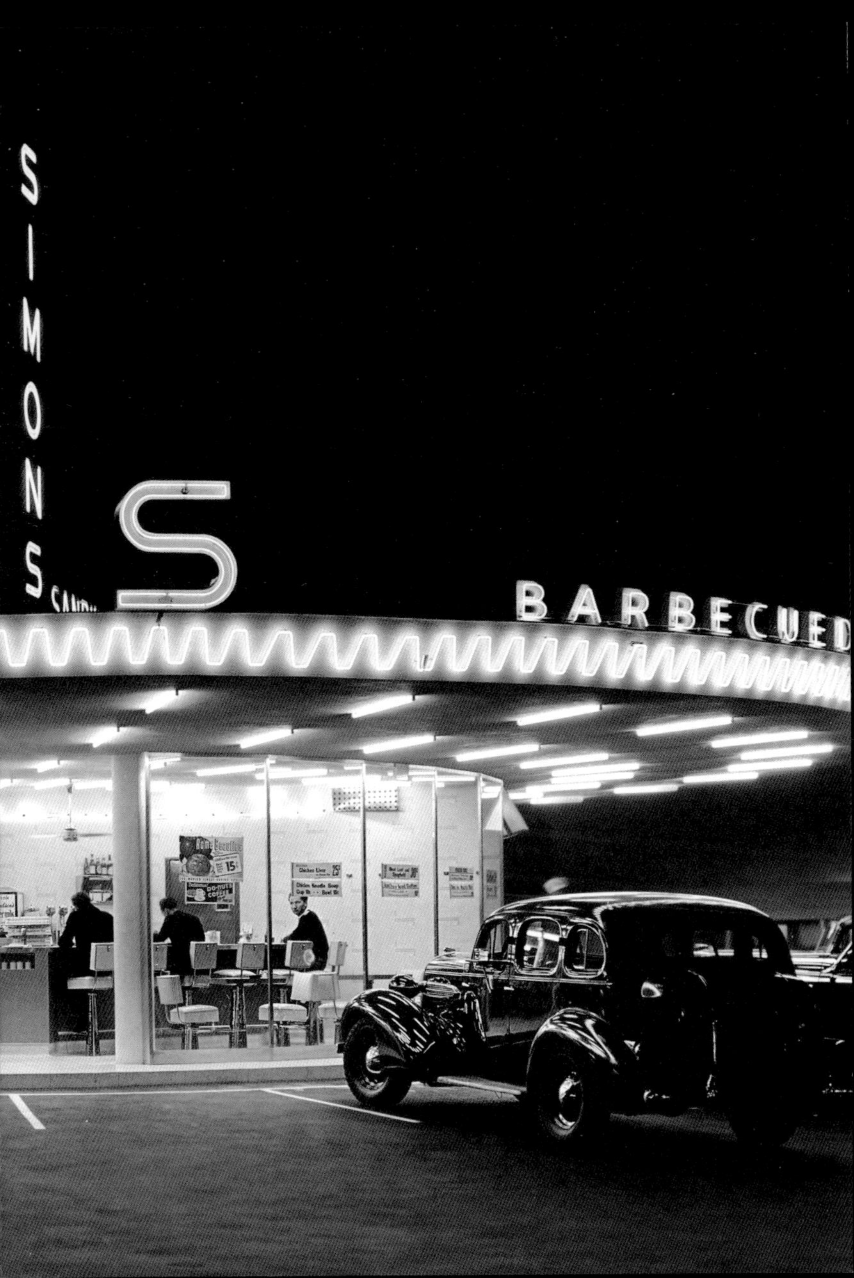
SIMONS
S
BARBECUED

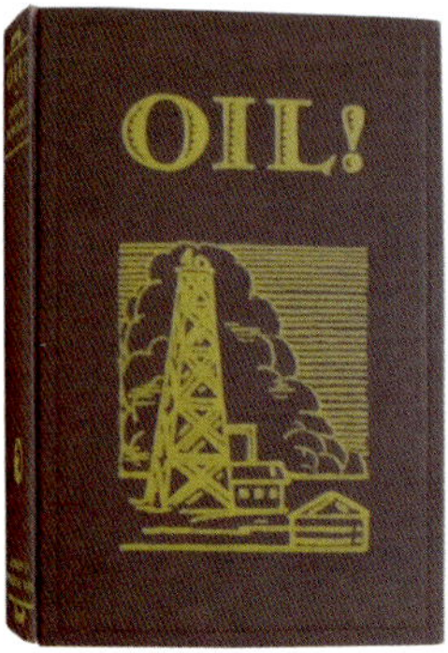

"By day you saw white puffs from the steam-engines, and by night you saw lights gleaming on the derricks, and day and night you heard the sound of heavy machinery turning, turning —'ump-um-ump-um-ump-um-ump-um.'"

„Tagsüber sah man die weißen Rauchwölkchen der Dampfmaschinen, nachts die funkelnden Lichter auf den Bohrtürmen, Tag und Nacht hörte man den Klang der sich drehenden, drehenden Maschinen – ‚amp-am-amp-am-amp-am-amp-am'."

« Dans la journée, on voyait des bouffées blanchâtres sortir des engins à vapeur, le soir, des lumières scintiller sur les derricks et, jour et nuit, on entendait le bruit des lourdes machineries qui tournaient, tournaient – "eump-heum-eump-heum-eump-heum-eump-heum". »

Upton Sinclair, *Oil!*, 1927

p. 88/89

Dick Whittington

Simon's drive-in, Wilshire Boulevard and Fairfax Avenue, c. 1939.

Das Drive-in-Restaurant Simon's, Ecke Wilshire Boulevard und Fairfax Avenue, um 1939.

Le drive-in Simon's, au coin de Wilshire Boulevard et de Fairfax Avenue, vers 1939.

→

John Swope

An oil derrick stands in the middle of La Cienega Boulevard, 1938.

Ein Bohrturm unmittelbar am La Cienega Boulevard, 1938.

Un derrick se dresse au milieu de La Cienega Boulevard, 1938.

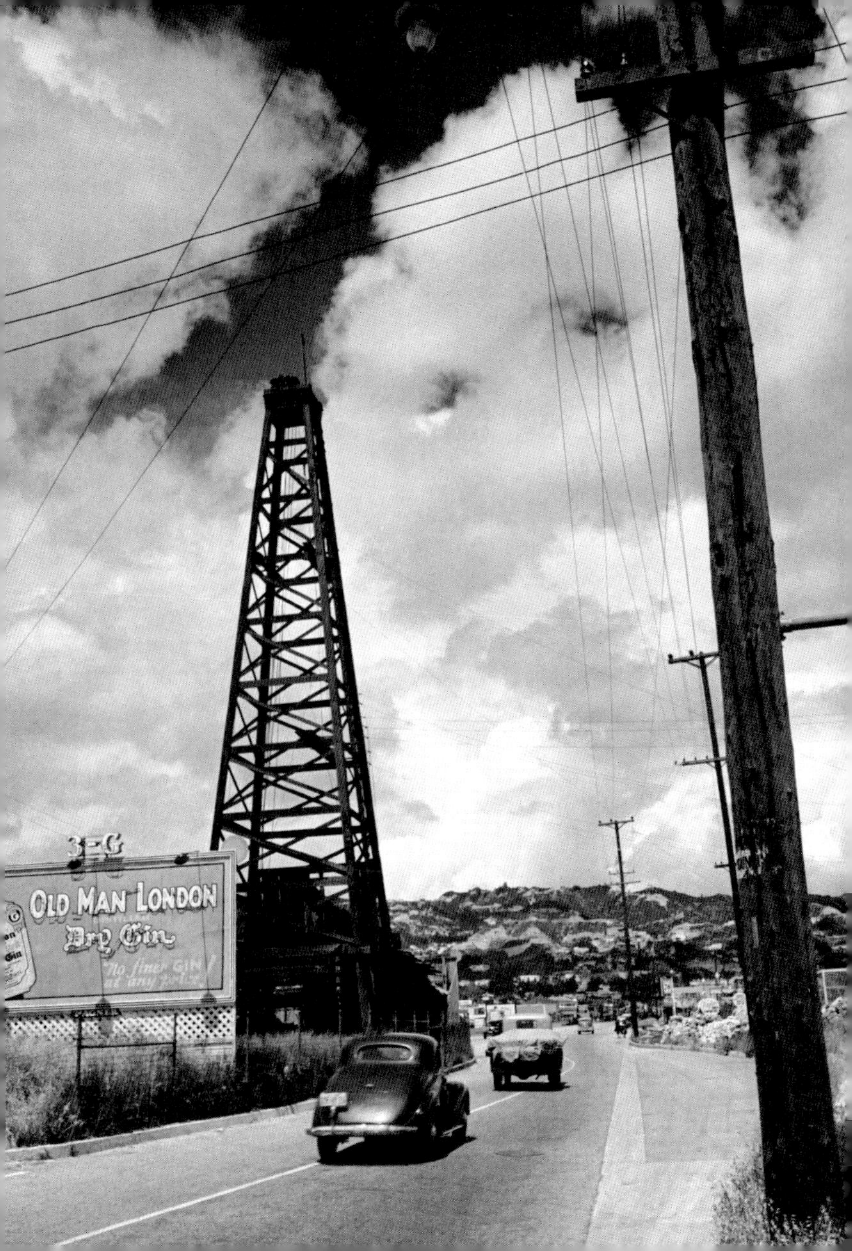
3-G
OLD MAN LONDON
Dry Gin
"No finer GIN!

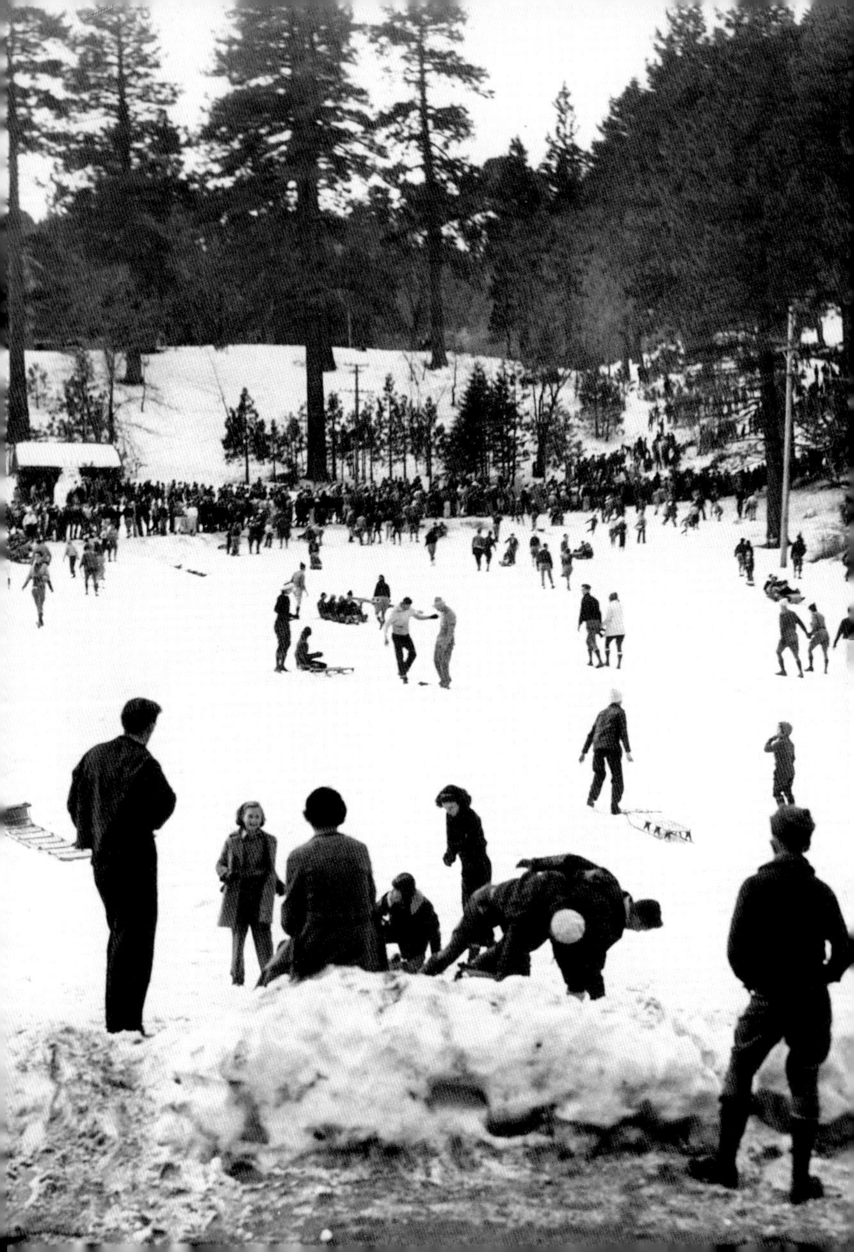

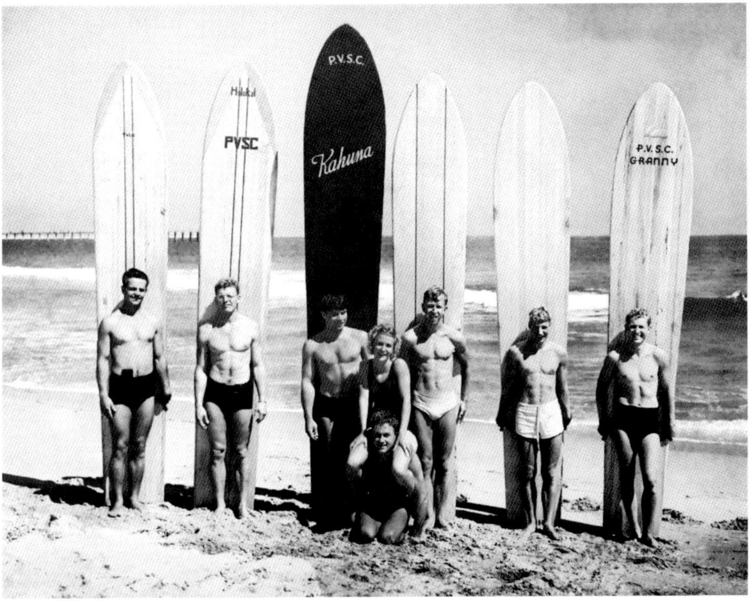

←

Anonymous

Tobogganers at Big Pines mountain camp, c. 1930. Although Southern California is mostly known for sun and surf, its mountains offer up a perfect venue for winter sports.

Schlittenfahrer in Big Pines, um 1930. Obwohl Südkalifornien in erster Linie für sein sonniges Klima und seine Strände bekannt ist, sind seine Berge hervorragend für Wintersport geeignet.

Lugeurs dans la station de Big Pines, vers 1930. Bien que la Californie du Sud soit surtout connue pour ses plages ensoleillées et ses surfeurs, ses montagnes sont parfaitement adaptées aux sports d'hiver.

↑

LeRoy Grannis

Surf culture, 1938. The members of the Palos Verdes Surf Club pose with their 12-foot longboards.

Surfkultur, 1938. Mitglieder des Palos Verdes Surf Club posieren mit ihren 3,6 Meter langen Longboards.

Culture surf, 1938. Les membres du club de surf Palos Verdes posent avec leurs planches de 3,60 m.

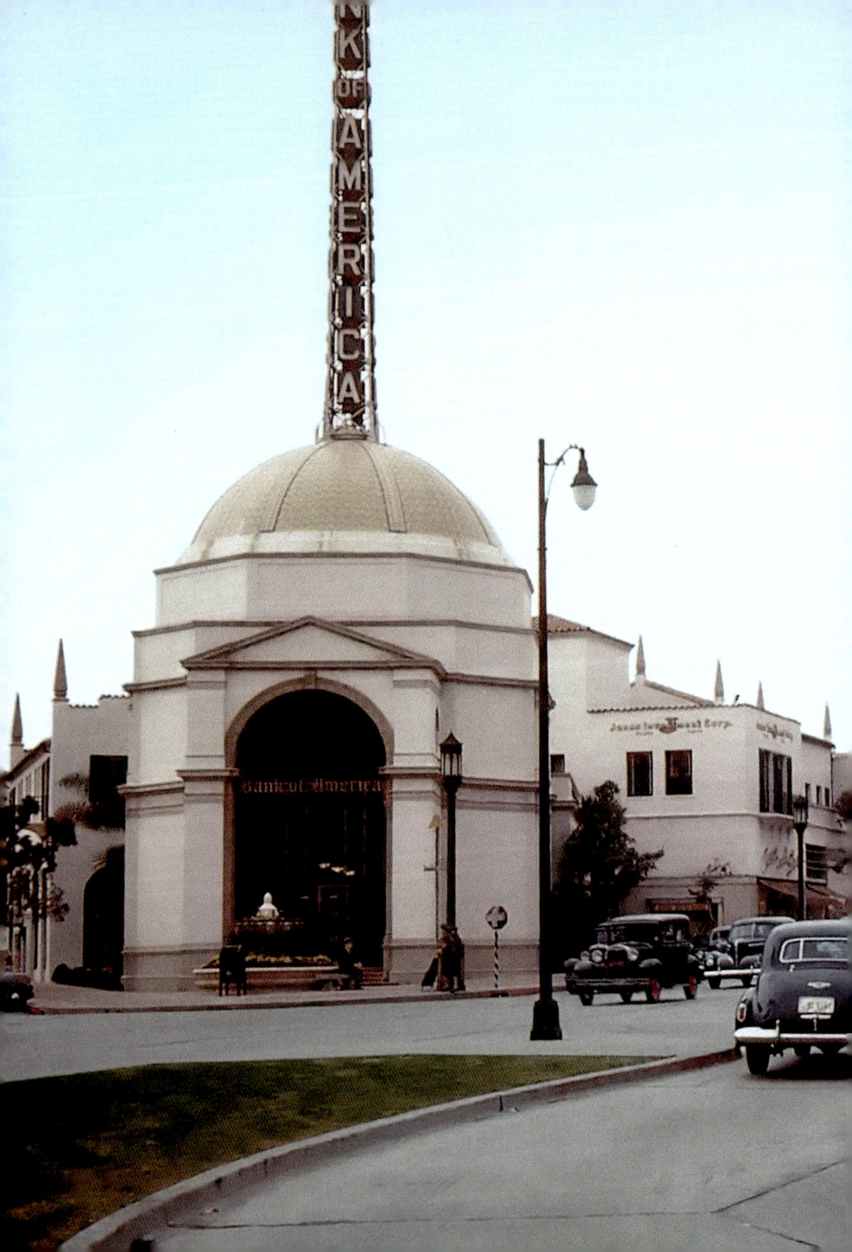
NK OF AMERICA
Bank of America

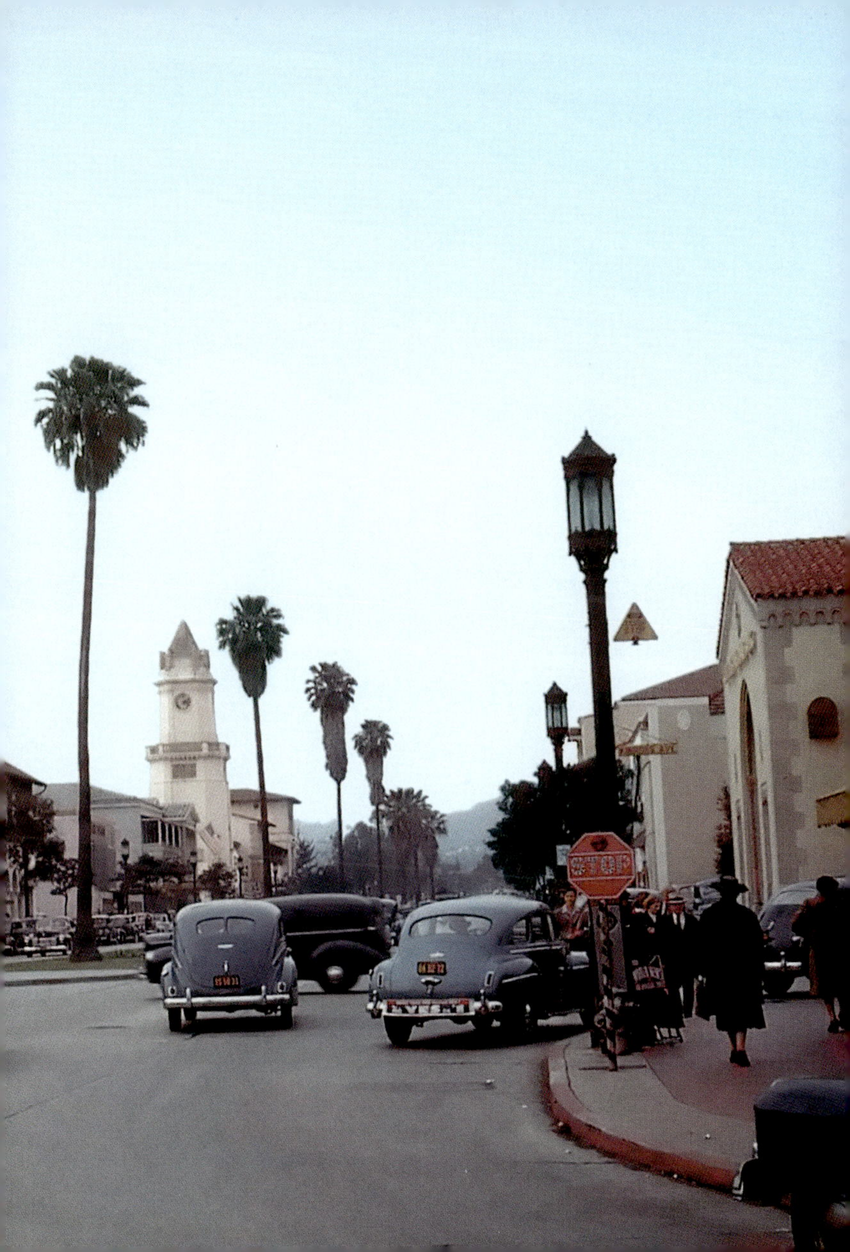
STOP

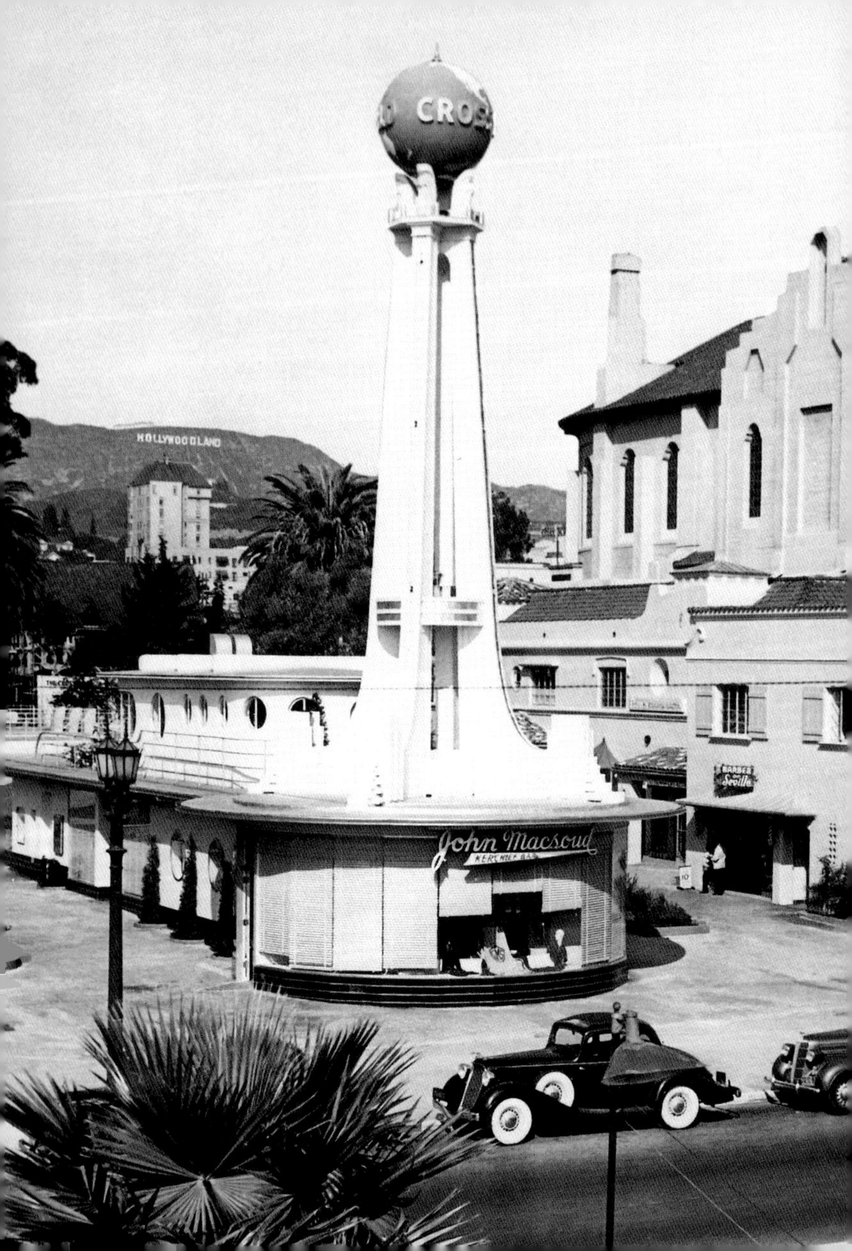
CROS
HOLLYWOODLAND
John Macsoud
Seville

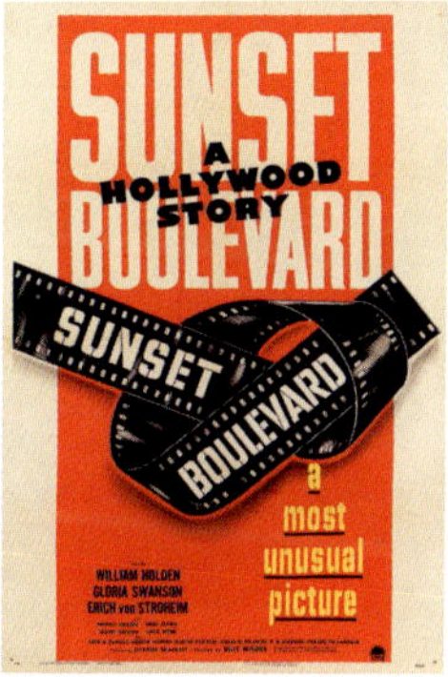

"You see, this is my life! It always will be! Nothing else! Just us, the cameras, and those wonderful people out there in the dark!…All right, Mr. DeMille, I'm ready for my close-up."

„Sehen Sie, das ist mein Leben! Das wird es immer sein! Nichts anderes! Nur wir, die Kameras und jene wunderbaren Menschen dort im Dunkeln!… Und jetzt, Mr. DeMille, bin ich bereit für meine Großaufnahme."

« Vous voyez, c'est ça ma vie ! Et pour toujours ! Rien d'autre ! Juste nous, les caméras, et ces gens merveilleux, là-bas dans le noir !… Ça y est, M. DeMille, je suis prête pour le gros plan… »

***Sunset Boulevard,* 1950**

p. 94/95
Anonymous
Westwood Village, 1941.

←
Anonymous
Crossroads of the World, Hollywood, 1937. The Streamline Moderne shopping complex, designed by Robert V. Derrah and built in 1936 on Sunset Boulevard, is now home to TASCHEN's Los Angeles office.

Das Crossroads of the World, Hollywood, 1937. Der 1936 im Stil der Streamline-Moderne am Sunset Boulevard erbaute Komplex war ein Entwurf von Robert V. Derrah und beherbergt heute TASCHENs Büro in Los Angeles.

Crossroads of the World, Hollywood, 1937. Ce complexe de style paquebot, dessiné par Robert V. Derrah, et édifié en 1936 sur Sunset Boulevard, comprend aujourd'hui le bureau de TASCHEN à Los Angeles.

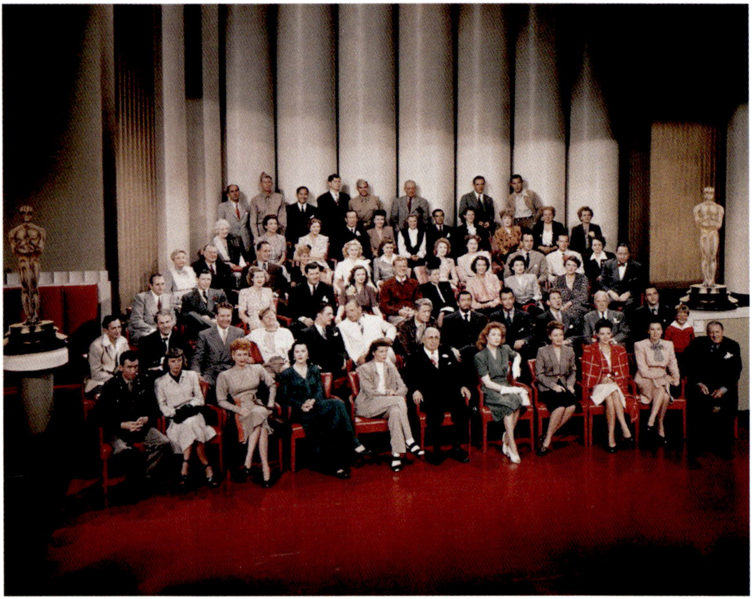

↑
Walter Sanders
MGM studio head Louis B. Mayer and stars sit for a photograph celebrating the studio's 20th anniversary, 1943.

MGM-Studiochef Louis B. Mayer und seine Stars posieren für eine Aufnahme zum 20. Jubiläum des Studios, 1943.

Le grand patron de la MGM, Louis B. Mayer pose avec ses stars pour une photographie célébrant le 20e anniversaire du studio, 1943.

→
Walter Sanders
Tanner the lion performs the MGM trademark roar, 1943. Tanner was the third lion to serve as the studio's mascot, "Leo the Lion," a role he held from 1934 to 1956.

Tanner, der Löwe, präsentiert sein Brüllen, das MGM-Markenzeichen. Tanner war der dritte Löwe, der als Studiomaskottchen „Leo, der Löwe" diente, eine Rolle, die er von 1934 bis 1956 spielte.

Le célèbre rugissement du lion Tanner, emblème de la MGM, 1943. Tanner fut le troisième lion à servir de mascotte au studio sous le nom de « Leo, le Lion », rôle qu'il tint de 1934 à 1956.

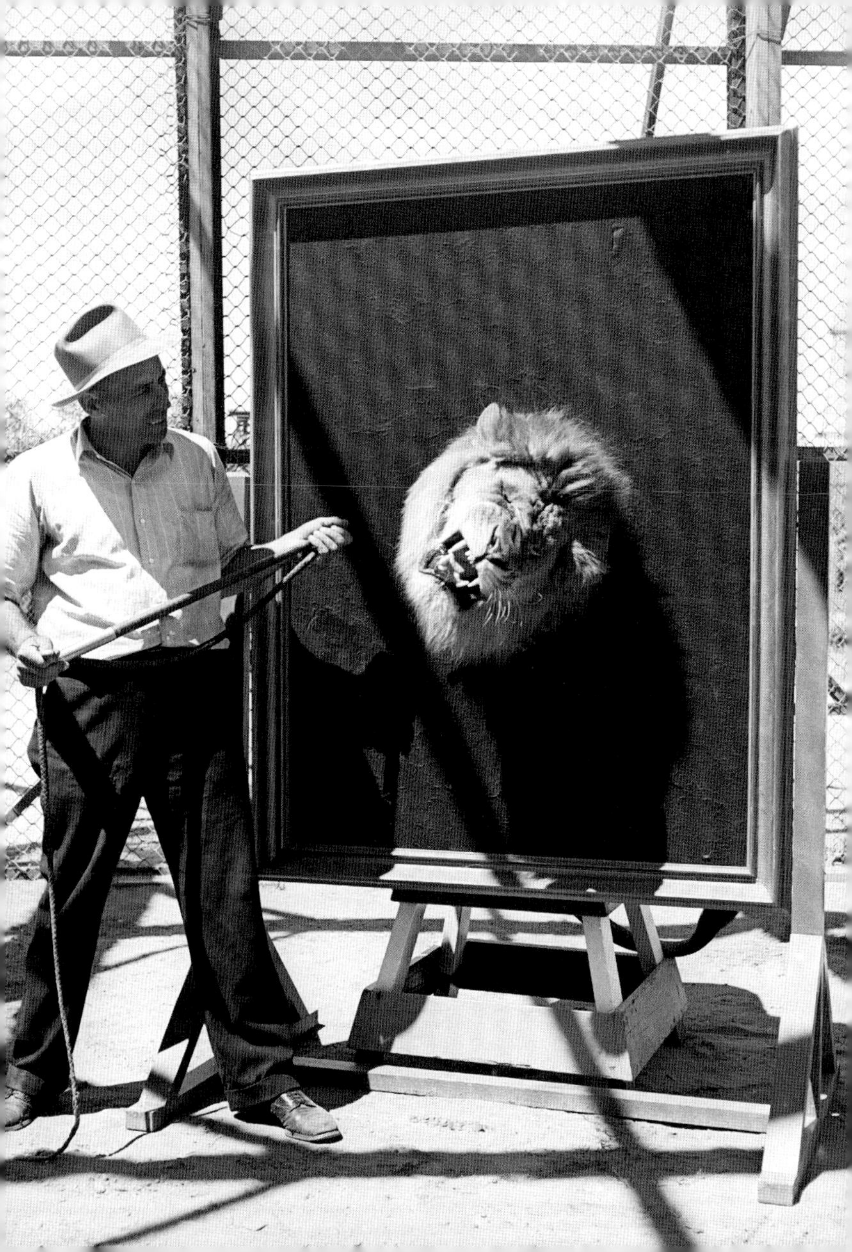

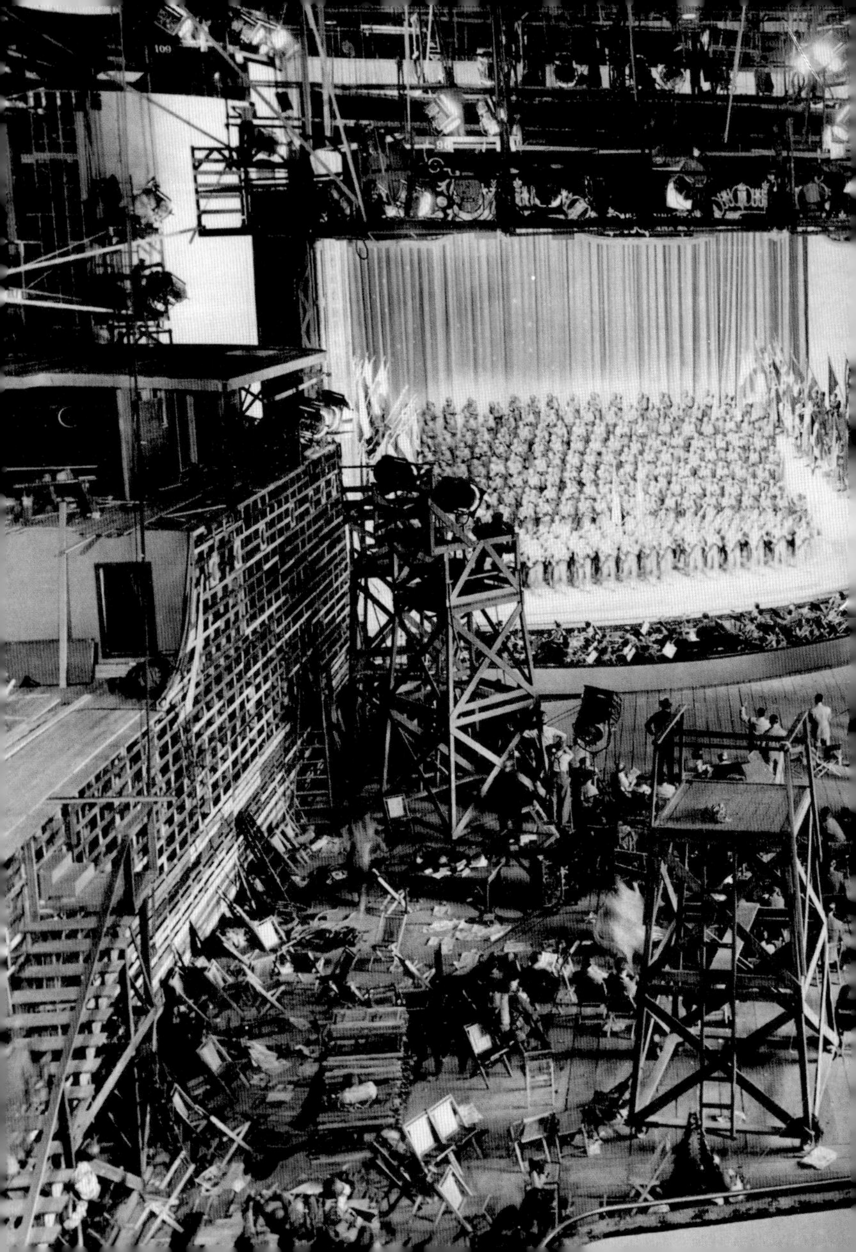

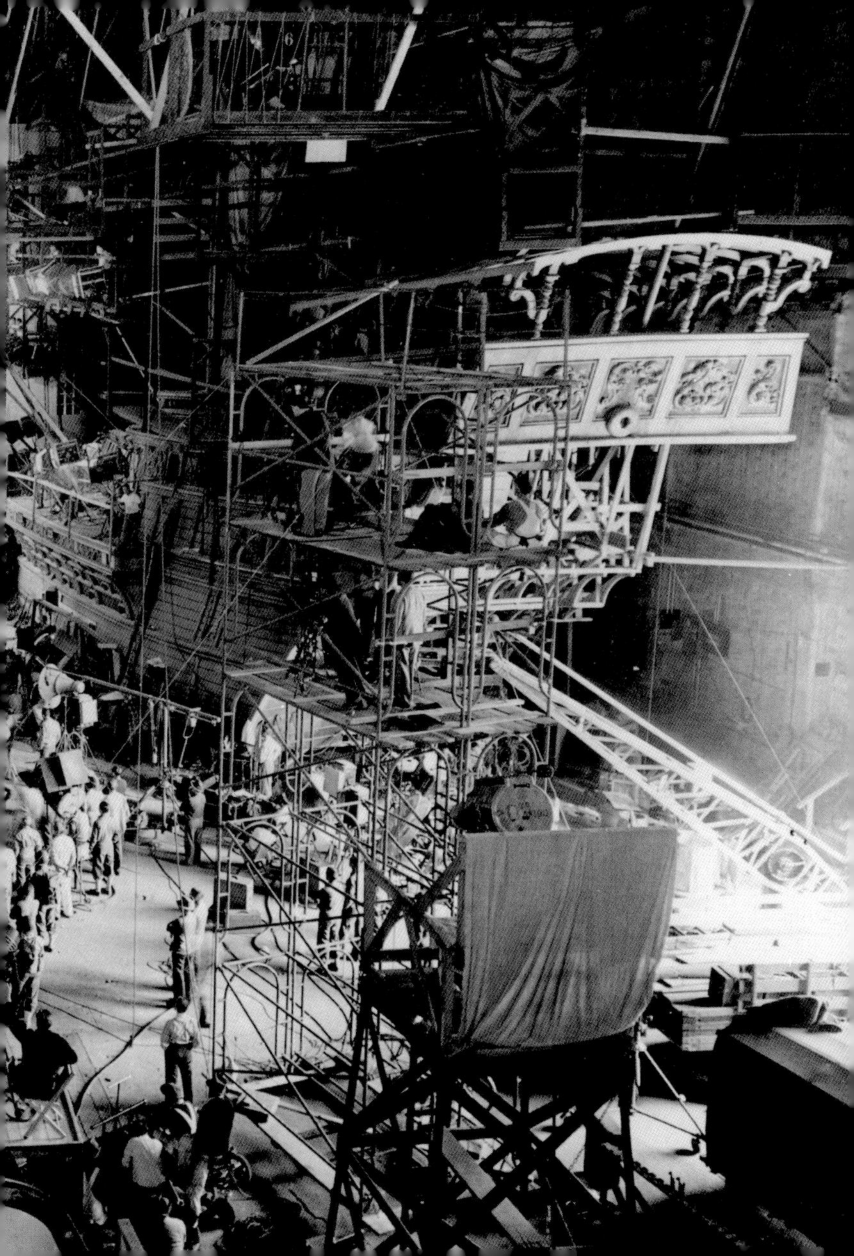

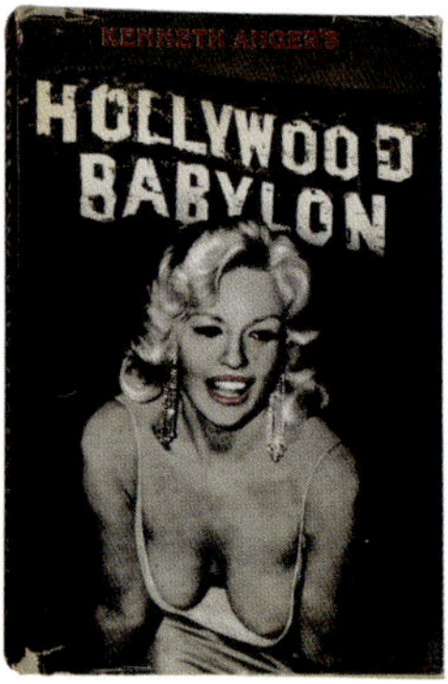

"The fans worshipped, but the fans also could be fickle, and if their deities proved to have feet of clay, they could be cut down without compassion."

„Die Fans verehrten ihre Stars, doch sie konnten auch launisch sein; wenn sich zeigte, dass ihre Gottheiten auf tönernen Füßen standen, stürzten sie sie durchaus ohne jedes Mitleid."

« Les fans idolâtraient, mais les fans pouvaient aussi se montrer inconstants, et, si leurs divinités avaient des pieds d'argile, elles pouvaient être jetées à terre sans compassion. »

Kenneth Anger, *Hollywood Babylon,* 1965

p. 100/101
Anonymous
A set for the movie This Is the Army, *in full production mode, with director, cast, and crew, c. 1942.*

Ein Filmset für die Produktion von This Is the Army *in vollem Betrieb, samt Regisseur, Schauspielern und Filmcrew, um 1942.*

Un décor du film This Is the Army *avec l'équipe de tournage au grand complet, le réalisateur, les acteurs et les techniciens, vers 1942.*

→
John Swope
The famous gates of Paramount Pictures, Hollywood, 1939.

Das berühmte Eingangstor von Paramount Pictures, Hollywood, 1939.

Le célèbre portail de la Paramount, Hollywood, 1939.

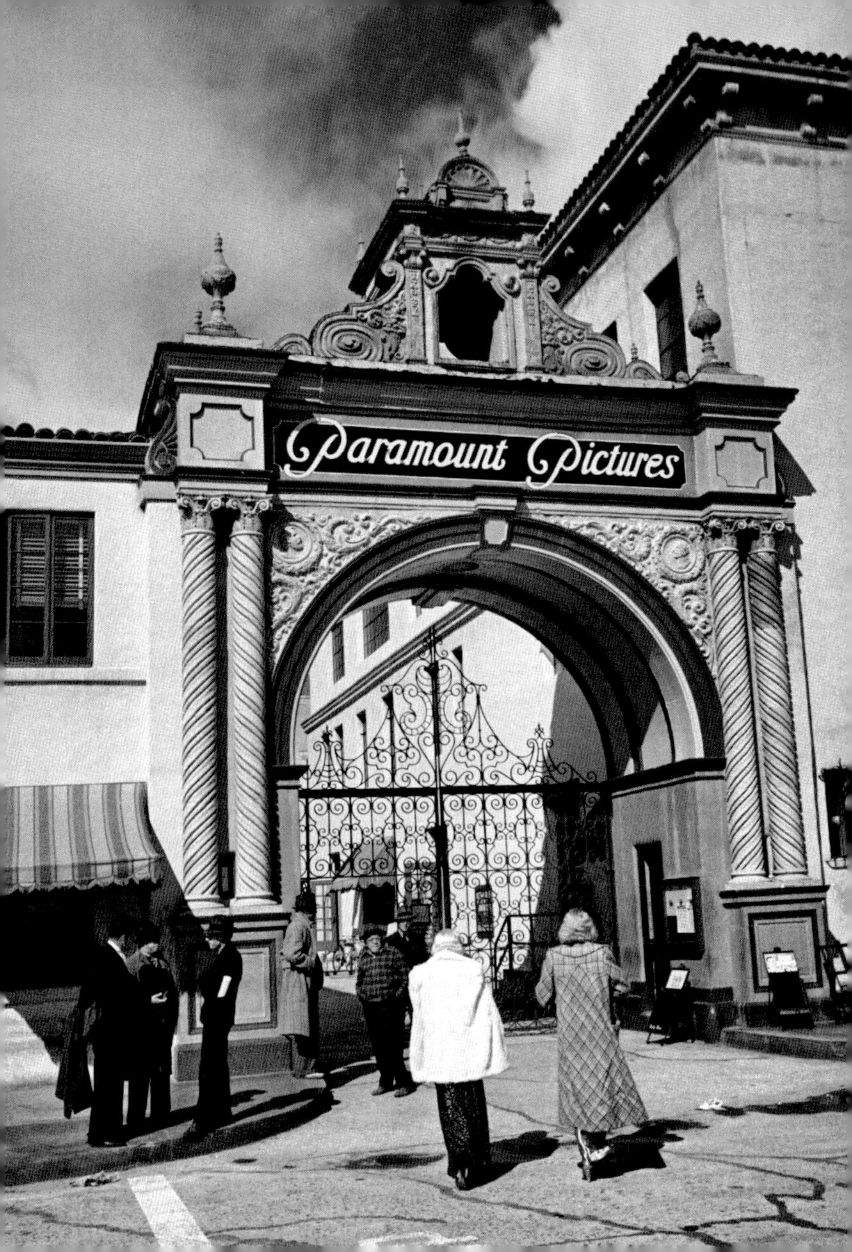
Paramount Pictures

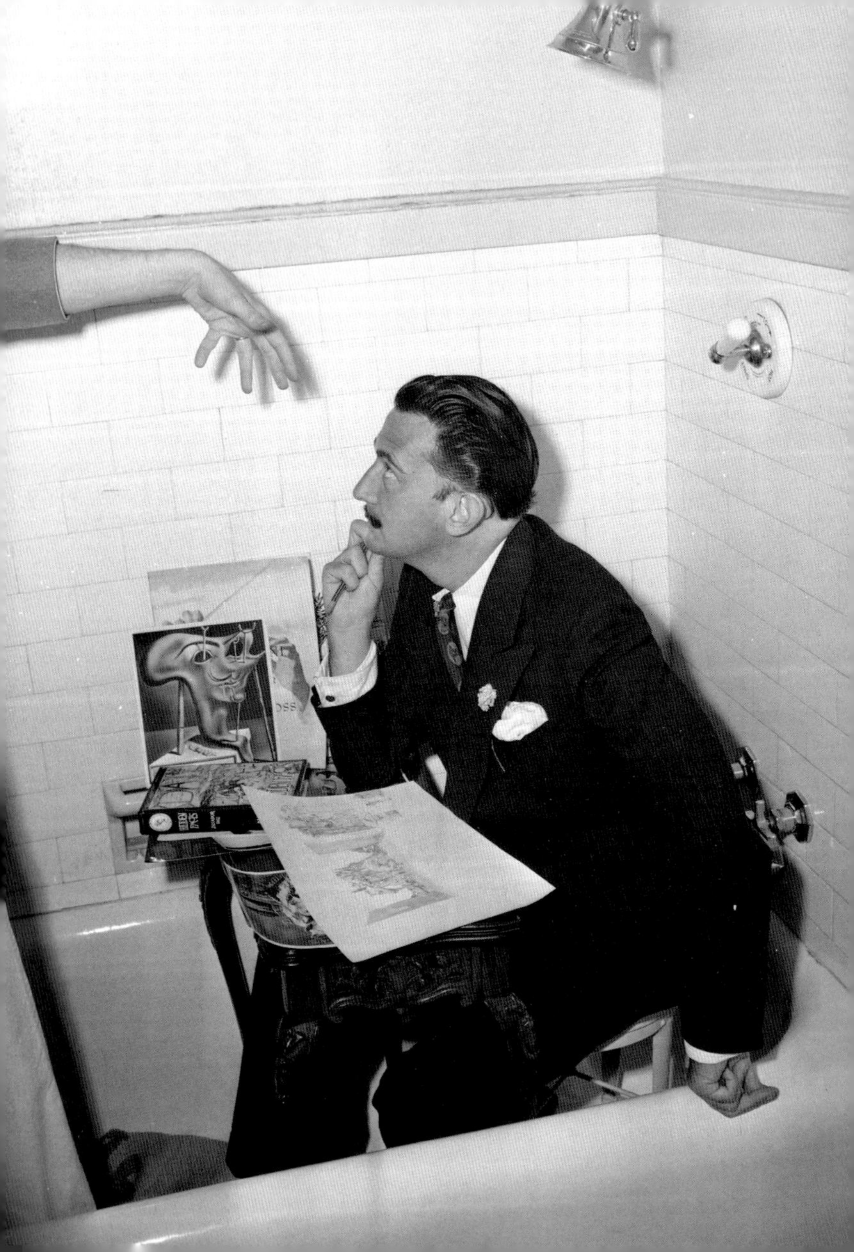

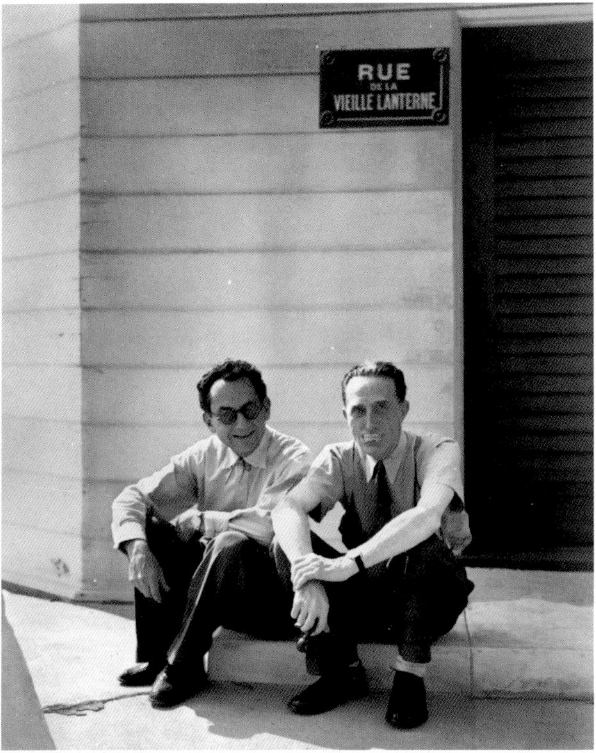

←
Anonymous
Salvador Dalí draws in the bath, the Ambassador Hotel, c. 1944.

Salvador Dalí zeichnet in der Badewanne, Ambassador Hotel, um 1944.

Salvador Dalí dessinant dans une baignoire, hôtel Ambassador, vers 1944.

↑
Anonymous
Surrealists in Hollywood. Man Ray and Marcel Duchamp at a studio back lot, c. 1945.

Surrealisten in Hollywood. Man Ray und Marcel Duchamp hinter einem Studio, um 1945.

Les surréalistes à Hollywood. Man Ray et Marcel Duchamp dans les coulisses d'un studio, vers 1945.

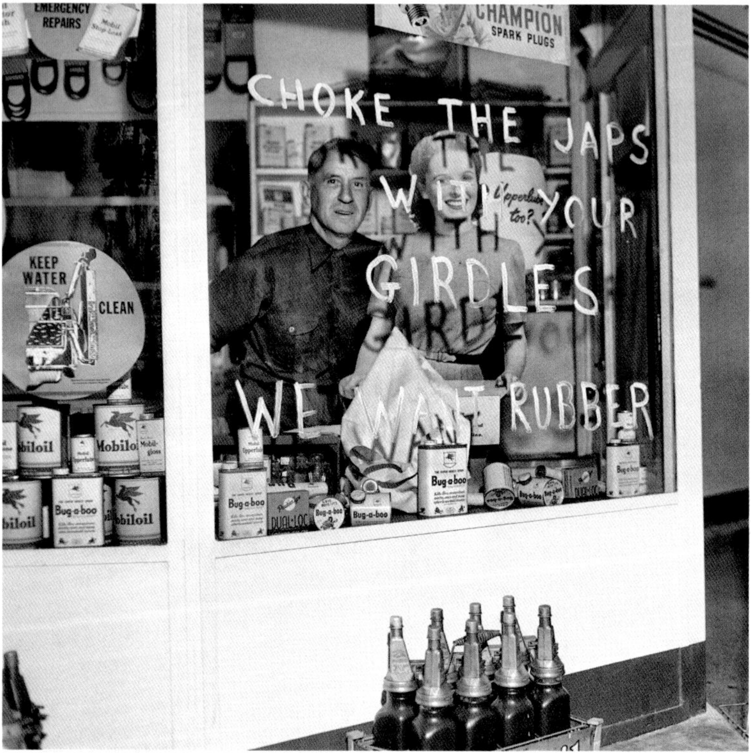

↑
Anonymous
A Los Angeles gas station makes a loaded plea for rubber, 1942. Casual racism in support of the war effort was common.

Eine Tankstelle in Los Angeles ruft auf drastische Weise zum Spenden von Gummi auf, 1942. Im Zuge der Kriegsvorbereitungen war alltäglicher Rassismus, wie hier gegen die Japaner, weit verbreitet.

Une station-service de Los Angeles appelle les citoyens à recycler leur caoutchouc, 1942. Les propos racistes (ici, anti-Japonais) en soutien à l'effort de guerre étaient courants.

→
Alfred T. Palmer
Lunchtime for "Rosie the Riveter," 1942.

Mittagspause für „Rosie the Riveter", so der Spitzname für Arbeiterinnen in der Rüstungsindustrie, 1942.

L'heure du déjeuner pour « Rosie, la riveteuse », 1942.

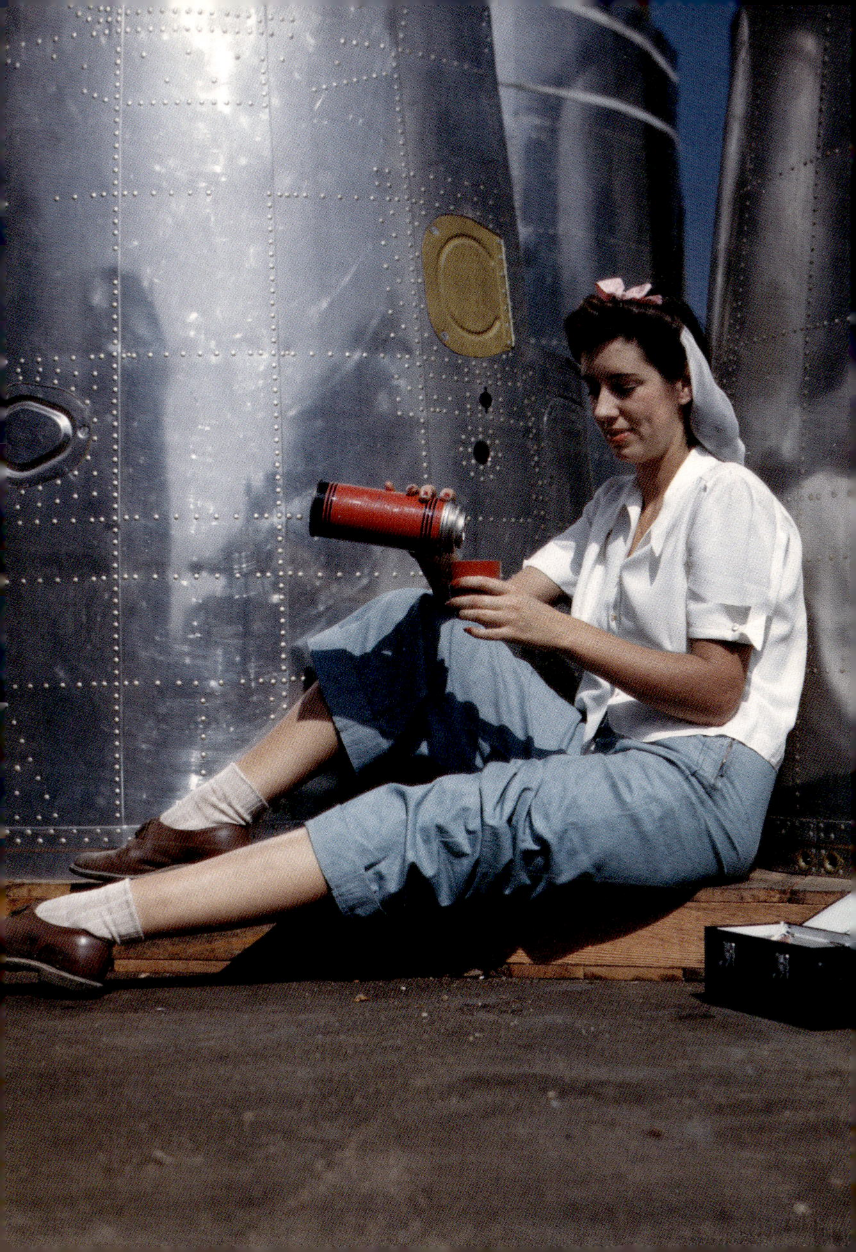

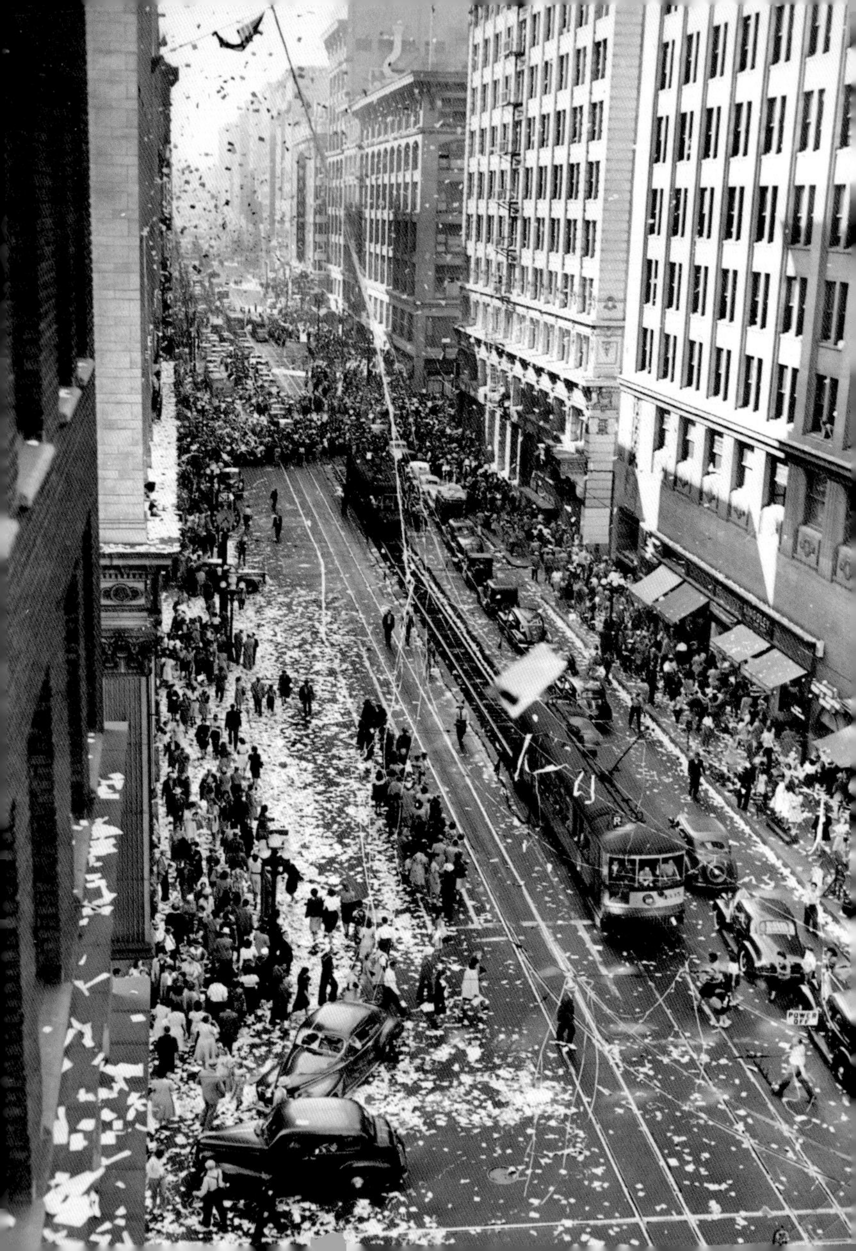
POWER OFF

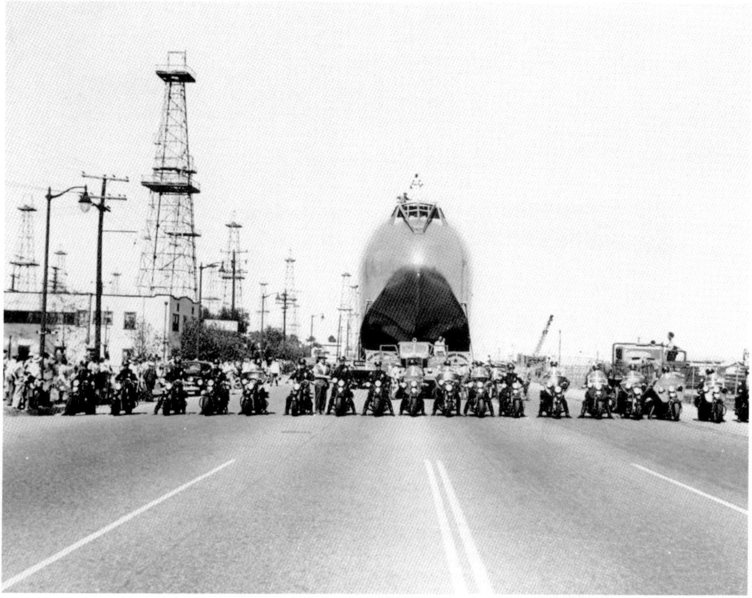

←

Anonymous

Los Angeles celebrates V-J Day and the end of World War II, Sixth Street, August 15, 1945.

Los Angeles feiert den V-J Day (den Sieg über Japan) und das Ende des Zweiten Weltkriegs, Sixth Street, 15. August 1945.

Los Angeles célèbre le V-J Day et la fin de la Seconde Guerre mondiale, sur la 6ᵉ Rue, le 15 août 1945.

↑

Anonymous

Accompanied by a phalanx of police officers, Howard Hughes's experimental flying boat, derisively dubbed the "Spruce Goose," is transported to Long Beach Harbor, where it flew only once, for a single minute, 1947.

Das spöttisch „Schmucke Gans" genannte experimentelle Flugschiff von Howard Hughes wird zum Hafen von Long Beach transportiert und von einer Phalanx von Polizisten begleitet. Es flog dort nur ein einziges Mal – eine ganze Minute lang, 1947.

Accompagné d'une imposante escorte policière, le bateau volant expérimental d'Howard Hughes, surnommé par dérision l'« oie pimpante », est acheminé jusqu'au port de Long Beach où il ne volera qu'une fois, pendant une seule minute, 1947.

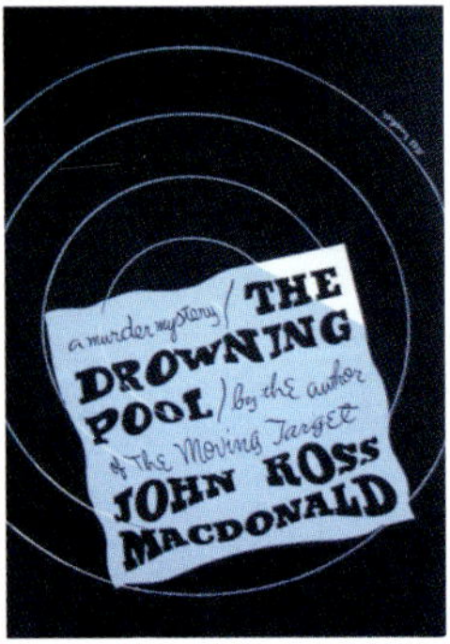

"I stopped at a lunch-bar…and watched the sidewalk roamers. The young hep-cats high on music or weed, the middle-aged men on the town, the tourists waiting for something to fulfill their fantasies…"

„Ich setzte mich in eine Lunchbar…und sah den Menschen auf den Gehwegen zu. Den jungen Hipstern, high von Musik oder Gras, den Männern mittleren Alters, unterwegs in der Stadt, den Touristen, die darauf warteten, dass etwas ihre Träume erfüllte …"

«Je me suis arrêté dans un snack… et j'ai regardé les badauds sur le trottoir. Les jeunes "musicos" défoncés à la musique ou à l'herbe, les hommes mûrs de la ville, les touristes attendant quelque chose qui viendrait combler leurs attentes…»

Ross MacDonald, *The Drowning Pool,* 1950

→
Max Yavno
The city's pop-architecture tradition continued after World War II with this surrealistic rotating leg, which advertised the Sanderson hosiery company in West Los Angeles, 1949.

Auch nach dem Zweiten Weltkrieg setzte sich die Tradition der Pop-architektur in der Stadt fort, etwa mit diesem surrealen, rotierenden Bein, das in West Los Angeles für die Strumpfwaren von Sanderson warb, 1949.

La tradition d'architecture « pop » de la ville continua après la Seconde Guerre mondiale, comme le montre cette jambe pivotante surréaliste, accessoire publicitaire pour le fabricant de bas et chaussettes Sanderson, situé à West Los Angeles, 1949.

p. 112/113
Ralph Crane
Crowds pack the ballroom floor of the Palladium, Hollywood, 1946.

Dichtes Gedränge auf der Tanzfläche im Ballsaal des Palladium, Hollywood, 1946.

Une foule compacte remplit la salle de bal du Palladium, Hollywood, 1946.

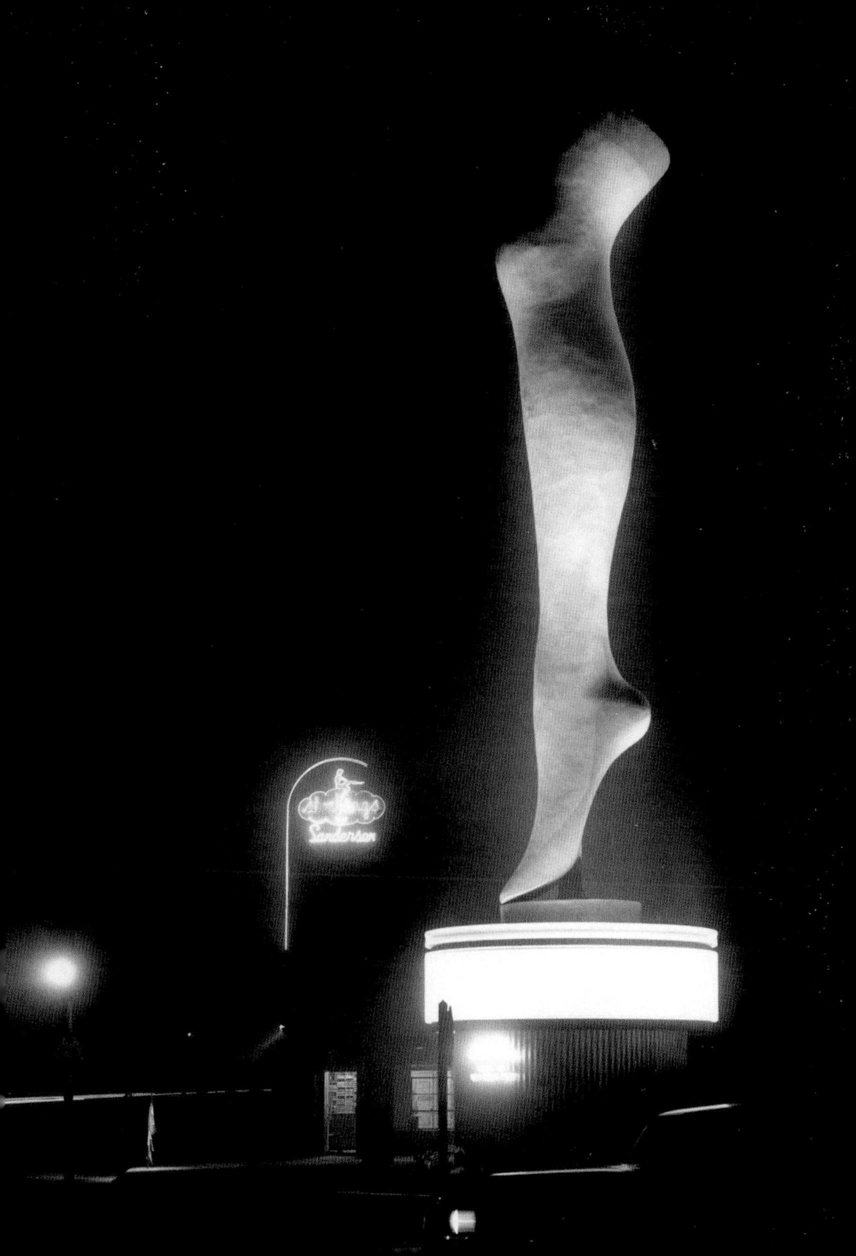
Sanderson

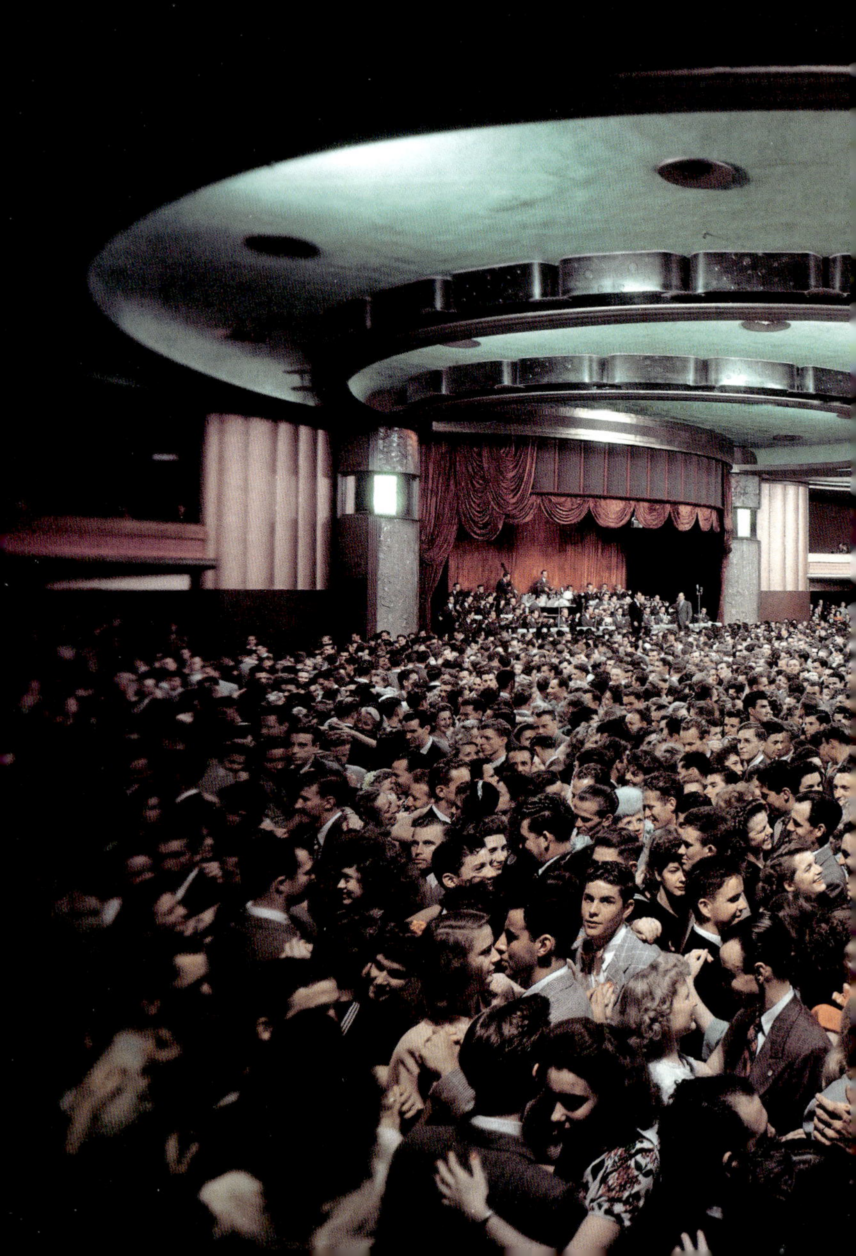

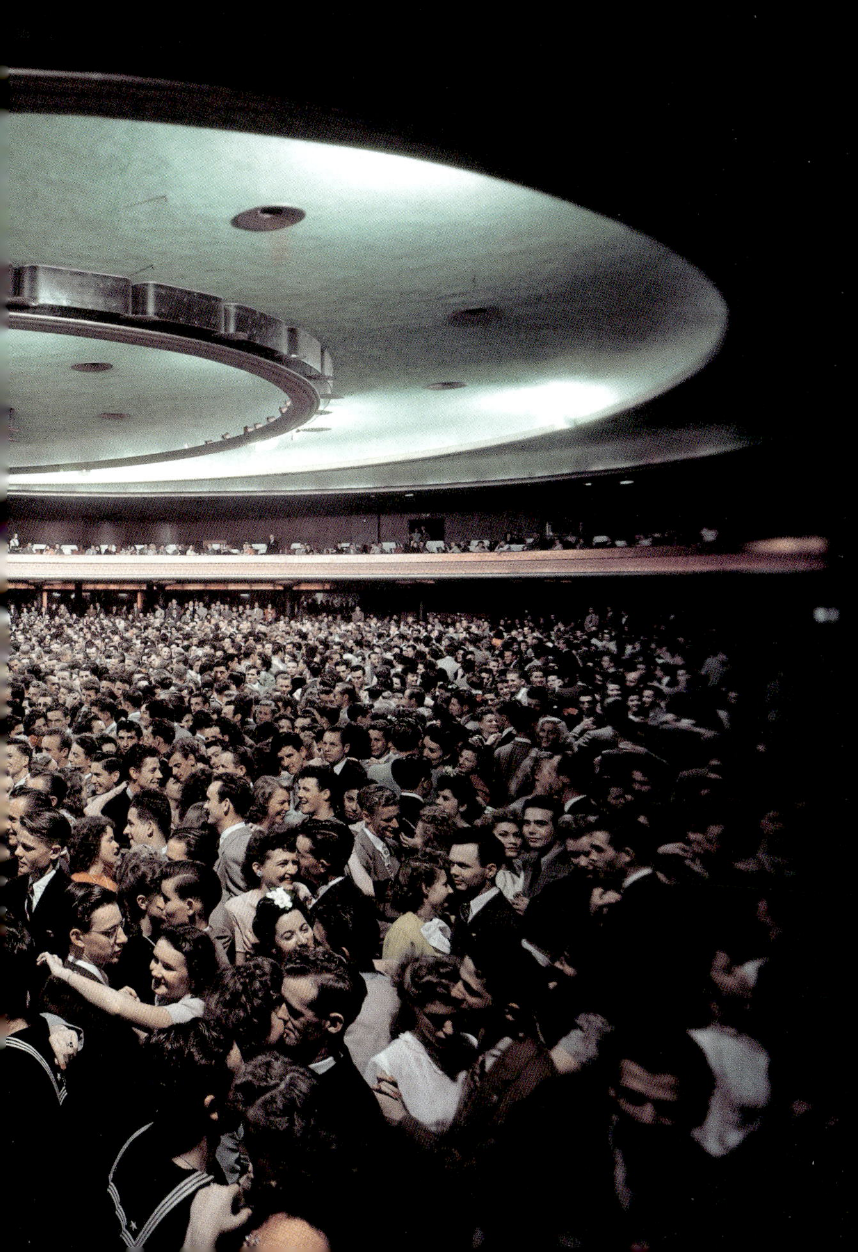

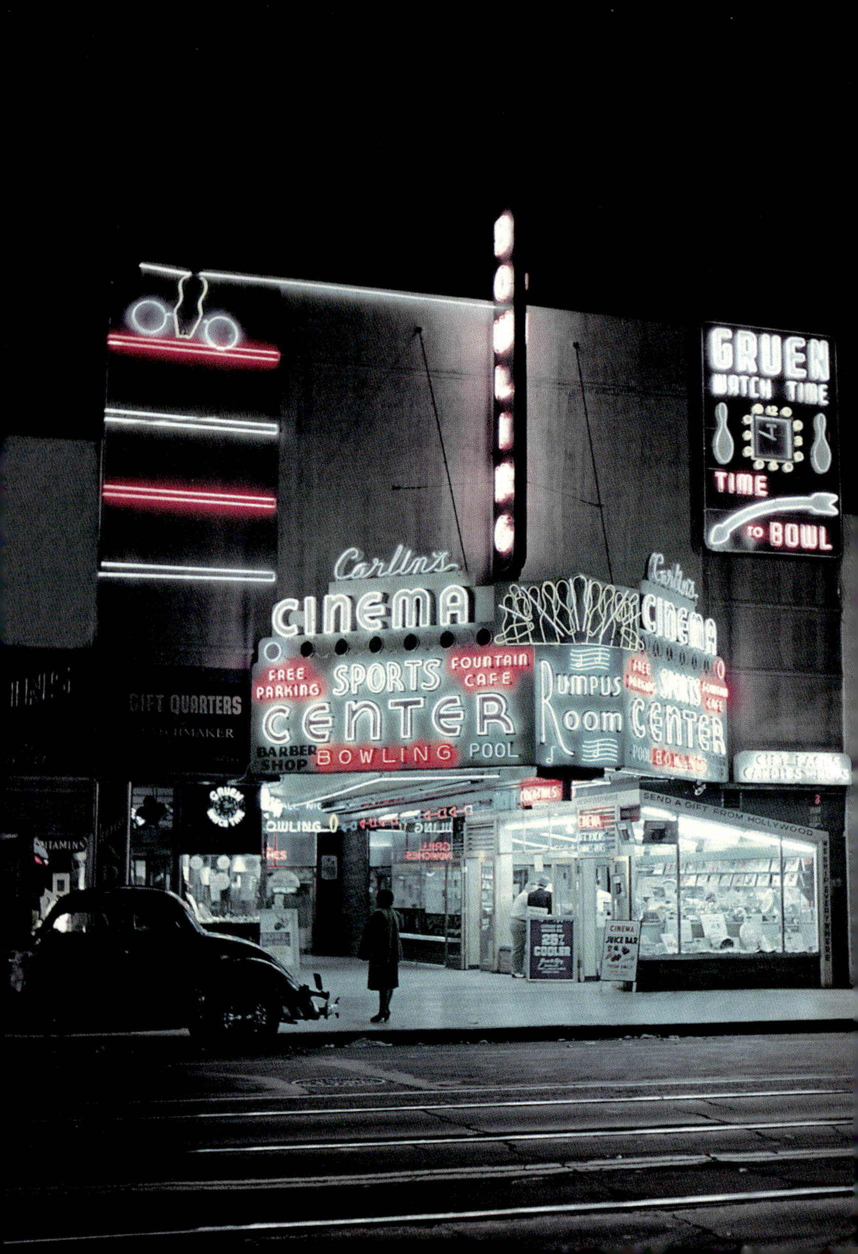

Carlin's
CINEMA
FREE PARKING
SPORTS
FOUNTAIN CAFE
CENTER
BARBER SHOP
BOWLING
POOL
Rumpus Room
GRUEN
WATCH TIME
TIME
TO BOWL
GIFT QUARTERS
SEND A GIFT FROM HOLLYWOOD
VITAMINS
CINEMA
JUICE BAR
25¢ COOLER

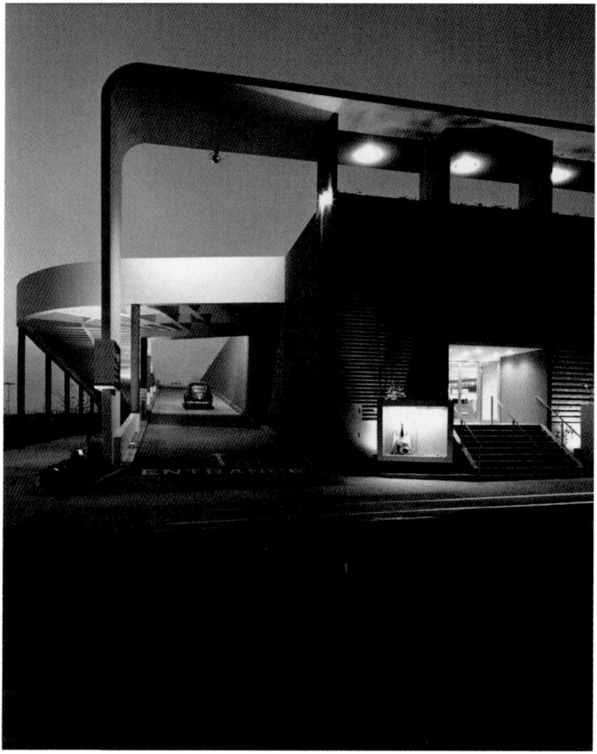

←

Richard C. Miller

The neon facade of an entertainment multiplex lights up Hollywood Boulevard, c. 1950.

Die Leuchtreklame an der Fassade eines Vergnügungskomplexes taucht den Hollywood Boulevard in Neonlicht, um 1950.

La façade aux enseignes lumineuses d'un multiplexe illumine Hollywood Boulevard, vers 1950.

↑

Julius Shulman

The graceful ramps of the Milliron's department store, in the community of Westchester, led cars up to rooftop parking, 1949.

Über elegante Rampen konnten Autos auf den Dachparkplatz des Milliron-Kaufhauses in Westchester fahren, 1949.

Les rampes élégantes du grand magasin Milliron, dans le quartier de Westchester, menaient les voitures jusqu'au parking situé sur le toit, 1949.

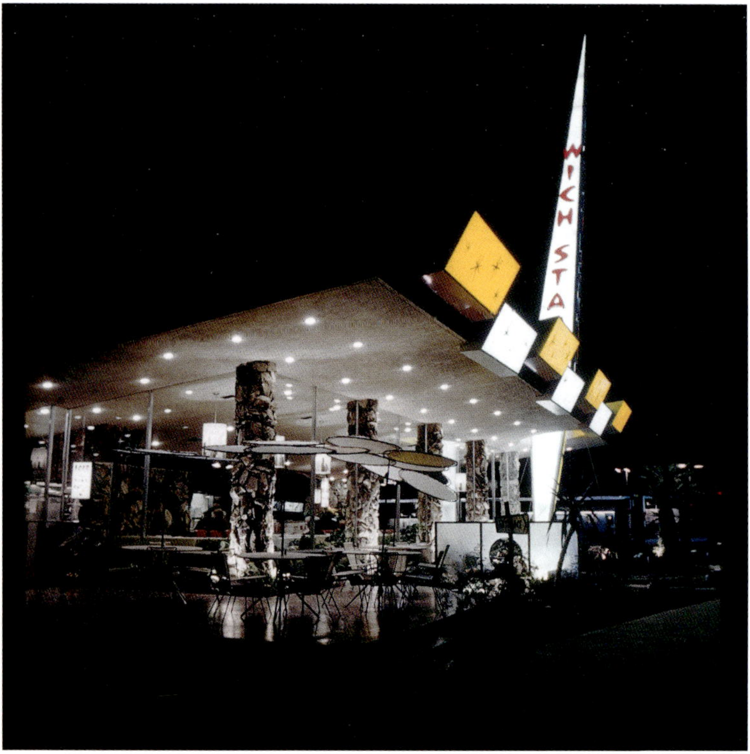

↑
Jack Laxer
The 'Wich Stand was an exponent of the exuberant Googie style, Slauson Avenue and Overhill Drive, 1957.

Das 'Wich Stand war ein Beispiel für den quirligen Googie-Stil, Slauson Avenue und Overhill Drive, 1957.

Le 'Wich Stand, un exemple notable du style Googie, à l'angle de Slauson Avenue et d'Overhill Drive, 1957.

→
Peter Stackpole
The original Googies Coffee Shop, designed in 1948 by John Lautner, at Crescent Heights and Sunset boulevards inspired a genre of eateries after which a casual architectural style was named.

Der 1948 von John Lautner entworfene Googies Coffee Shop, Ecke Crescent Heights und Sunset Boulevard, begründete ein Genre lässiger Restaurantarchitektur, das nach ihm benannt wurde.

Le Googies Coffee Shop, créé en 1948 par John Lautner, au coin de Crescent Heights et Sunset Boulevard a influencé de nombreux cafés-restaurants qui ont adopté son style architectural décontracté.

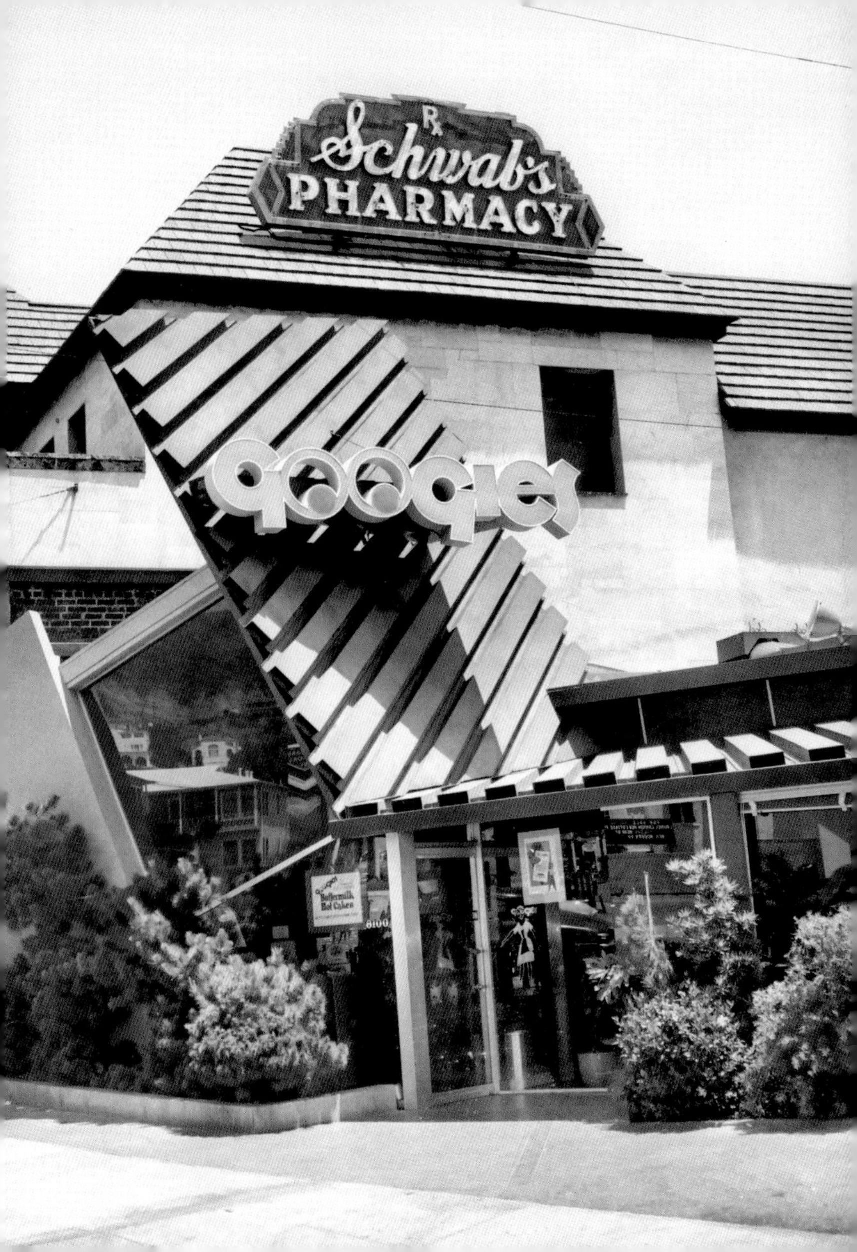
Rx
Schwab's
PHARMACY
Googies
Buttermilk Hot Cakes
8100

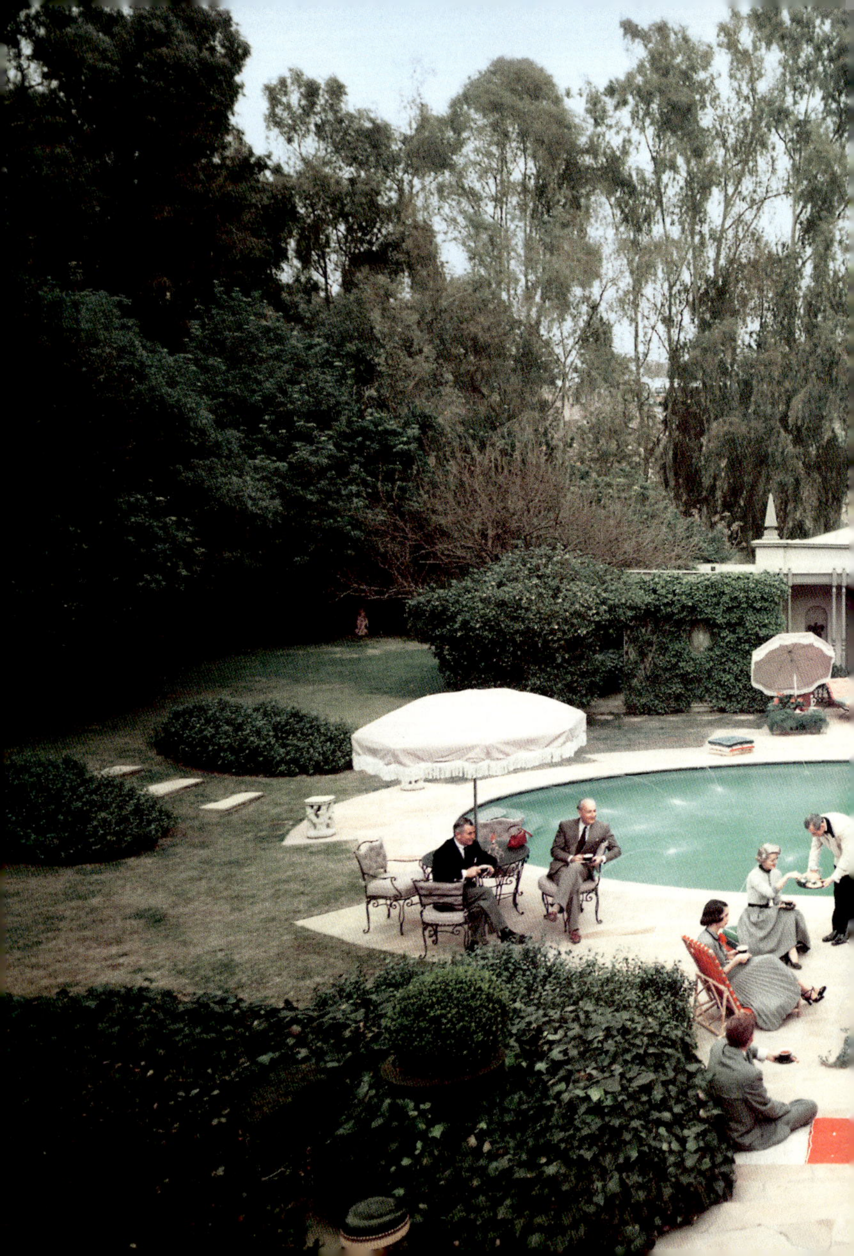

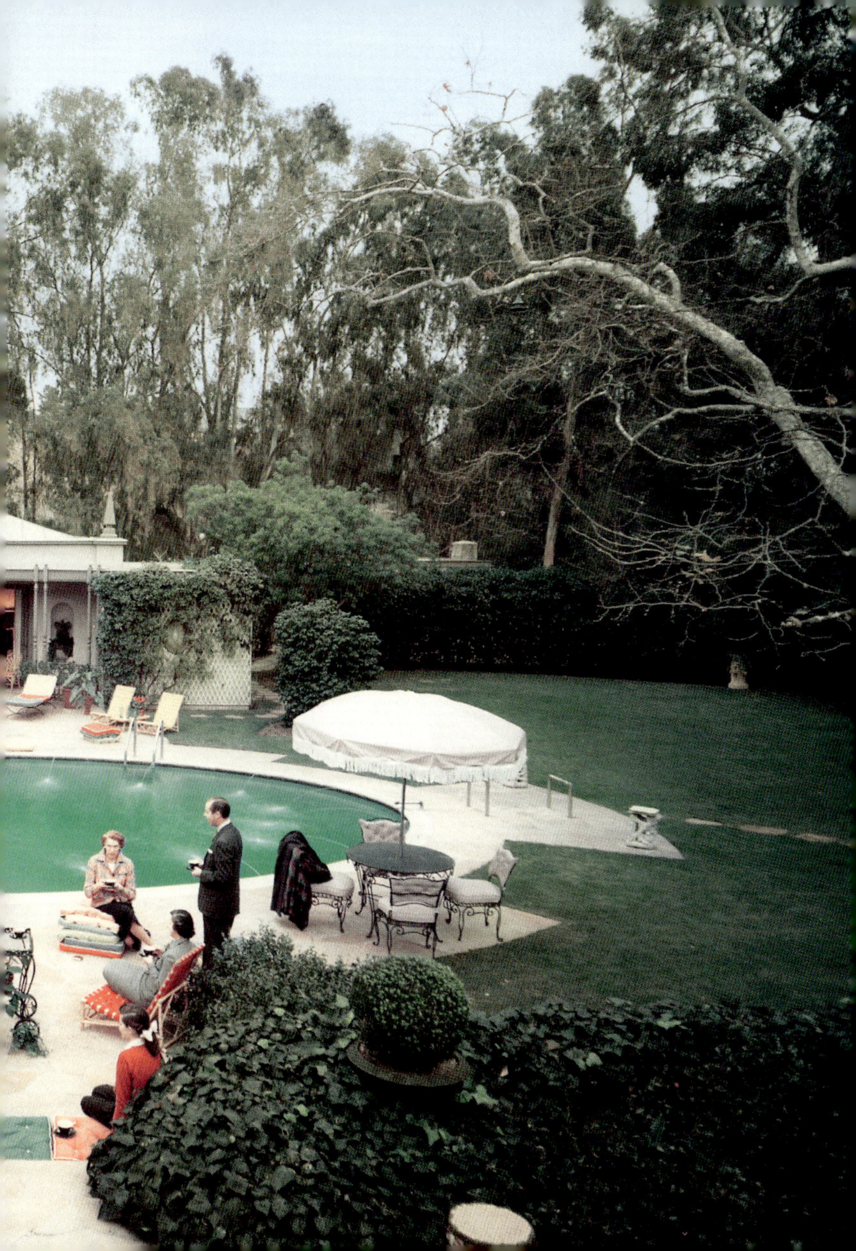

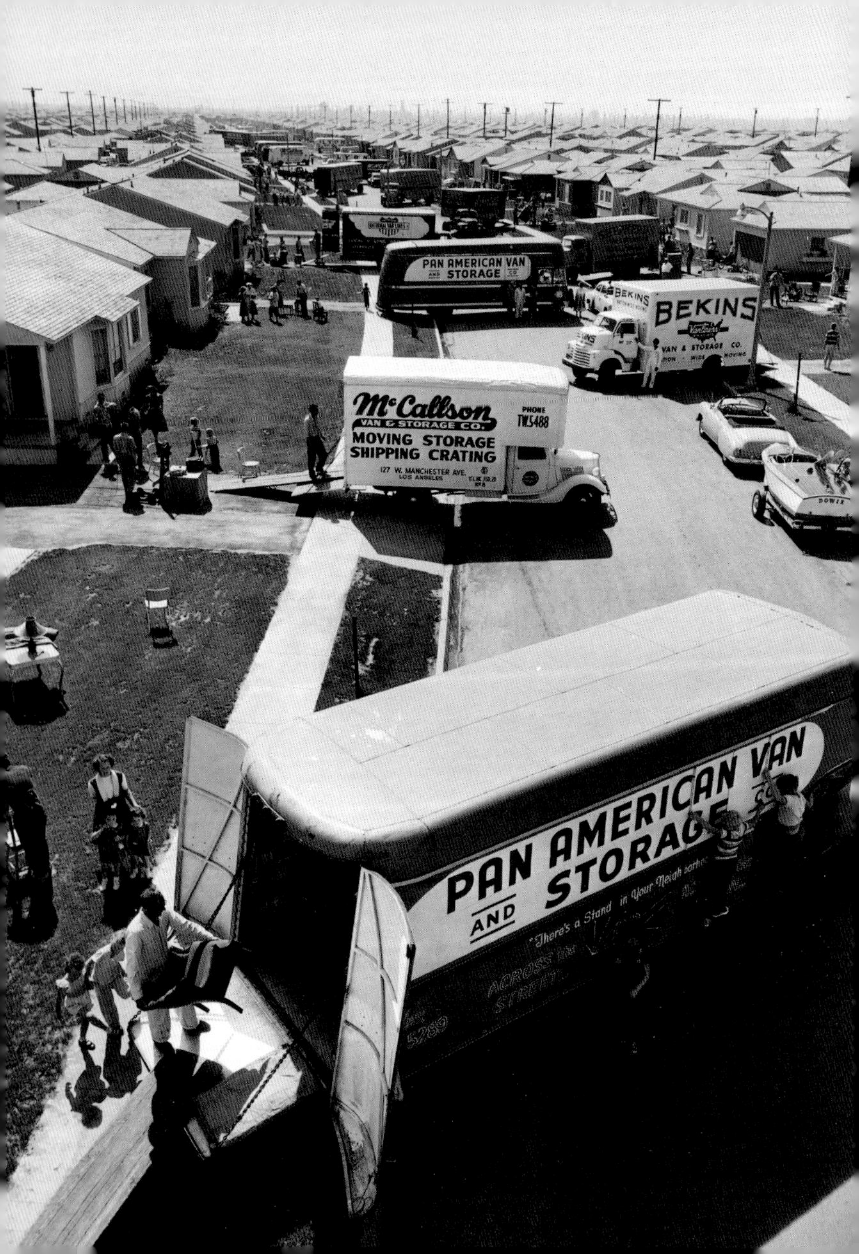
PAN AMERICAN VAN AND STORAGE CO
BEKINS
VAN & STORAGE CO.
McCallson VAN & STORAGE CO.
PHONE TW.5488
MOVING STORAGE SHIPPING CRATING
127 W. MANCHESTER AVE. LOS ANGELES
PAN AMERICAN VAN AND STORAGE CO

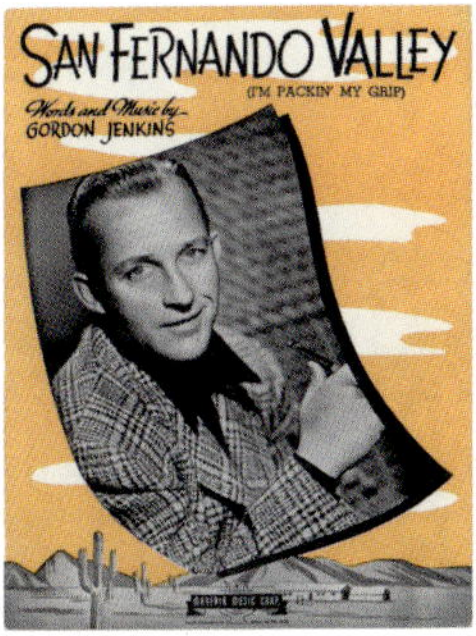

"Oh! I'm packing my grip
And I'm leavin' to-day,
Cause I'm takin' a trip Cal-i-for-nia way.
I'm gonna settle down and never more roam
And make the San Fernando Valley my home."

Gordon Jenkins, "San Fernando Valley," performed by Bing Crosby, 1943

p. 118/119

Slim Aarons

The backyard residence of the art dealer and interior decorator James Pendelton and his wife, Mary Frances, Beverly Hills, 1952. The Pendelton estate was designed in the Hollywood Regency style by society/celebrity architect John Woolf in 1942.

Das Gartenhaus des Kunsthändlers und Inneneinrichters James Pendelton und seiner Frau Mary Frances, Beverly Hills, 1952. Das Anwesen der Pendletons war 1942 vom Society- und Prominentenarchitekten John Woolf im Hollywood-Regency-Stil entworfen worden.

Le jardin de la résidence du marchand d'art et décorateur d'intérieur, James Pendelton, et son épouse, Mary Frances, Beverly Hills, 1952. La demeure des Pendelton avait été conçue dans un style « Régence Hollywood » par John Woolf, l'architecte de la bonne société et des célébrités en 1942.

←

J. R. Eyerman

Moving day in the Southland, 1952. A picture for Life *magazine illustrates the region's rabid suburbanization.*

Umzugstag im Umland von Los Angeles, 1952. Das Foto für das Life Magazine *zeigt das rabiate Wachstum der Vorstädte in der Region.*

Jour d'emménagement dans le sud de l'État, 1952. Cette photo du magazine Life *illustre l'urbanisation accélérée du sud de la Californie.*

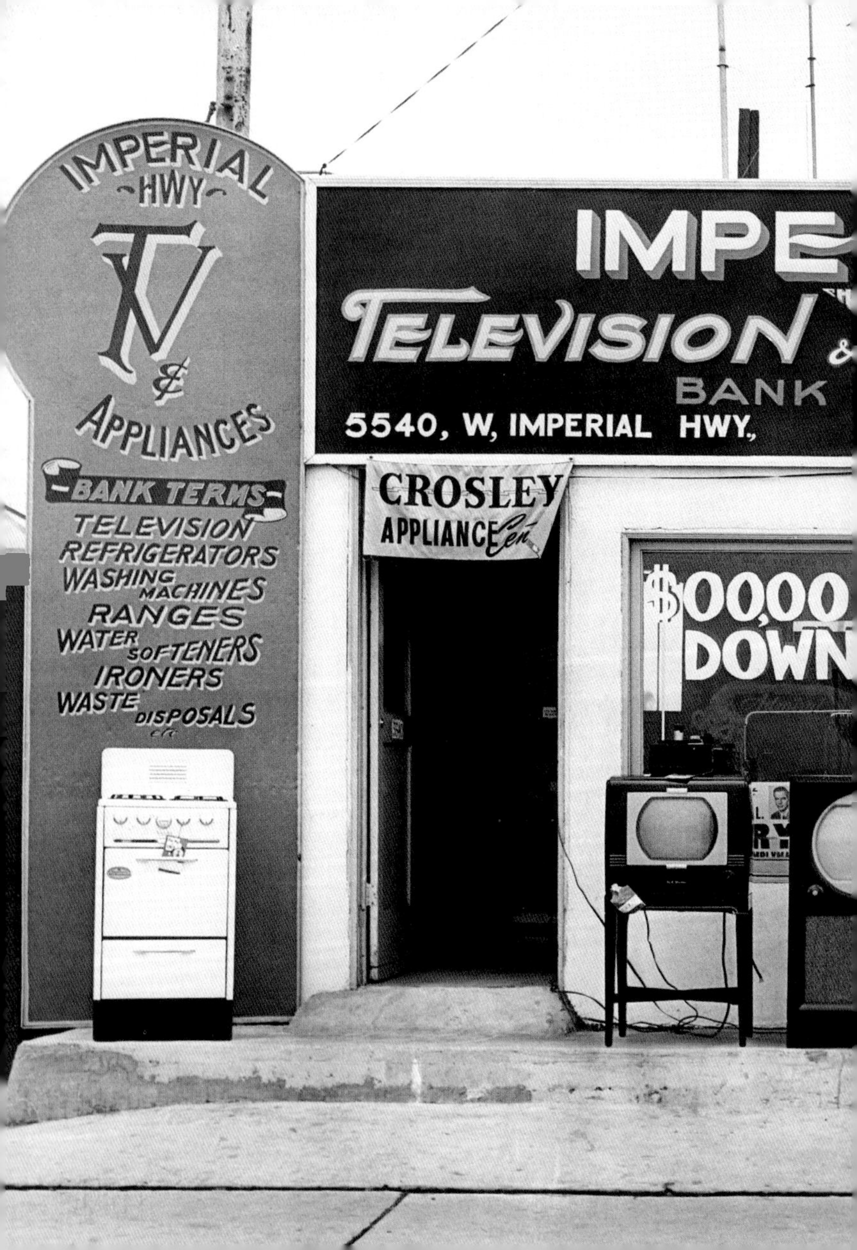
IMPERIAL
HWY
TV
&
APPLIANCES
BANK TERMS
TELEVISION
REFRIGERATORS
WASHING MACHINES
RANGES
WATER SOFTENERS
IRONERS
WASTE DISPOSALS
IMPE
TELEVISION &
BANK
5540, W, IMPERIAL HWY.,
CROSLEY
APPLIANCE Cen
$00,00
DOWN

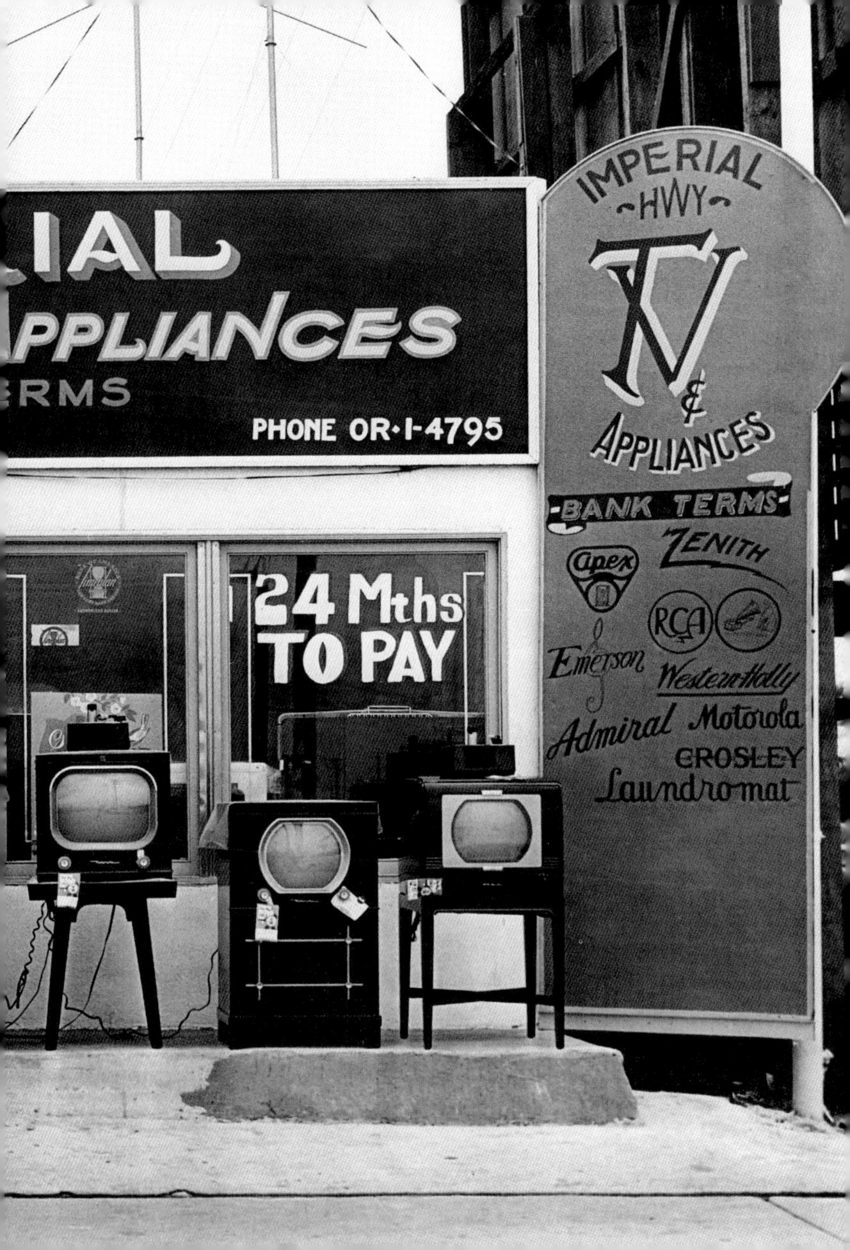
IAL
PPLIANCES
RMS
PHONE OR-1-4795
24 Mths
TO PAY
IMPERIAL
HWY
TV
&
APPLIANCES
BANK TERMS
Apex
ZENITH
RCA
Emerson
Western Holly
Admiral
Motorola
CROSLEY
Laundromat

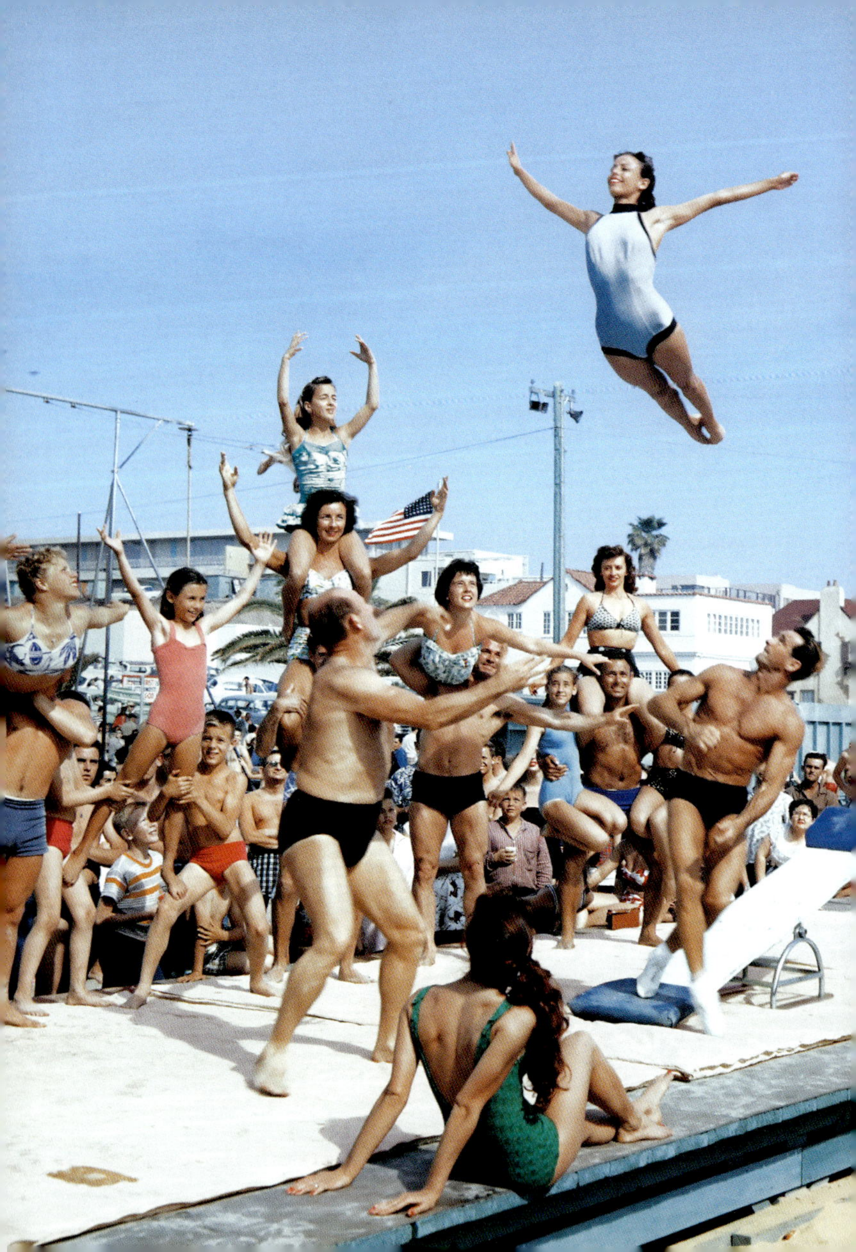

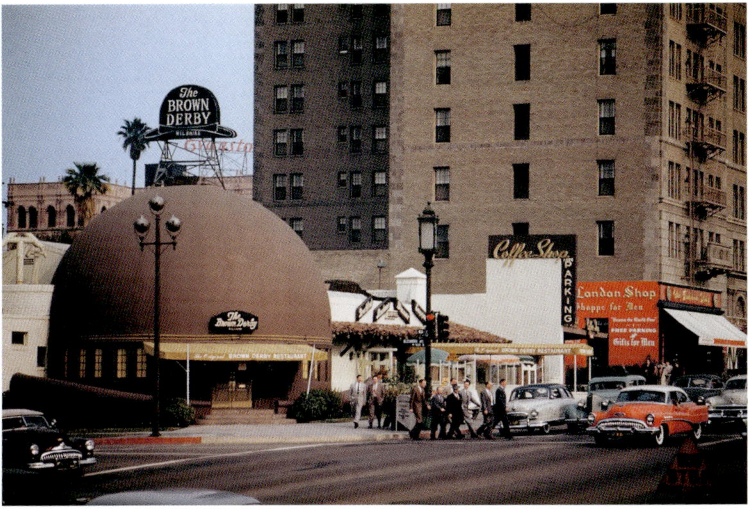

p. 122/123
Anonymous
An early vendor of the new entertainment technology displays his wares streetside in Los Angeles, c. 1952.

Eines der ersten Geschäfte für die neuartige Unterhaltungstechnologie präsentiert seine Waren am Straßenrand in Los Angeles, um 1952.

L'un des premiers magasins à proposer la nouvelle technologie de divertissement expose ses marchandises sur un trottoir de Los Angeles, vers 1952.

←
Frank J. Thomas
Muscle Beach, c. 1954.

Muscle Beach, um 1954.

Muscle Beach, vers 1954.

↑
Joseph Baylor Roberts
The Brown Derby, a fashionable restaurant in the Wilshire District, 1954.

The Brown Derby, ein angesagtes Restaurant im Stadtviertel Wilshire, 1954.

Le Brown Derby, *restaurant à la mode dans le quartier de Wilshire, 1954.*

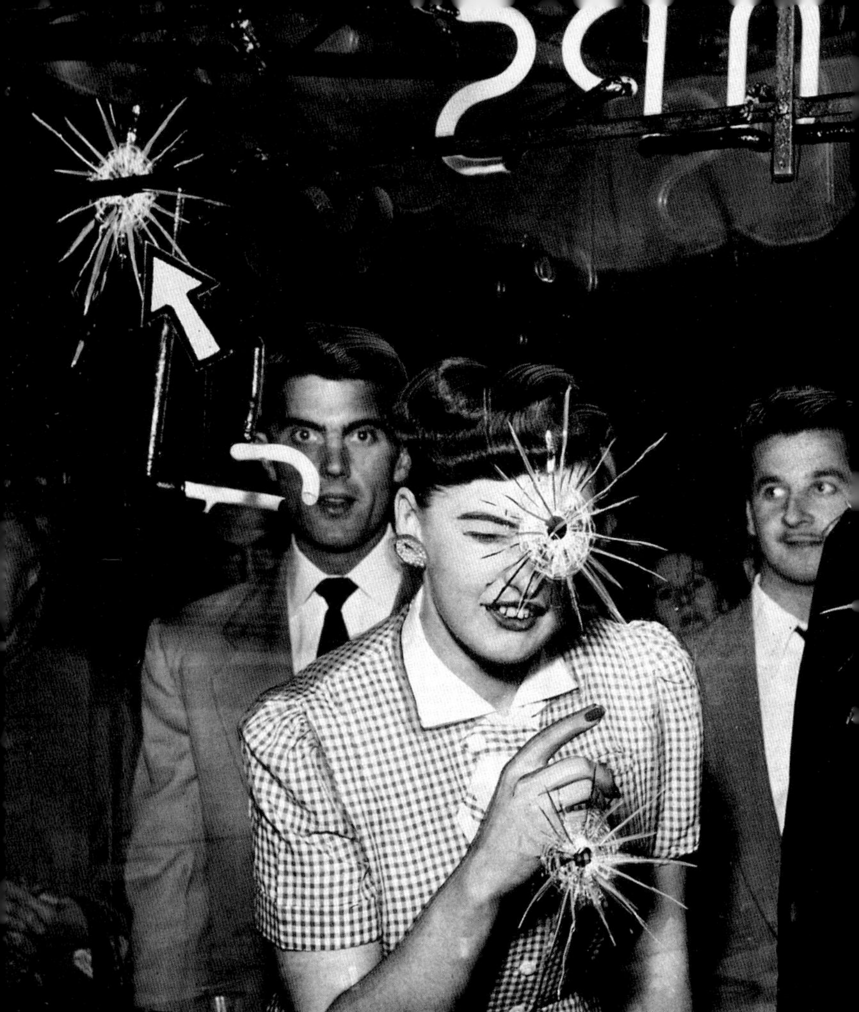

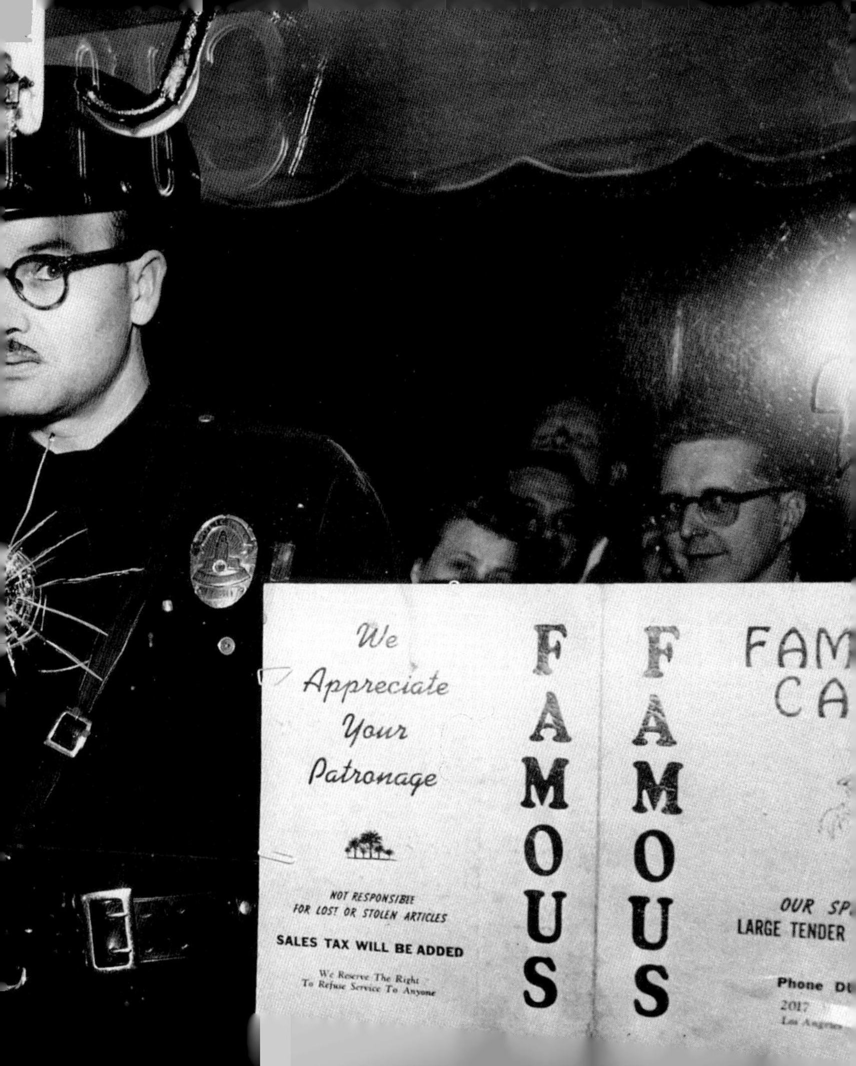
We
Appreciate
Your
Patronage
NOT RESPONSIBLE
FOR LOST OR STOLEN ARTICLES
SALES TAX WILL BE ADDED
We Reserve The Right
To Refuse Service To Anyone
FAMOUS
FAMOUS
FAM
CA
OUR SP
LARGE TENDER
Phone D
2017

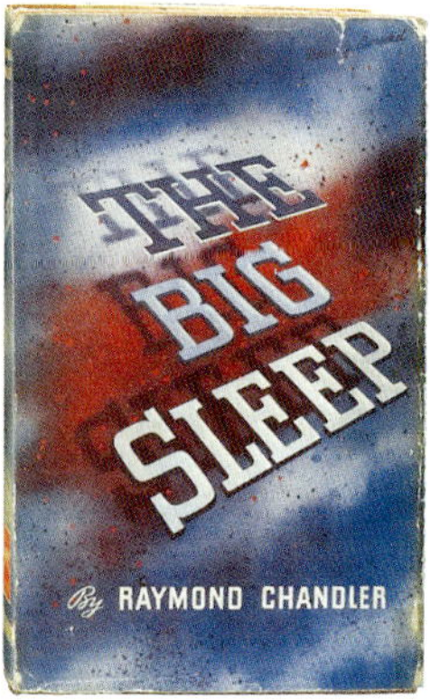

"'Give me the money.' The motor of the gray Plymouth throbbed under her voice.... The violet light at the top of Bullock's green-tinged tower was far above us, serene and withdrawn from the dark, dripping city."

„,Geben Sie mir das Geld.' Der Motor des grauen Plymouth pochte unter ihrer Stimme...Das lila Licht auf dem grün illuminierten Turm von Bullocks war hoch über uns, klar und von der dunklen, triefenden Stadt abgesetzt."

« "Donne-moi l'argent." Le moteur de la Plymouth grise vrombissait sous sa voix... La lumière violette au sommet de la tour Bullock teintée de vert planait loin au-dessus de nous, sereine et dégagée de la ville sombre et dégoulinante. »

Raymond Chandler, *The Big Sleep,* 1939

p. 126/127

Anonymous

Spectators join police at the aftermath of a shootout, 1953.

Nach einer Schießerei; Schaulustige gesellen sich am Tatort zur Polizei, 1953.

Badauds agglutinés autour de policiers après une fusillade, 1953.

→

Ed Clark

The gangster Mickey Cohen sitting amid the front pages of newspapers that helped make him the city's most infamous citizen, 1953.

Der Gangster Mickey Cohen zwischen den Zeitungsschlagzeilen, die dazu beigetragen haben, ihn zum berüchtigtsten Bürger der Stadt zu machen, 1953.

Le gangster Mickey Cohen assis au milieu des unes des journaux qui ont contribué à faire de lui le citoyen le plus honni de la ville, 1953.

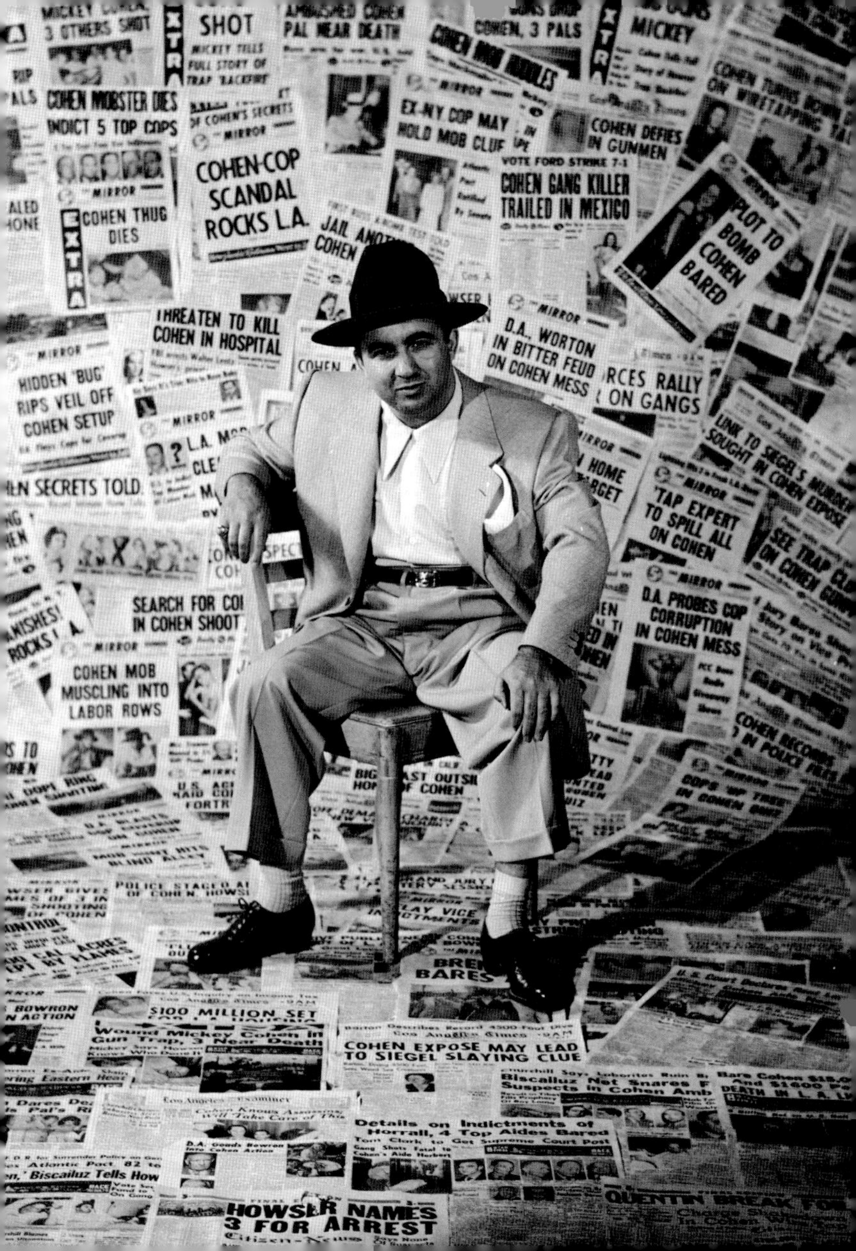
3 OTHERS SHOT
SHOT
MICKEY TELLS FULL STORY OF TRAP 'BACKFIRE'
PAL NEAR DEATH
COHEN, 3 PALS
MICKEY
COHEN MOBSTER DIES
INDICT 5 TOP COPS
OF COHEN'S SECRETS
EX-NY COP MAY HOLD MOB CLUE
COHEN DEFIES IN GUNMEN
COHEN TURNS DOWN ON WIRETAPPING
COHEN-COP SCANDAL ROCKS L.A.
VOTE FORD STRIKE 7-1
COHEN GANG KILLER TRAILED IN MEXICO
EXTRA
COHEN THUG DIES
PLOT TO BOMB COHEN BARED
THREATEN TO KILL COHEN IN HOSPITAL
D.A., WORTON IN BITTER FEUD ON COHEN MESS
HIDDEN 'BUG' RIPS VEIL OFF COHEN SETUP
RCES RALLY ON GANGS
LINK TO SIEGEL'S MURDER SOUGHT IN COHEN EXPOSE
'TAP EXPERT TO SPILL ALL ON COHEN
SEE TRAP CL ON COHEN
SEARCH FOR CO IN COHEN SHOOT
D.A. PROBES COP CORRUPTION IN COHEN MESS
COHEN MOB MUSCLING INTO LABOR ROWS
COPS 'UP TREE' IN COHEN
POLICE STAGED A OF COHEN, HOWSE
$100 MILLION SET
Wound Mickey Cohen in Gun Trap, 3 Near Death
COHEN EXPOSE MAY LEAD TO SIEGEL SLAYING CLUE
Biscailuz Net Snares F Suspects in Cohen Amb
Details on Indictments of Horrall, 4 Top Aides Bared
D.A. Goads Bowron Into Cohen Action
QUENTIN BREAK FO
HOWSER NAMES 3 FOR ARREST

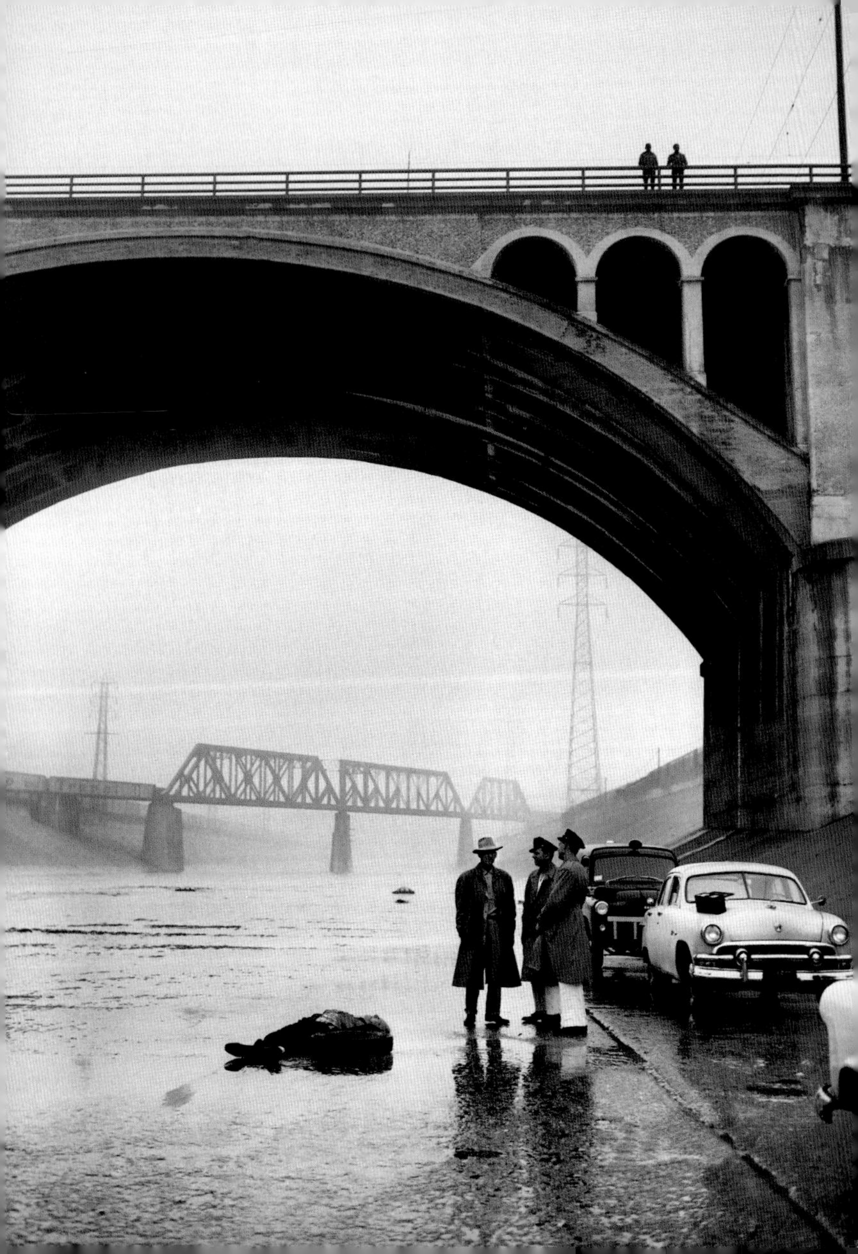

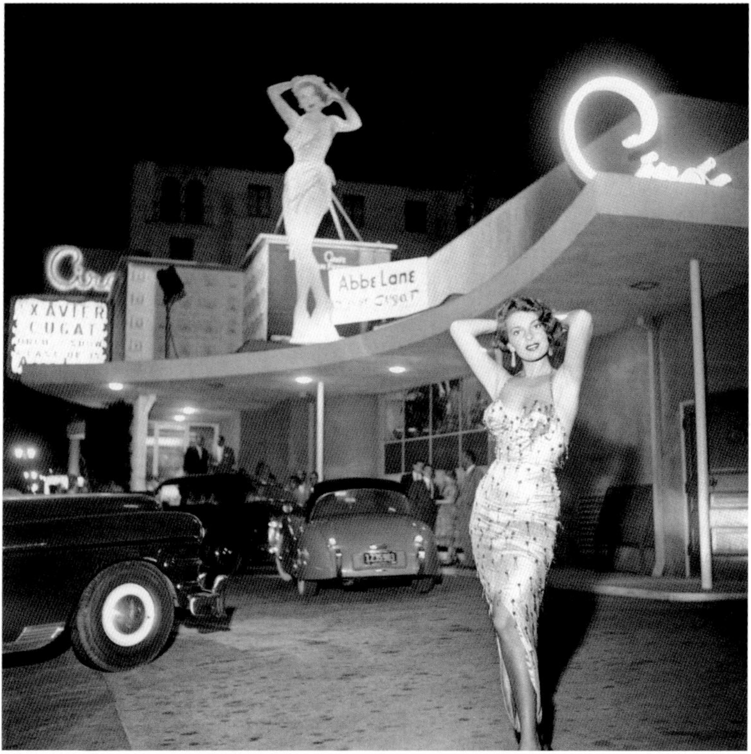

←
R. Rittenhouse
Noir incarnate — an abandoned body in the concrete bed of the Los Angeles River, 1955.

Ein Fleisch gewordener Film noir – eine im Betonbett des Los Angeles River abgelegte Leiche, 1955.

Une image sinistre : un cadavre abandonné sur le lit de béton de la rivière Los Angeles, 1955.

↑
Earl Leaf
Singer Abbe Lane, voluptuous wife of orchestra leader Xavier Cugat, poses in front of Ciro's night club, a top spot for nightlife on the Sunset Strip, 1954.

Die Sängerin Abbe Lane, sinnliche Ehefrau des Orchesterleiters Xavier Cugat, posiert vor dem Nachtklub Ciro's, einer der ersten Adressen im Nachtleben auf dem Sunset Strip, 1954.

La chanteuse Abbe Lane, épouse voluptueuse du chef d'orchestre Xavier Cugat, pose devant la discothèque Ciro's, l'un des hauts lieux de la vie nocturne du Sunset Strip, 1954.

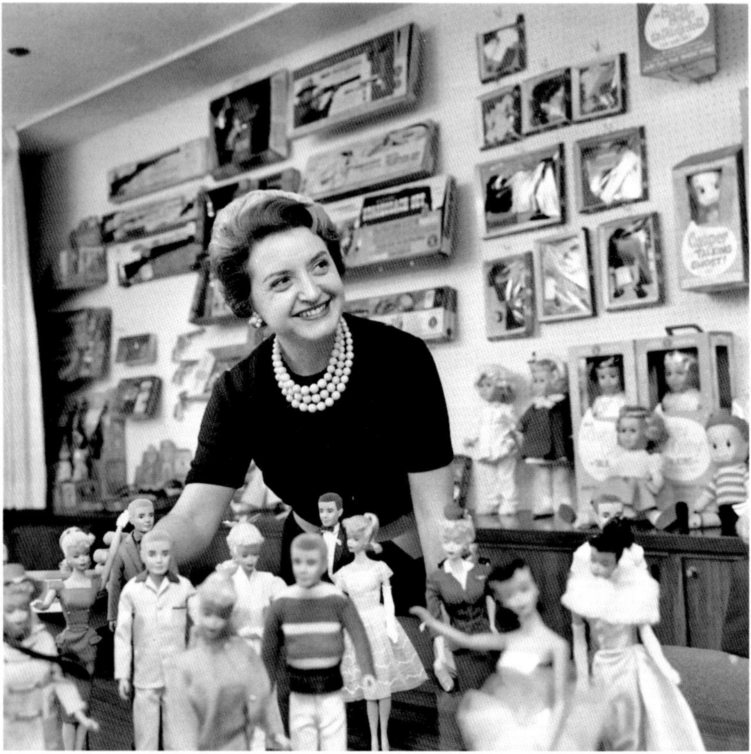

↑
Anonymous
Ruth Handler, who introduced Barbie in 1959. The doll became a worldwide phenomenon for Handler's Mattel toy company, based in the Los Angeles suburb of Hawthorne.

Ruth Handler, Erfinderin der Barbie, um 1959. Für Handlers Firma Mattel (mit Sitz im Vorort Hawthorne von Los Angeles) sollte die Puppe zum internationalen Phänomen werden.

Ruth Handler, qui a introduit la poupée Barbie, vers 1959. C'est devenu un succès mondial pour Mattel, la fabrique de jouets de Handler, basée à Hawthorne dans la banlieue de Los Angeles.

→
Allan Grant
Jayne Mansfield floats amid novelty bottles made in her image, c. 1958.

Jayne Mansfield schwimmt inmitten von Flaschen nach ihrem Ebenbild, um 1958.

Jayne Mansfield flottant parmi des bouteilles à son effigie, vers 1958.

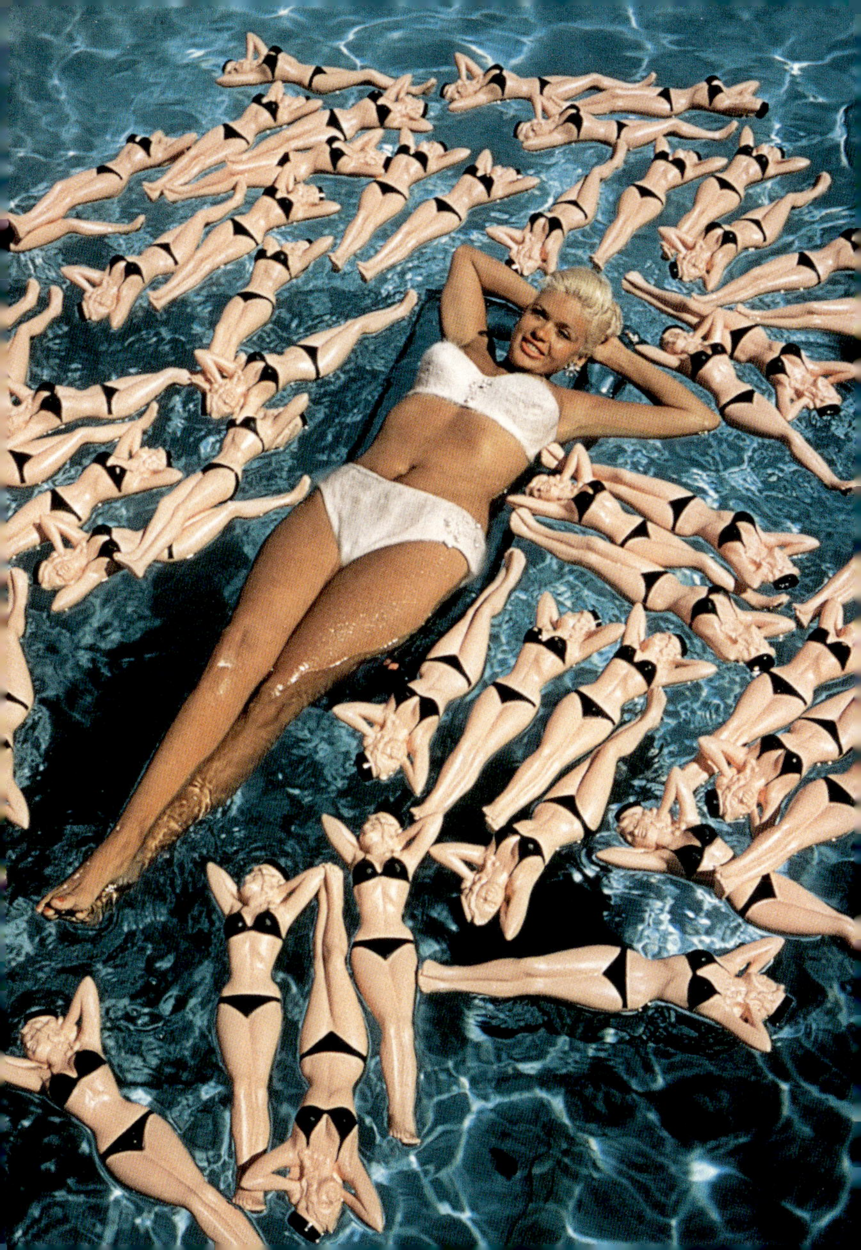

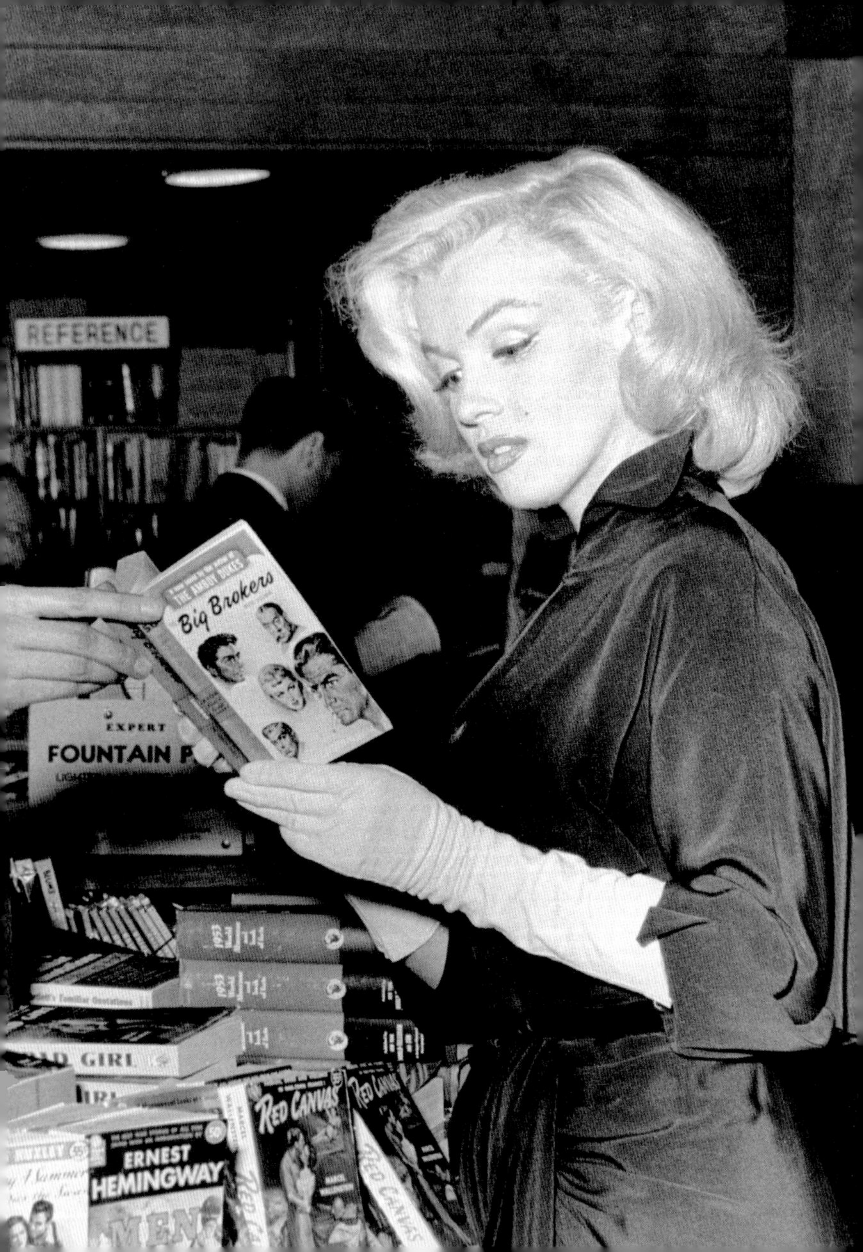
REFERENCE
Big Brokers
THE AMBOY DUKES
EXPERT
FOUNTAIN
RED CANVAS
RED CANVAS
ERNEST
HEMINGWAY
GIRL

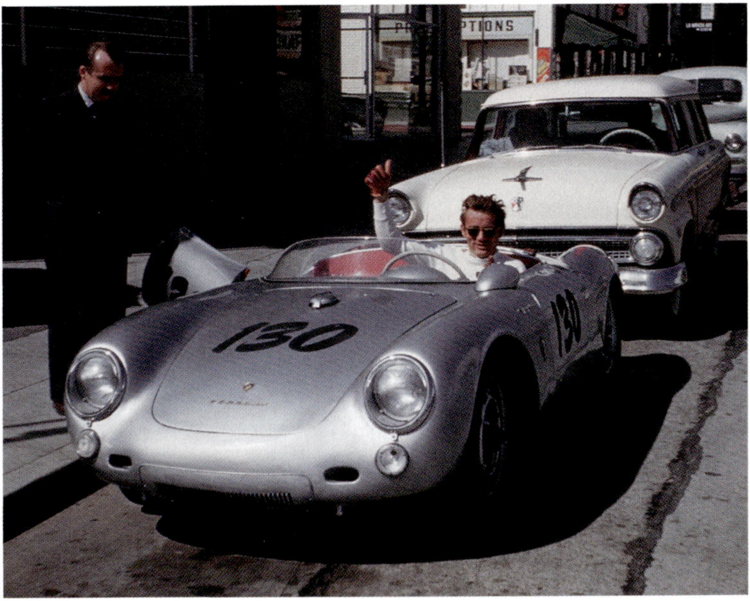

←

André de Dienes

Marilyn Monroe in a Beverly Hills bookstore, 1953.

Marylin Monroe in einem Buchladen in Beverly Hills, 1953.

Marilyn Monroe dans une librairie de Beverly Hills, 1953.

↑

Anonymous

James Dean, in his Porsche Spyder 550—one of only 90 produced—the car in which he would meet his death, in 1955.

James Dean in seinem Porsche Spyder 550 – einem von insgesamt nur 90 hergestellten Modellen – dem Auto, in dem er 1955 ums Leben kam.

James Dean, dans sa Porsche Spyder 550 – l'un des 90 exemplaires fabriqués – la voiture dans laquelle il devait trouver la mort en 1955.

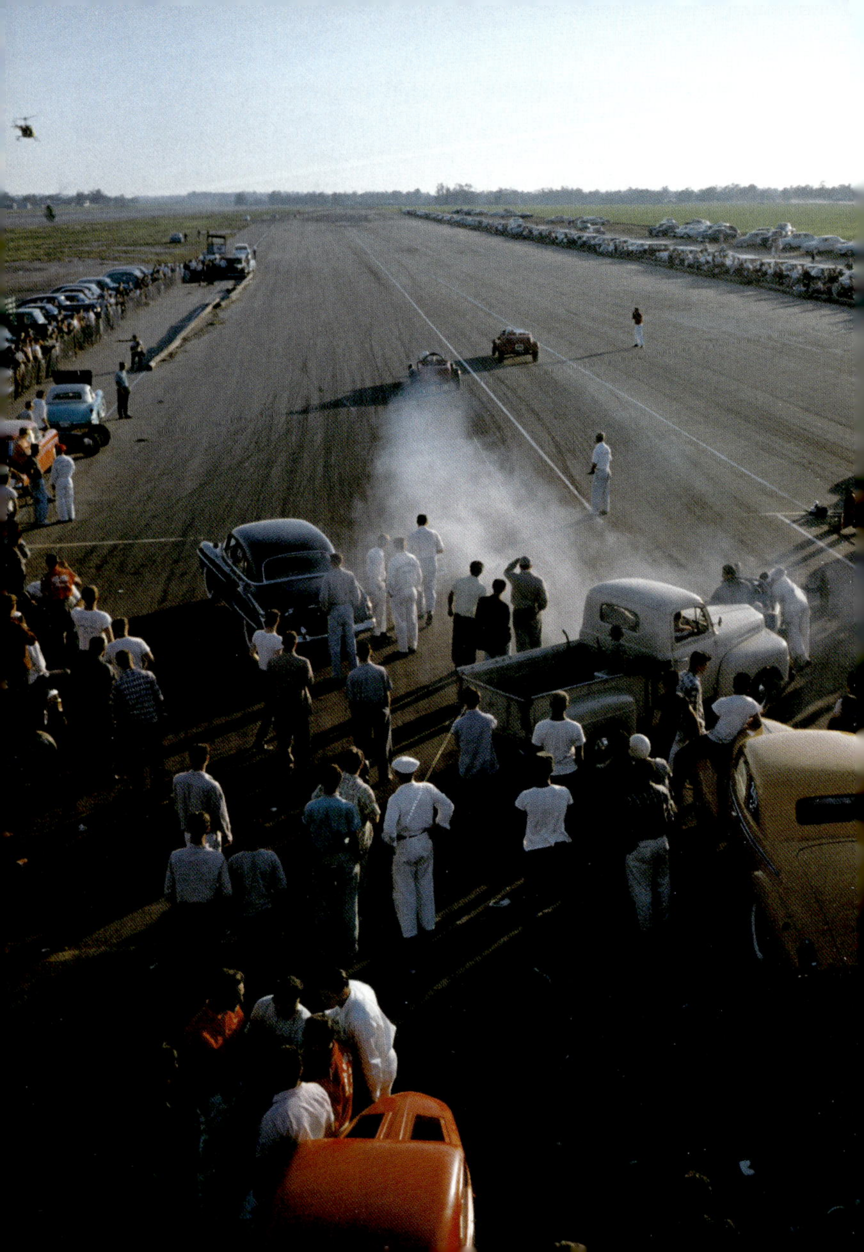

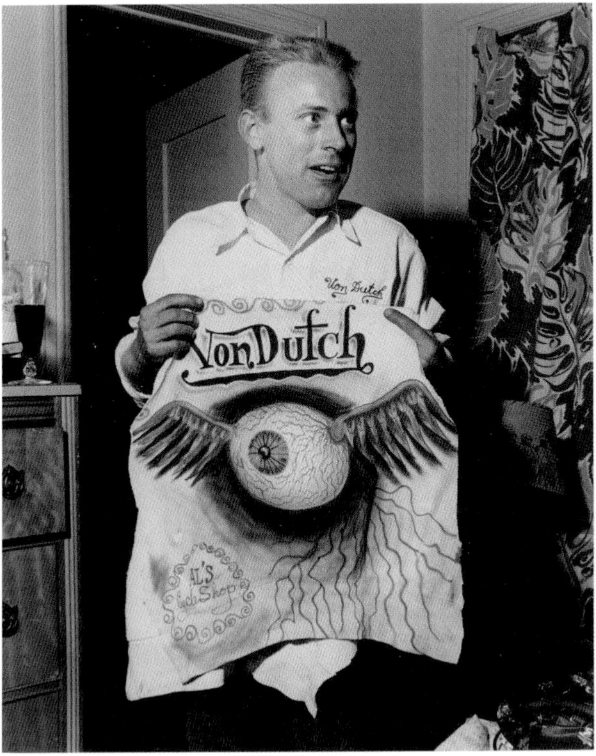

←

Ralph Crane

Drag meet, 1957. Drag racing's birth in Southern California was followed by a full-blown scene in which both amateur and professional drivers took to the streets.

Ein Beschleunigungsrennen (Drag Race) in Santa Ana, 1957. Nach der Erfindung dieser Sportart in Kalifornien entwickelte sich Drag Racing zu einer eigenen Szene; an den Rennen nahmen Amateur- ebenso wie Profifahrer teil.

Rassemblement de dragsters, 1957. À leurs débuts, les courses de dragsters en Californie du Sud étaient suivies d'un moment d'invasion urbaine au cours duquel les pilotes amateurs comme professionnels s'égayaient dans les rues.

↑

Robert Lee Behme

Master pinstriper Von Dutch capitalized on a beatnik persona while decorating hot rods and custom cars, 1965.

Von Dutch, Meister des Pinstripings, stilisierte sich zum Beatnik und lackierte Hotrods und spezialangefertigte Autos, 1965.

Von Dutch, maître de la décoration, a basé sa réussite sur son personnage de beatnik, peignant des voitures trafiquées et customisées, 1965.

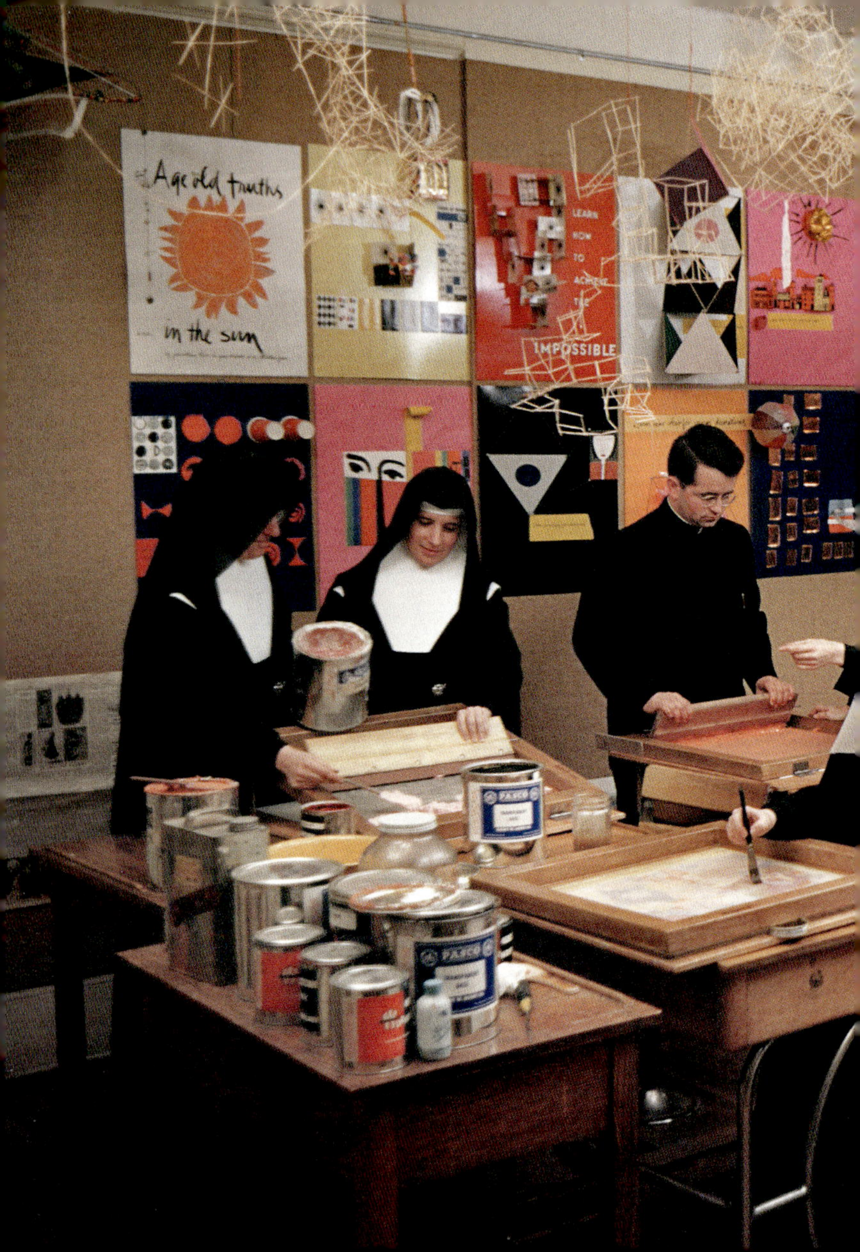
Age old truths
in the sun
LEARN
HOW
TO
IMPOSSIBLE

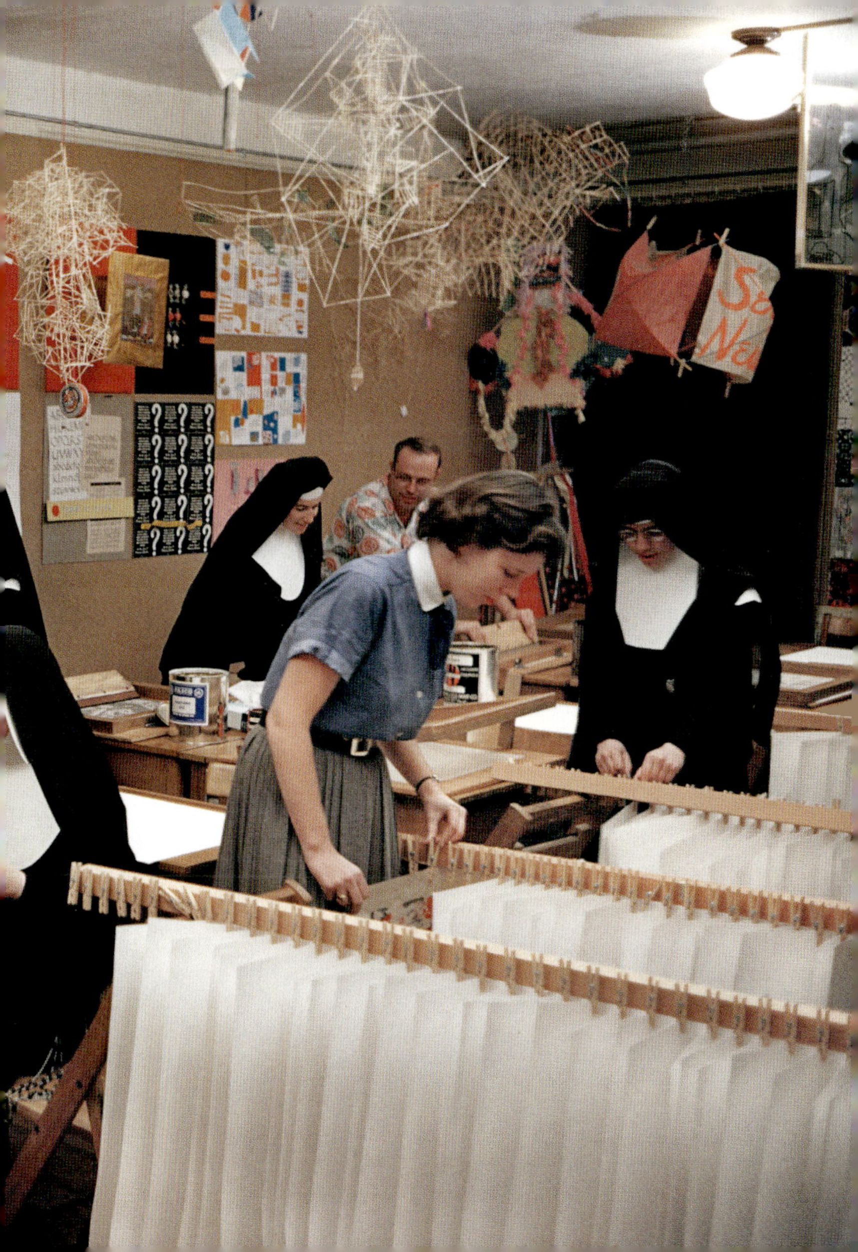

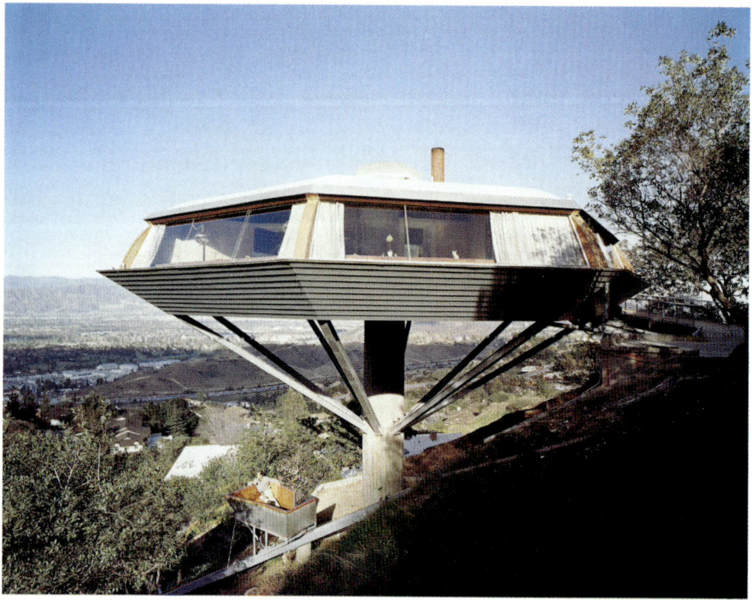

p. 138/139

Julie Ault

The local art scene received a creative shot in the arm with Sister Mary Corita Kent's groundbreaking serigraphs, c. 1955.

Die Kunstszene von Los Angeles bekam neue Impulse, als Schwester Mary Corita Kent ihre bahnbrechenden Siebdrucke realisierte, um 1955.

La scène artistique de Los Angeles reçut un choc créatif quand la sœur Mary Corita Kent réalisa ses sérigraphies révolutionnaires, vers 1955.

↑

Julius Shulman

Called "the most modern home built in the world," John Lautner's Chemosphere House championed a new lifestyle for the Space Age, 1960.

Das Chemosphere House von John Lautner wurde als „modernstes Wohnhaus der Welt" bezeichnet und war der Inbegriff eines neuen Lebensstils im Zeitalter der Raumfahrt, 1960.

« Maison la plus moderne construite dans le monde » : selon un slogan de l'époque, la maison Chemosphere de John Lautner se voulait le cadre d'un nouveau mode de vie pour l'ère spatiale naissante, 1960.

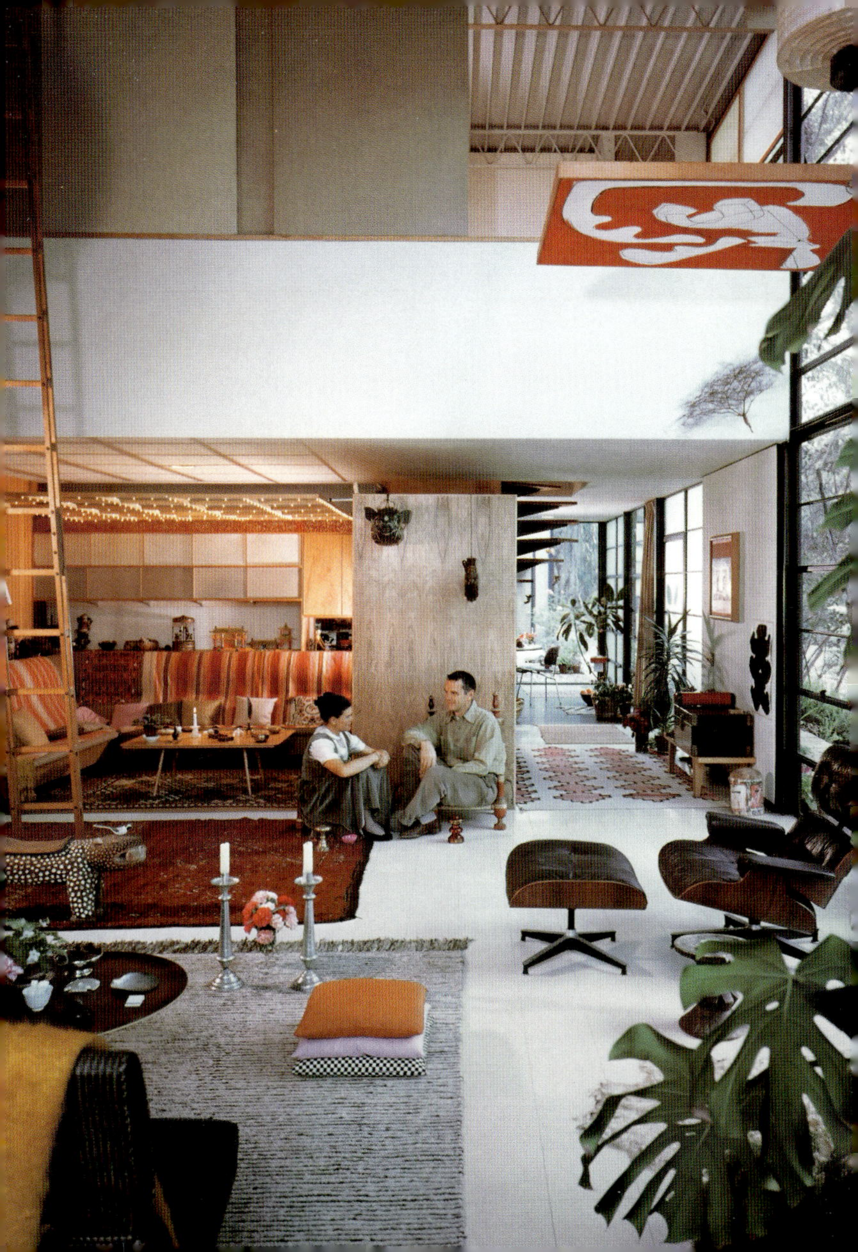

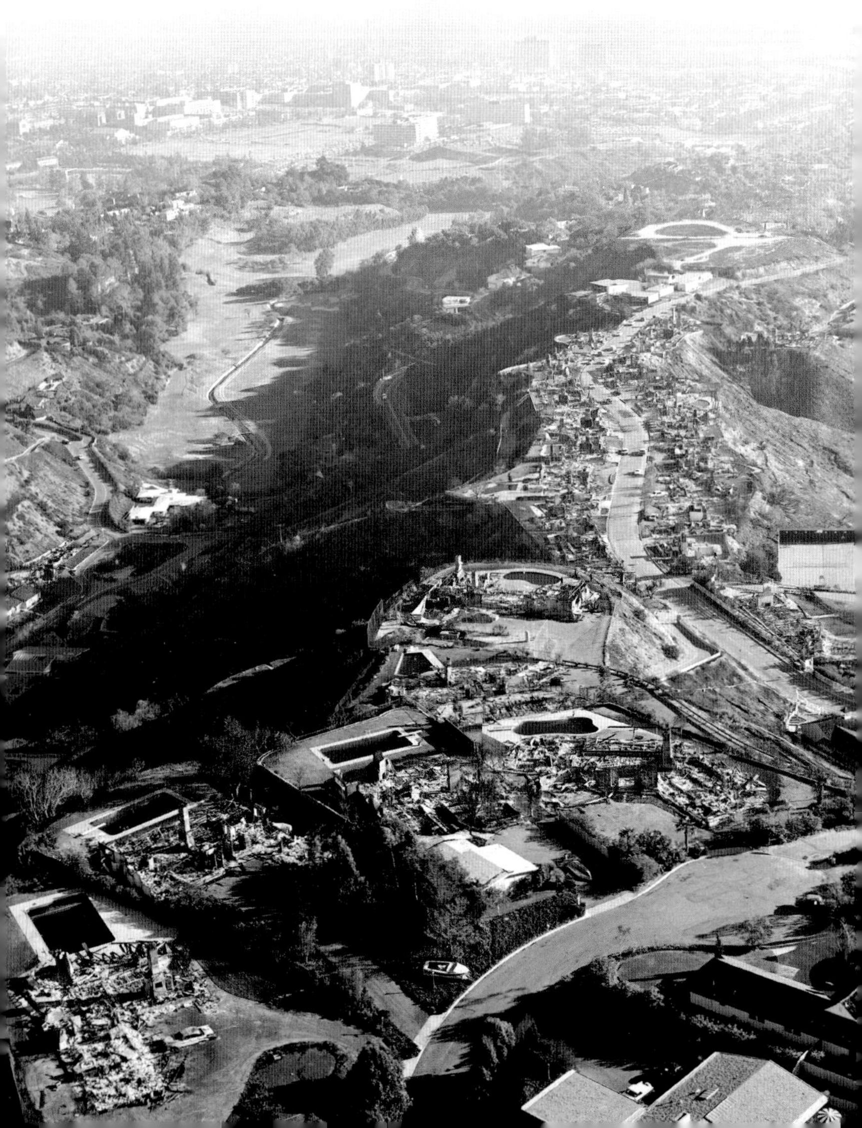

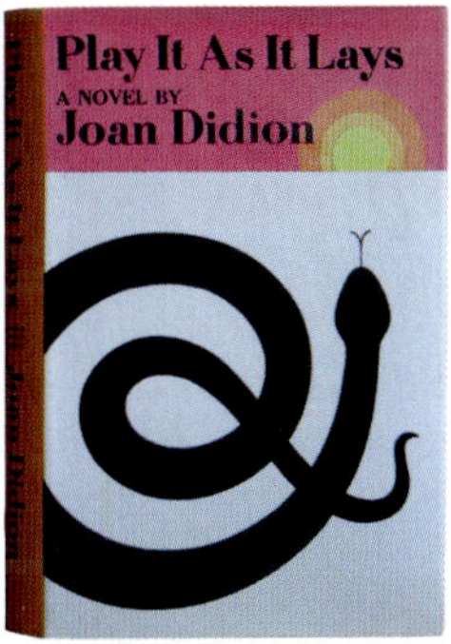

"She drove the San Diego to the Harbor, the Harbor up to the Hollywood, the Hollywood to the Golden State, the Santa Monica, the Santa Ana, the Pasadena, the Ventura."

„Sie fuhr den San Diego hoch bis zum Harbor, den Harbor bis hoch zum Hollywood, den Hollywood bis zum Golden State, den Santa Monica, den Santa Ana, den Pasadena, den Ventura."

« Elle roula de San Diego jusqu'au port, du port, elle remonta à Hollywood, d'Hollywood jusqu'à Golden State, Santa Monica, Santa Ana, Pasadena, Ventura. »

Joan Didion, *Play It As It Lays*, 1972

p. 141
Julius Shulman
Charles and Ray Eames relax in their Modernist residence in Pacific Palisades, 1958.

Charles und Ray Eames entspannen sich in ihrem modernistischen Haus in Pacific Palisades, 1958.

Charles et Ray Eames se détendent dans leur maison moderniste de Pacific Palisades, 1958.

←
J. R. Eyerman
Exclusive residential enclaves such as Bel Air were not immune to the perennial fires that consume the foothills of Los Angeles, November 1961. The "Tragedy Trimmed in Mink" burned more than 484 homes, many of them celebrity owned.

Auch exklusive Wohngebiete wie Bel Air waren nicht gefeit vor den ständigen Waldbränden, die die Bergausläufer von Los Angeles heimsuchten, November 1961. Bei der „Tragödie mit Nerzkragen" brannten über 484 Häuser aus, viele von ihnen gehörten Prominenten.

Les enclaves résidentielles les plus huppées comme Bel Air n'étaient pas à l'abri des incendies qui ravagent régulièrement les contreforts de Los Angeles, novembre 1961. La « tragédie qui a décimé les visons » a détruit plus de 484 maisons, dont beaucoup appartenant à des célébrités.

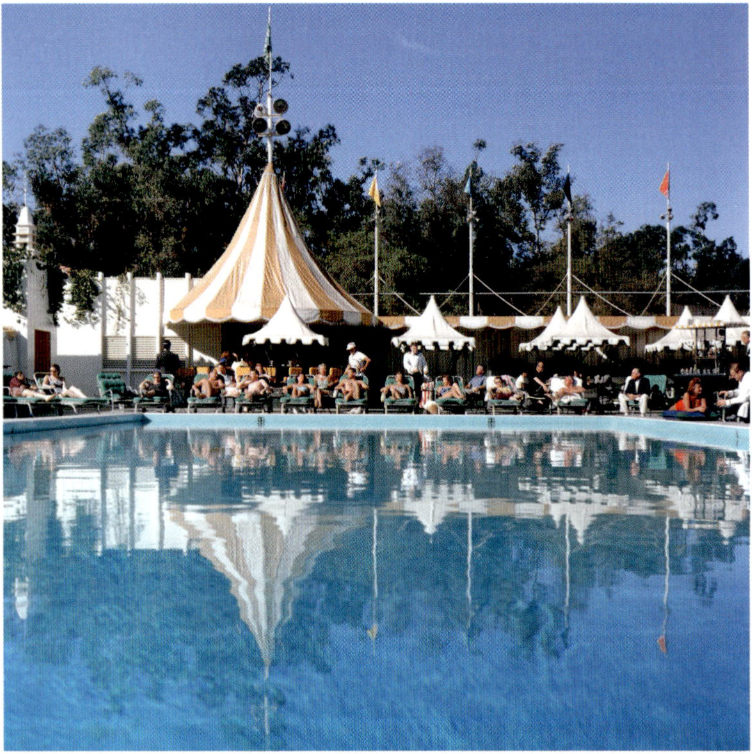

↑

Slim Aarons

Poolside at the posh Beverly Hills Hotel, 1957.

Am Pool des eleganten Hotels Beverly Hills, 1957.

Le bord de la piscine du très chic hôtel Beverly Hills, 1957.

→

Anonymous

The bane of Los Angeles, a layer of smog infiltrates and looms over the city center, 1957.

Ein Smogschleier, der Fluch von Los Angeles, schwebt über dem Stadtzentrum und durchdringt alles, 1957.

Le fléau de Los Angeles, une couche de smog qui s'insinue et plane au-dessus du centre-ville, 1957.

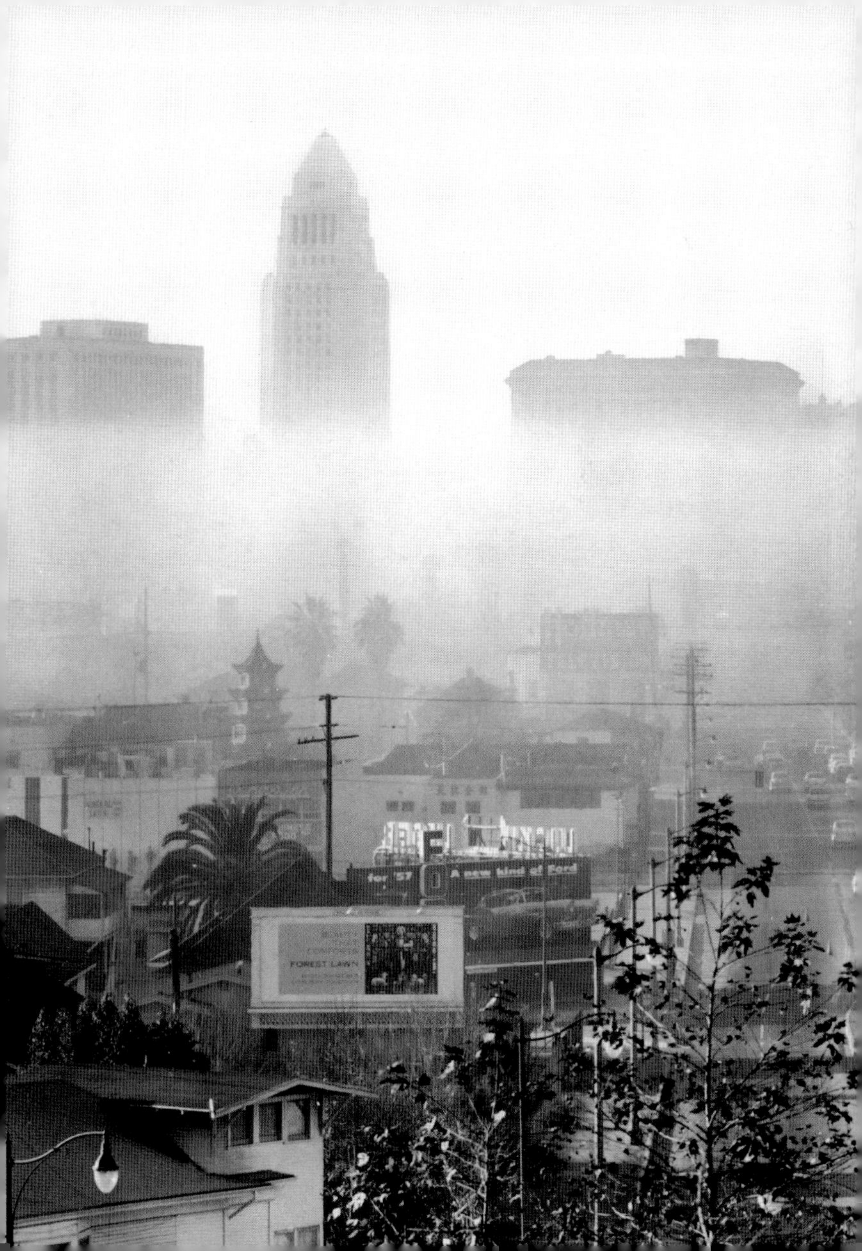
for '57
A new kind of Ford
FOREST LAWN

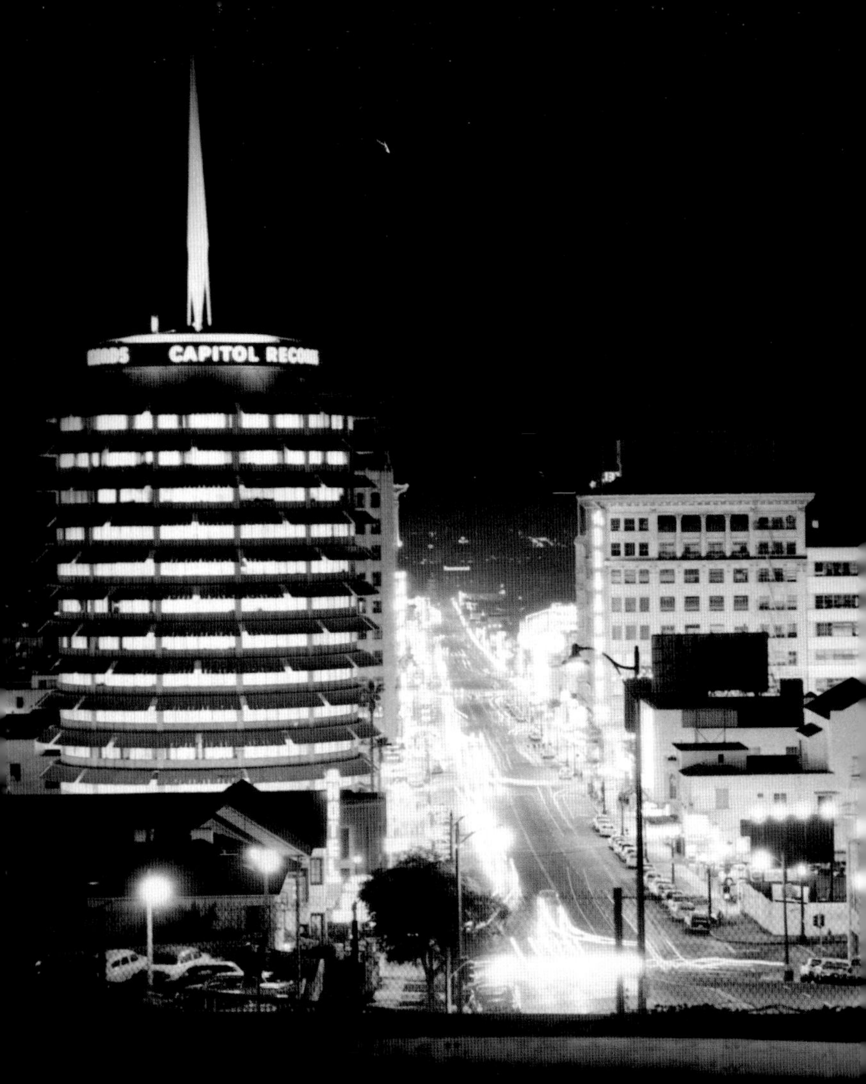
CAPITOL RECO

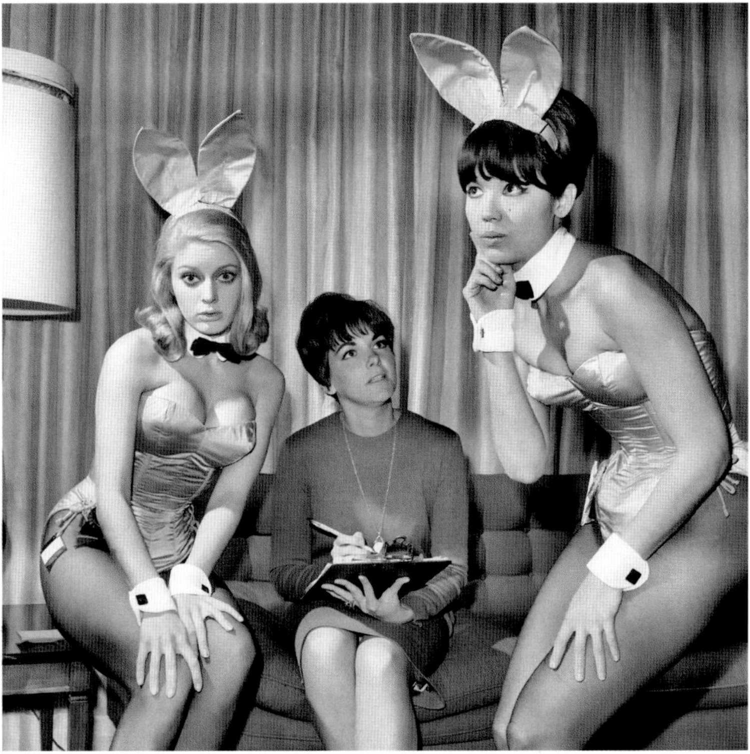

←
Roy Hankey
Welton Becket's Capitol Records building, world's first circular office building, c. 1960.

Das von Welton Becket entworfene Capitol-Records-Gebäude war das erste runde Bürogebäude der Welt, um 1960.

L'immeuble Capitol Records de Welton Becket fut le premier immeuble de bureaux circulaire du monde, vers 1960.

↑
Anonymous
Bunnies Anne and Diane with Mother Rabbit Alice Nichols at Hugh Hefner's Playboy Club, 1965.

Playboy-Häschen Anne und Diane mit „Mother Rabbit" (Hasenmutter) Alice Nichols in Hugh Hefners Playboy-Klub, 1965.

Les « Bunnies » Anne et Diane avec la « mère lapine » Alice Nichols dans le club Playboy de Hugh Hefner, 1965.

p. 148/149
William Claxton
Eating hot dogs in black tie — the cultural dichotomy of Los Angeles, 1961.

Hotdogs in Abendgarderobe – die kulturelle Dichotomie von Los Angeles, 1961.

Consommateurs de hot-dogs en tenue de soirée – la dichotomie culturelle de Los Angeles, 1961.

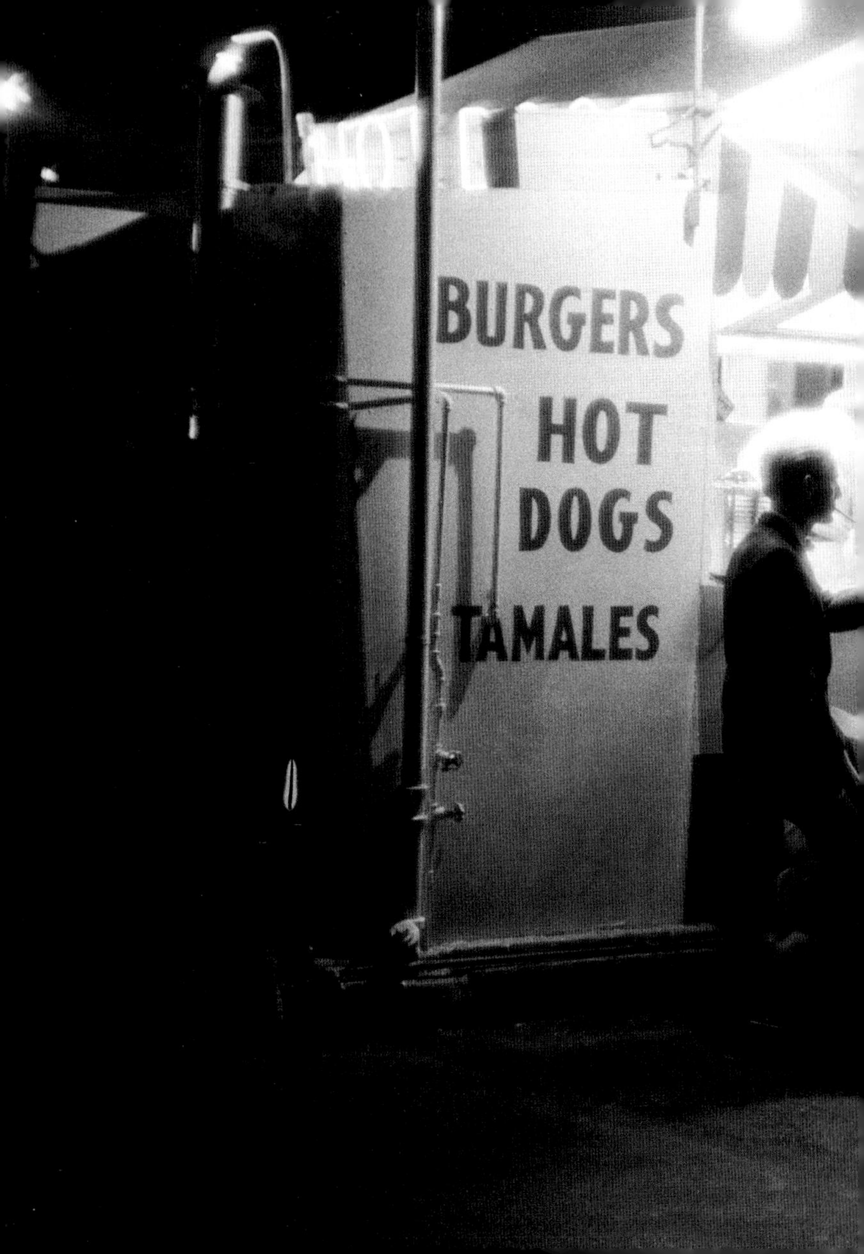
BURGERS
HOT
DOGS
TAMALES

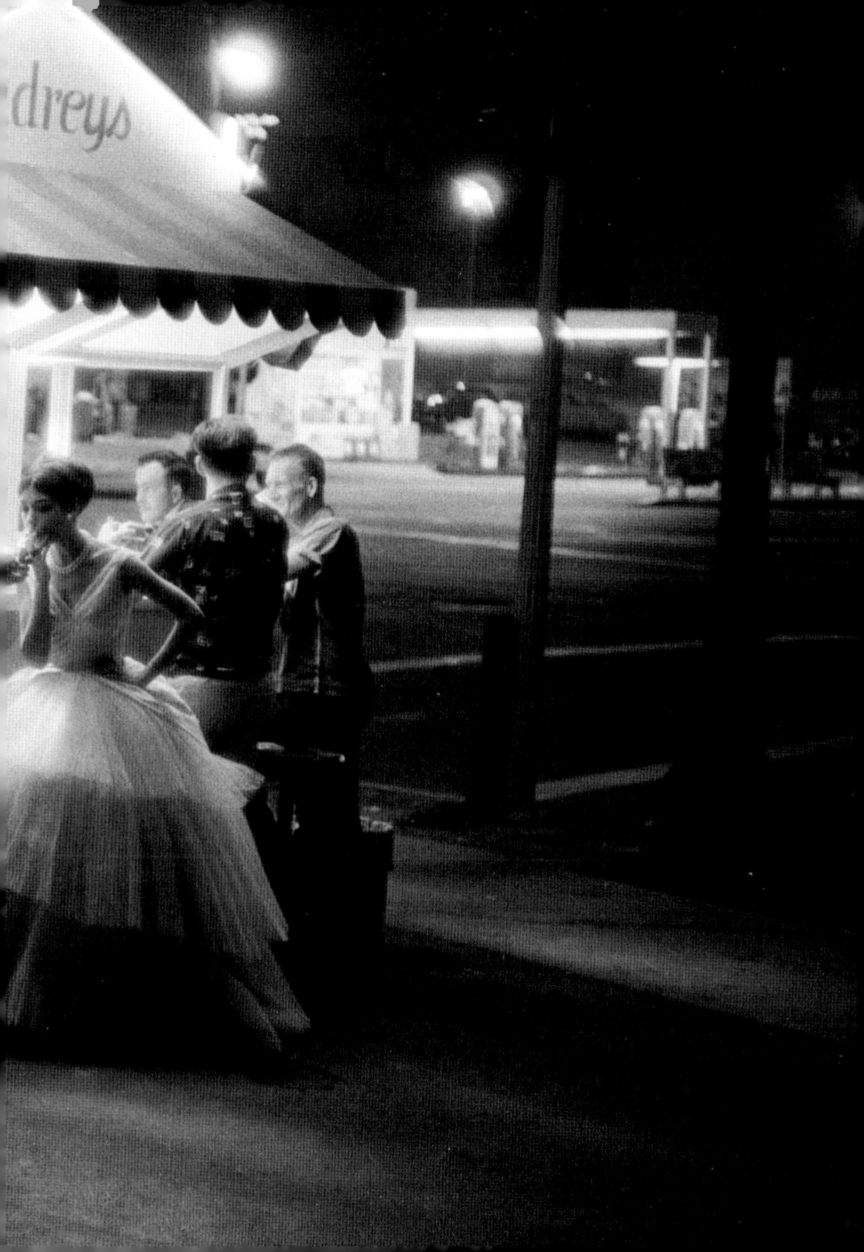
dreys

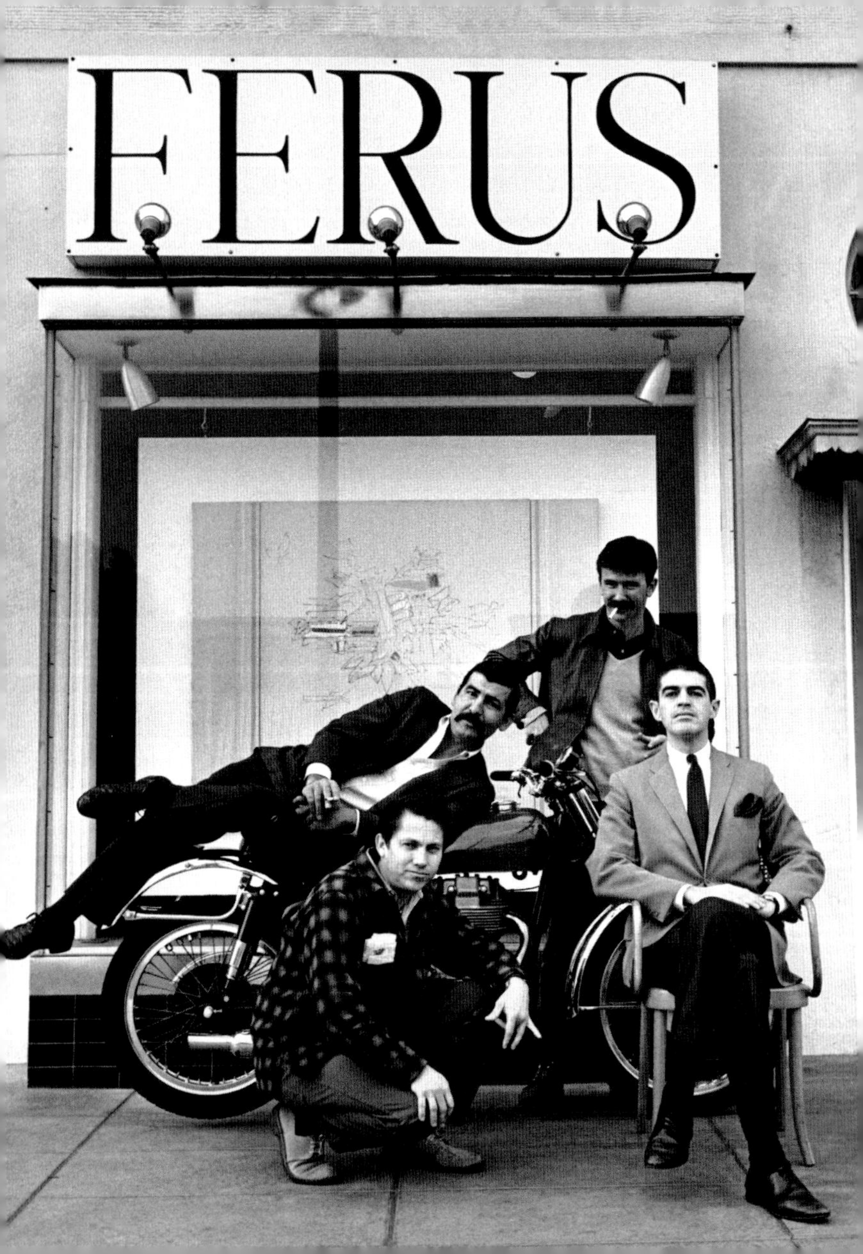
FERUS

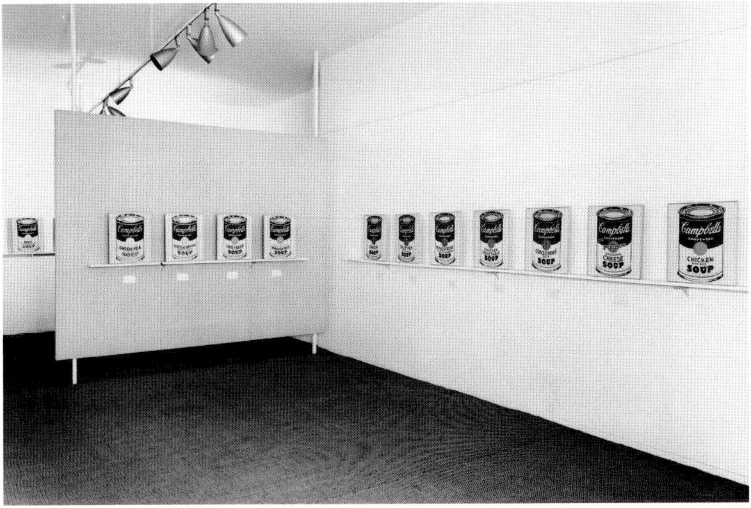

←

William Claxton

Artists Ed Moses, John Altoon, and Billy Al Bengston with gallery owner Irving Blum, Ferus Gallery, 1959.

Die Künstler Ed Moses, John Altoon und Billy Al Bengston mit dem Galeristen Irving Blum vor der Ferus Gallery, 1959.

Les artistes Ed Moses, John Altoon, et Billy Al Bengston avec le galeriste Irving Blum devant la galerie Ferus, 1959.

↑

Seymour Rosen

Andy Warhol's first solo show, at the Ferus Gallery, introduced Pop Art to the West Coast, July 9, 1962. "Andy agreed to sell the group of Soup Can Paintings for $1,000," said Irving Blum. "The rest, as they say, is history."

Andy Warhols erste Einzelausstellung am 9. Juli 1962 in der Ferus Gallery brachte die Pop-Art an die Westküste. „Andy erklärte sich bereit, die Serie von Campells Suppendosen für 1 000 Dollar zu verkaufen. Der Rest ist, wie man so sagt, Geschichte."

La première exposition personnelle d'Andy Warhol à la galerie Ferus le 9 juillet 1962, a lancé le pop art sur la côte Ouest. « Andy accepta de vendre la série de peintures des boîtes de soupe pour 1 000 $, déclara Irving Blum. Tout le monde connaît la suite. »

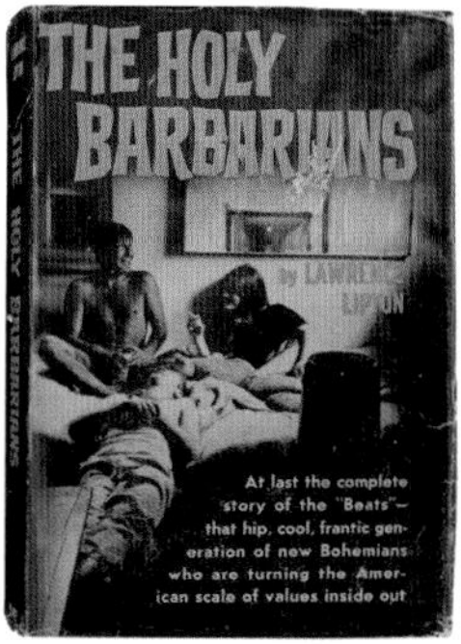

"All the impatient young-men-in-a-hurry, the lost, the seekers, the beat, the disaffiliated, the educated, diseducated, re-educated, in quest of a new vision…come to hole in for a while in a Venice pad."

„Alle ungeduldigen, ewig-eiligen jungen Männer, Verlorene, Suchende, Geschlagene, Ausgeschlossene, Gebildete, Ungebildete, Umerzogene, jeder auf der Suche nach neuen Visionen…kommt, um sich ein Weilchen in einer Bude in Venice zu verkriechen."

« Tous les jeunes hommes pressés impatients, les égarés, les chercheurs, les fatigués, les francs-tireurs, les éduqués, les dés-éduqués, les rééduqués, en quête d'une nouvelle vision… venaient passer un moment dans une crèche de Venice. »

Lawrence Lipton, *The Holy Barbarians*, 1950

→
Anonymous

Inspired by the West Hollywood chili joint and artist hangout, artist Ed Kienholz created an ode to pop commonplace in his three-dimensional tableau, shown here partially displayed in front of the actual Beanery, 1965.

Inspiriert vom Chili-Restaurant und Künstlertreffpunkt in West Hollywood, realisierte der Künstler Ed Kienholz mit seinem dreidimensionalen Tableau eine Hommage an die Alltagskultur; hier eine Teilansicht der Installation vor der echten Beanery, 1965.

Inspirée par la gargote de spécialités au chili de West Hollywood où se retrouvaient, entre autres, les artistes de l'époque, Ed Kienholz a créé une ode pop à la banalité avec ce tableau tridimensionnel, ici partiellement exposé devant la véritable Beanery, *1965.*

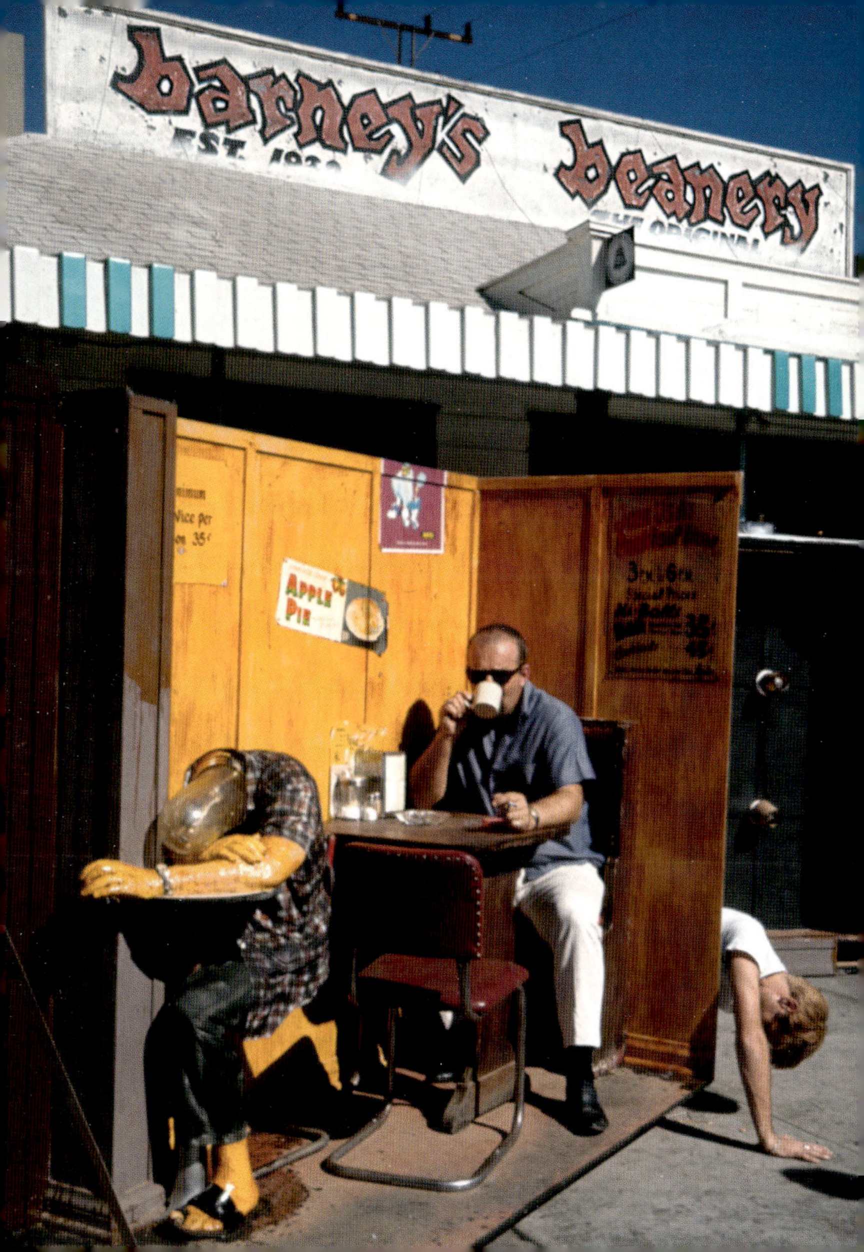
barney's beanery
APPLE PIE

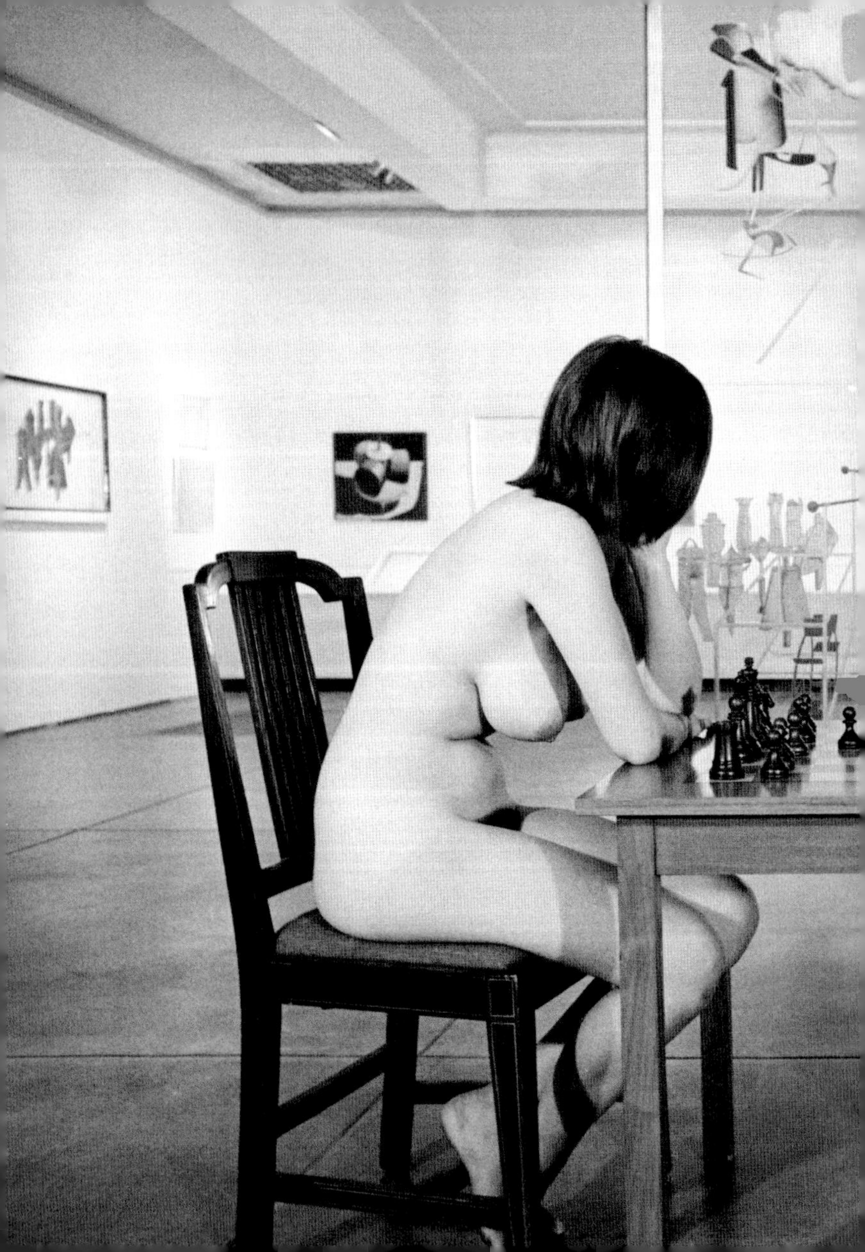

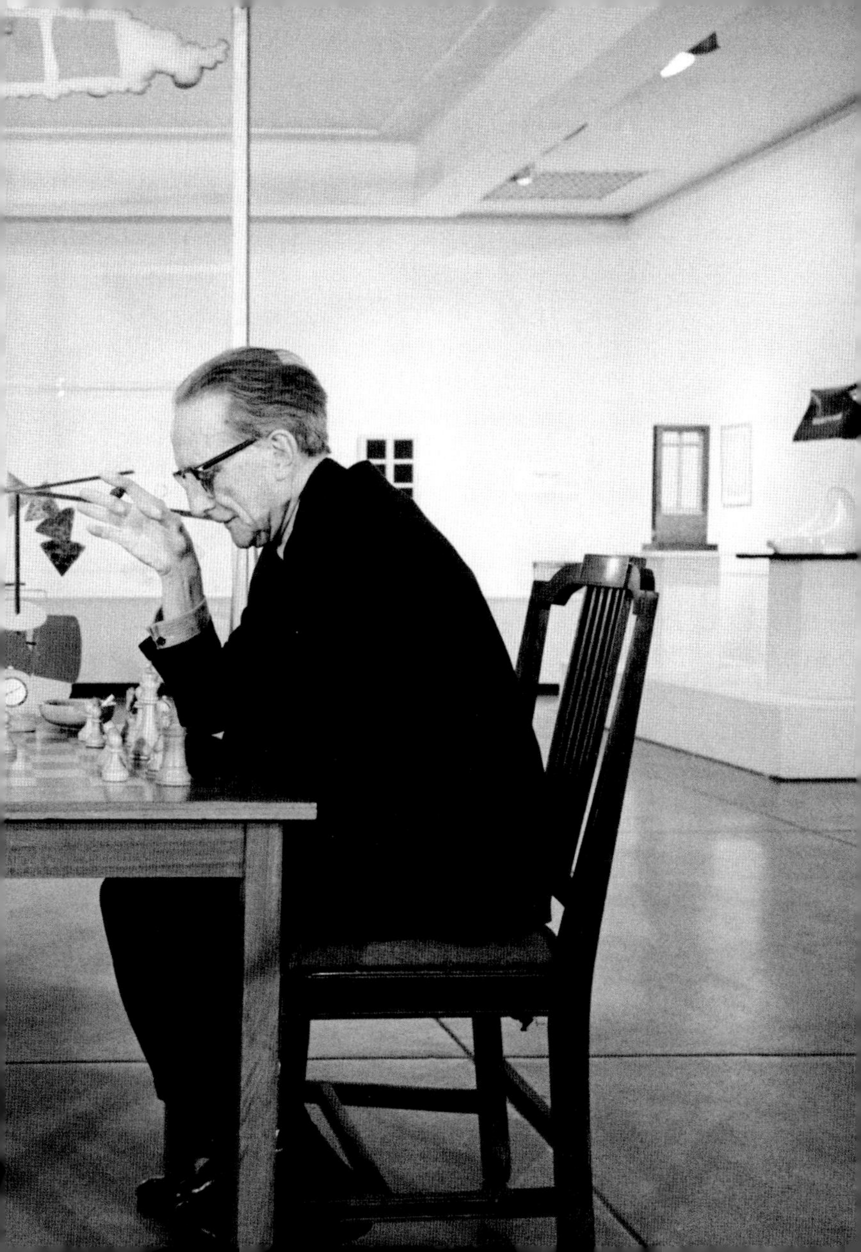

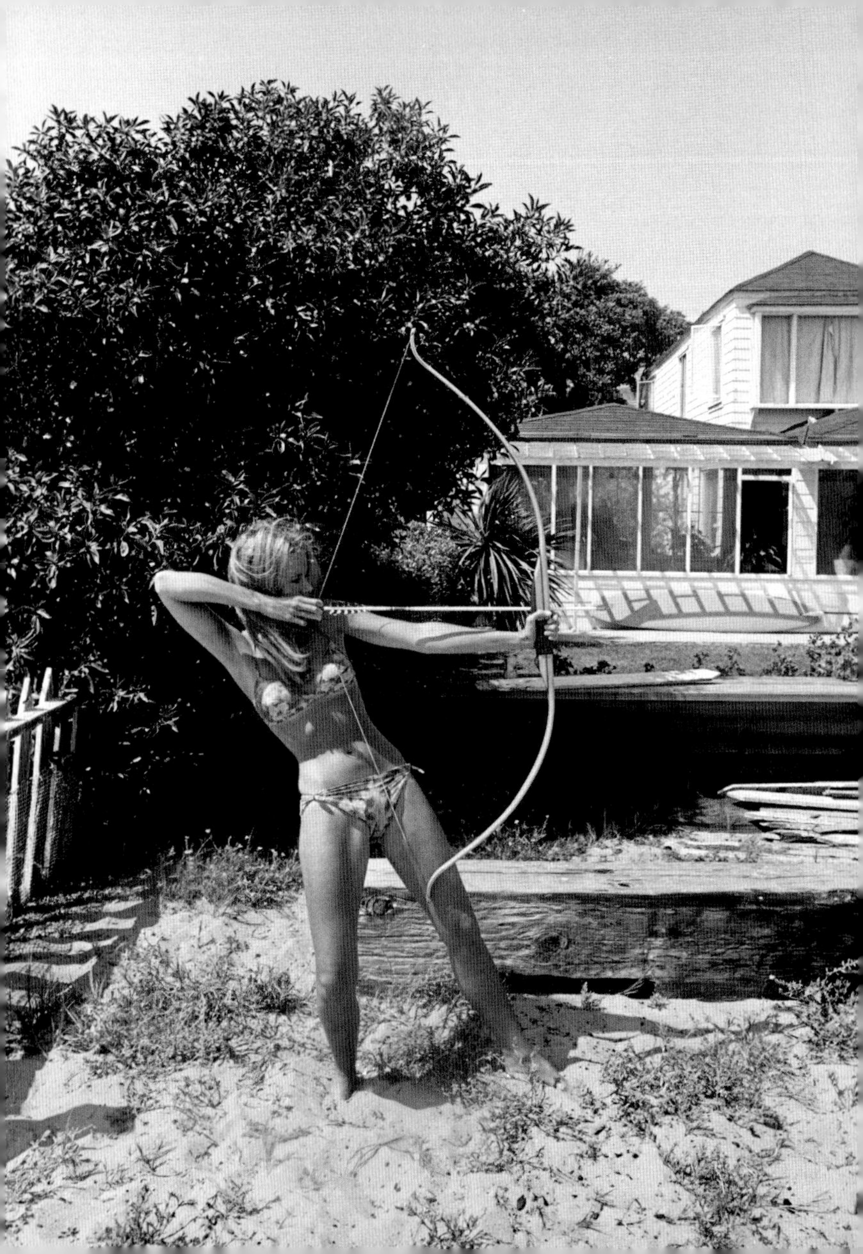

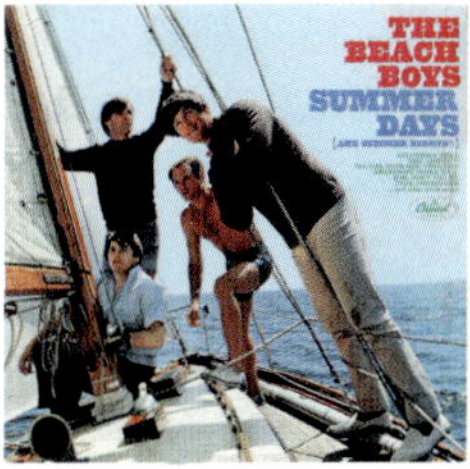

"Well East Coast girls are hip
I really dig those styles they wear
And the Southern girls with the way they talk
They knock me out when I'm down there.

"The West Coast has the sunshine
And the girls all get so tanned
I dig a French bikini on Hawai'i island
Dolls by a palm tree in the sand.

"I been all around this great big world
And I seen all kinds of girls
Yeah, but I couldn't wait to get back in the States
Back to the cutest girls in the world
I wish they all could be California girls."

The Beach Boys, "California Girls," 1965

p. 154/155
Julian Wasser

In a surreal piece of spontaneous performance art, a nude Eve Babitz engages Marcel Duchamp in a chess match at the Pasadena Museum of Art, 1963.

Eve Babitz bei einer surrealen, spontanen Performance, bei der sie nackt eine Partie Schach mit Marcel Duchamp spielte, Pasadena Museum of Art, 1963.

Dans une performance artistique surréaliste, Eve Babitz nue défie Marcel Duchamp aux échecs au Pasadena Museum of Art, 1963.

←
Dennis Hopper

A daughter of Hollywood royalty, Jane Fonda poses at a Malibu beach cottage, 1965.

Jane Fonda, Tochter einer Hollywood-Dynastie, posiert an einem Strandhaus in Malibu Beach, 1965.

Fille d'une star d'Hollywood, Jane Fonda pose dans le jardin d'une maison de plage de Malibu, 1965.

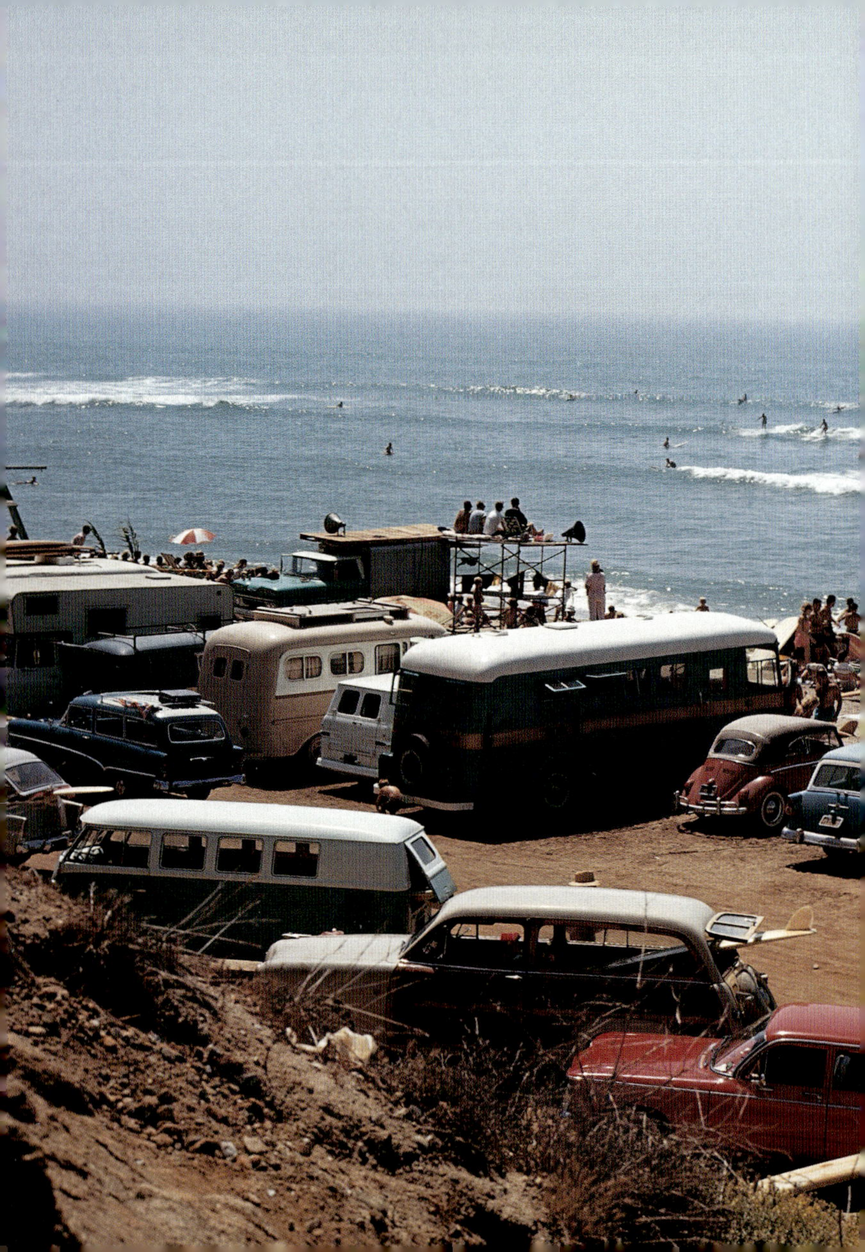

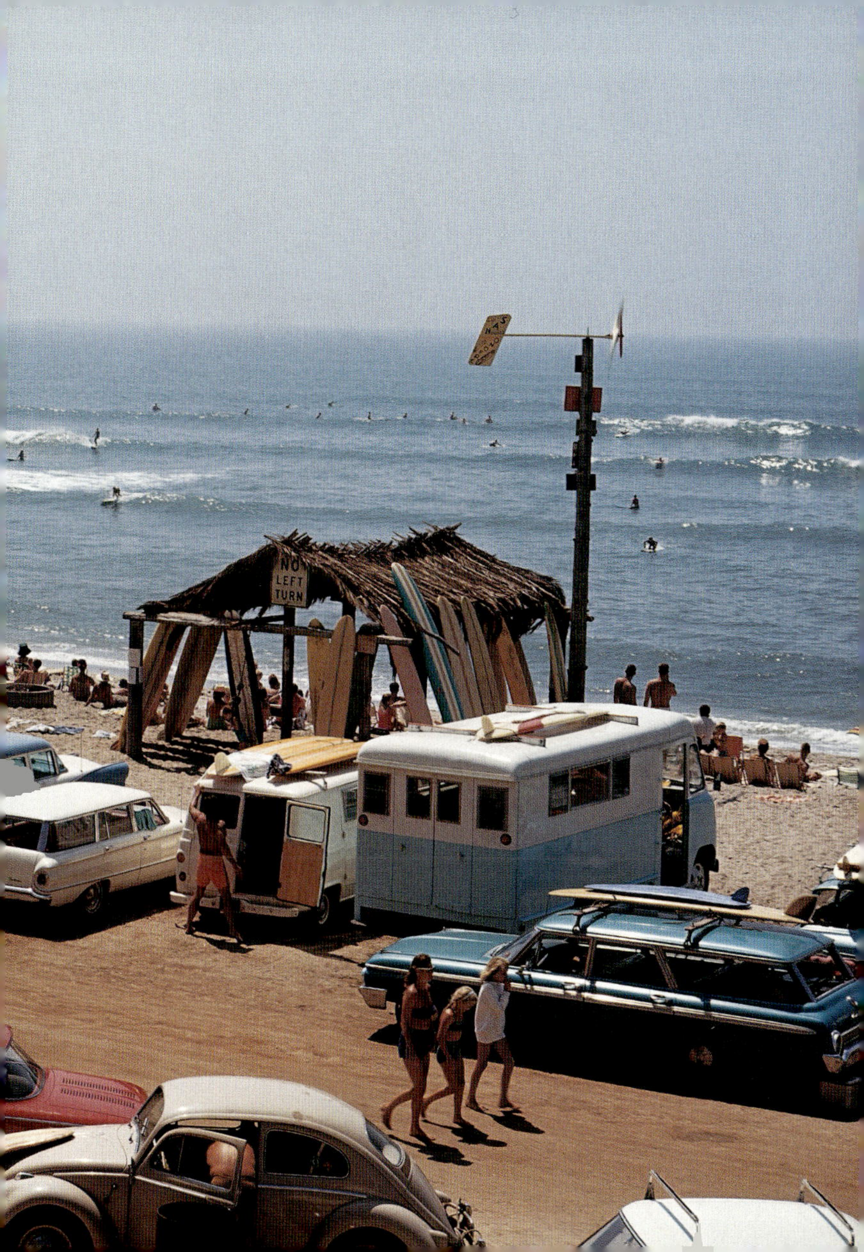
NO
LEFT
TURN

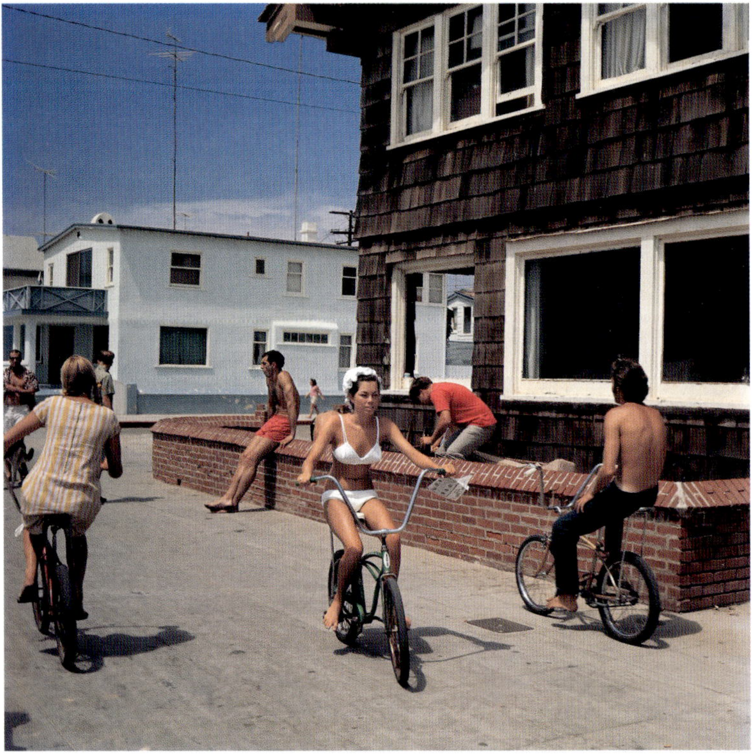

p. 158/159

LeRoy Grannis

*A typical Southern California surf scene, post-*Gidget *era, 1964.*

Eine typische südkalifornische Surferszene in der Zeit nach dem Film Gidget *(dt.* April entdeckt die Männer*), 1964.*

*Une scène de surf typique de la Californie du Sud, ère post-*Gidget*, 1964.*

↑

LeRoy Grannis

The boardwalk in Hermosa Beach, 1967.

Die Strandpromenade in Hermosa Beach, 1967.

La promenade longeant la plage d'Hermosa Beach, 1967.

→

Julius Shulman

Watts Towers, built by construction worker Simon Rodia in his spare time over a 30-year period, 1966.

Watts Towers war ein Projekt, das der Bauarbeiter Simon Rodia in über 30-jähriger Arbeit in seiner Freizeit errichtet hatte, 1966.

Les tours Watts, résultat de plus de trente ans de travail de l'ouvrier du bâtiment Simon Rodia pendant ses loisirs, 1966.

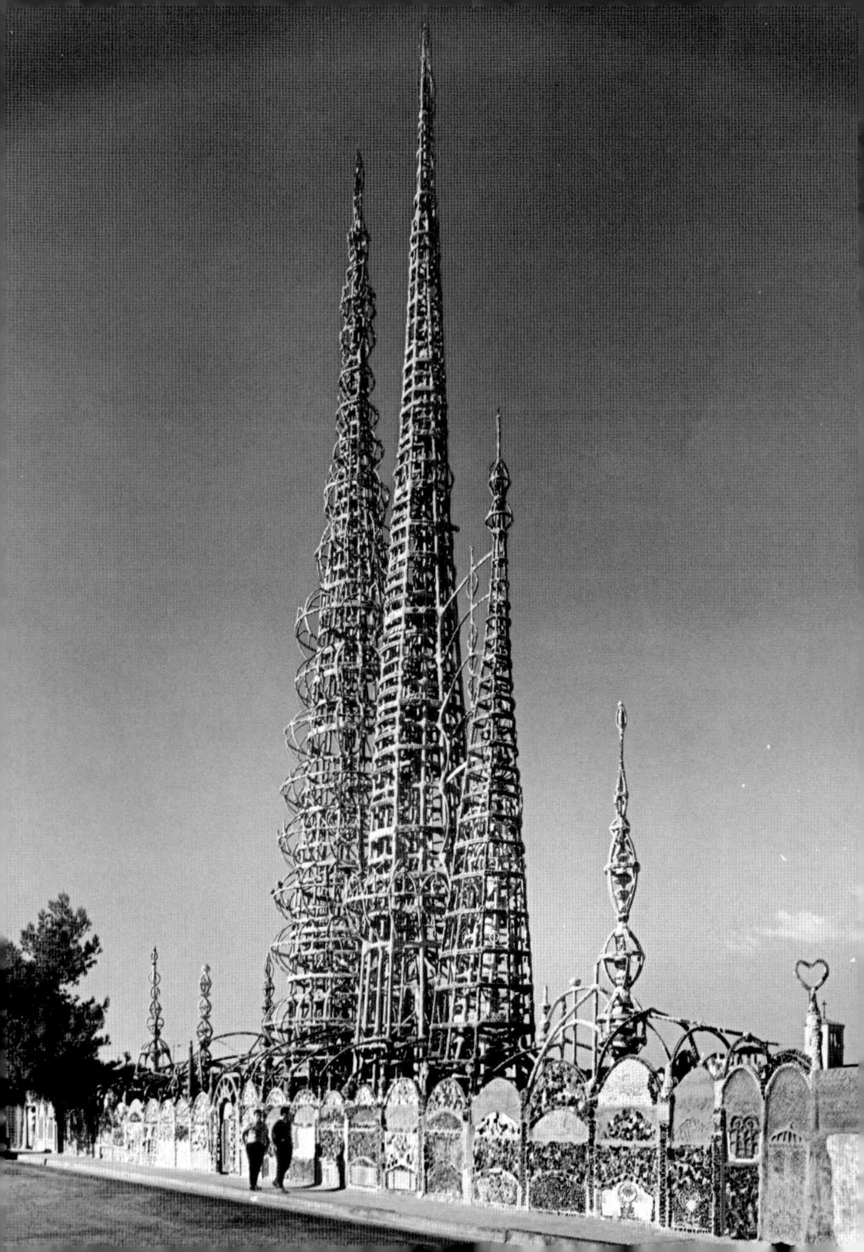

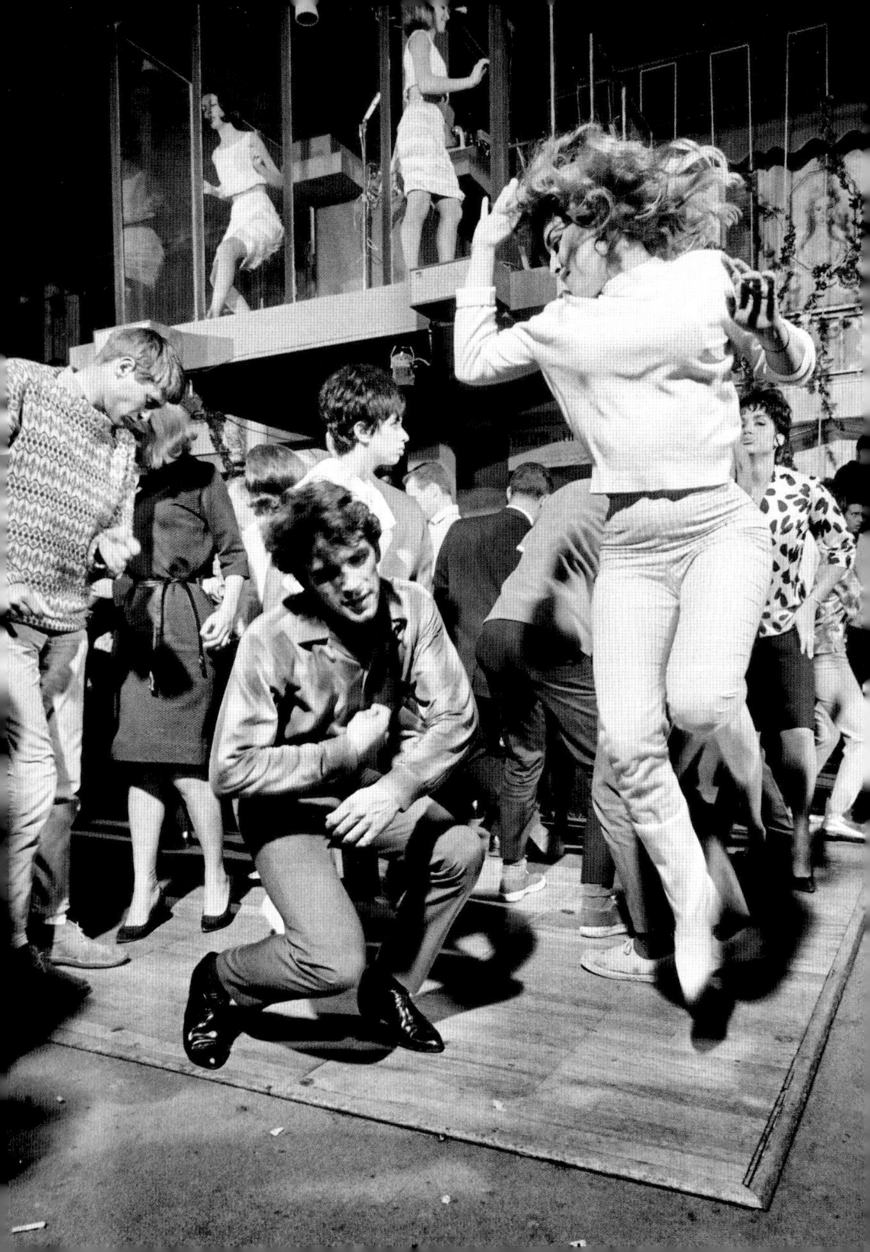

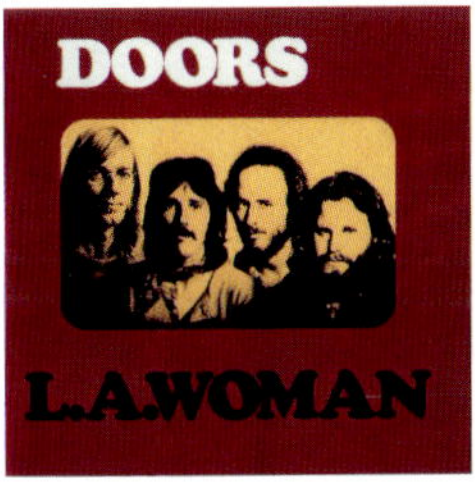

"Well, I just got into town about an hour ago
Took a look around, see which way the wind blows
Where the little girls in their Hollywood bungalows
Are you a lucky little lady in the city of light
Or just another lost angel
City of night.

"I see your hair is burnin'
Hills are filled with fire
If they say I never loved you
You know they are a liar
Drivin' down your freeways
Midnight alleys roam
Cops in cars, the topless bars
Never saw a woman…
So alone, so alone
Motel money murder madness
Let's change the mood from glad to sadness."

The Doors, "L. A. Woman," 1971

←
Julian Wasser
The Whisky A Go Go, 1964, with its signature go-go girls dancing in a cage. The Whisky was the kingpin of Sunset Strip nightclubs in the post-Hollywood-glamour days. Opened in January 1964, it was an instant success, drawing a celebrity crowd that included Jayne Mansfield, Steve McQueen, and Cary Grant.

Das Whisky A Go Go, 1964, mit seinem Markenzeichen, den tanzenden Go-go-Girls im Käfig. Das Whiskey war die Königin der Nachtklubs am Sunset Strip in der Zeit nach dem Hollywood-Glamour. Der 1964 eröffnete Klub hatte sofort Erfolg und zog prominente Gäste wie Jayne Mansfield, Steve McQueen und Cary Grant an.

Le Whisky A Go Go, *1964, avec ses fameuses* go-go girls *dansant dans une cage. Le Whisky était l'attraction numéro 1 des boîtes de nuit du Sunset Strip dans les années qui ont succédé à l'apogée du glamour hollywoodien. Ouvert en janvier 1964, il connut un succès instantané, drainant une foule de célébrités, dont Jayne Mansfield, Steve McQueen et Cary Grant.*

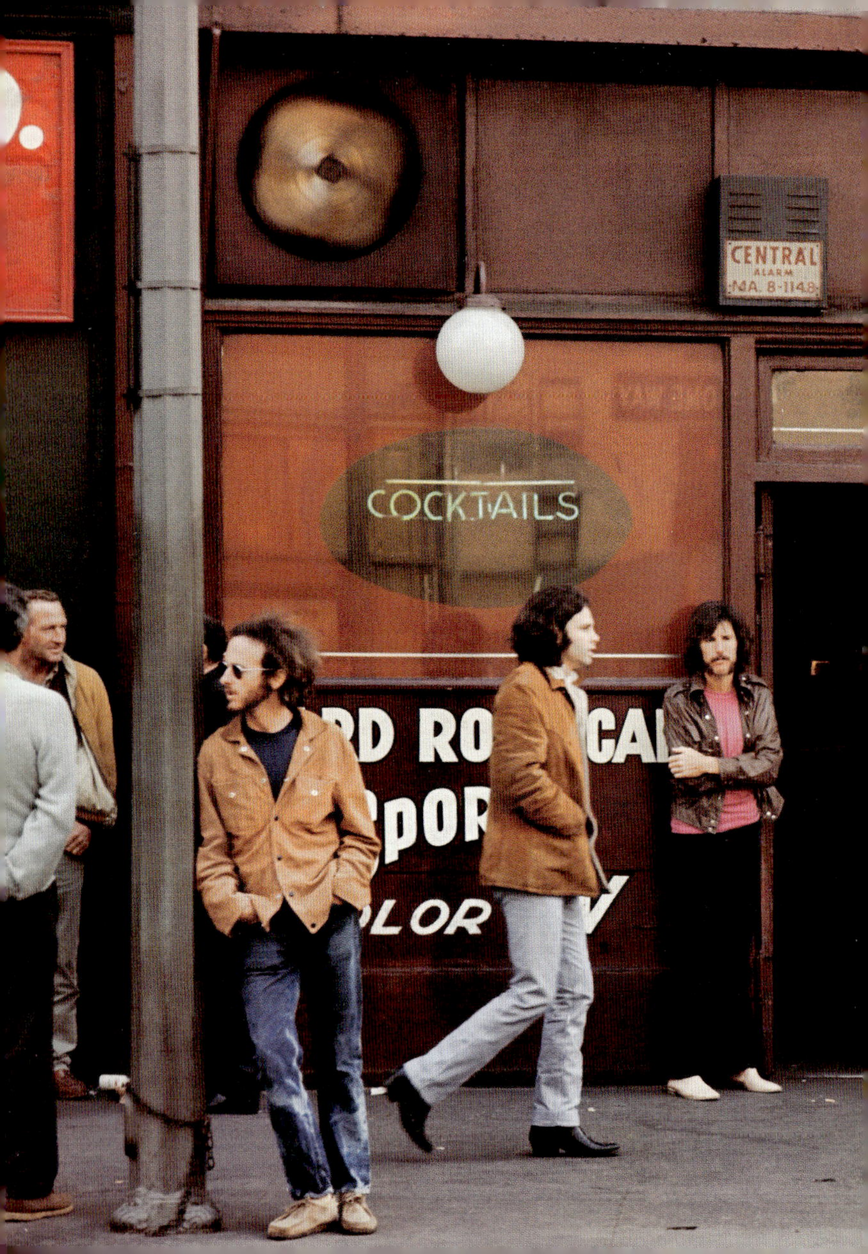
CENTRAL
ALARM
MA 8-1148
COCKTAILS

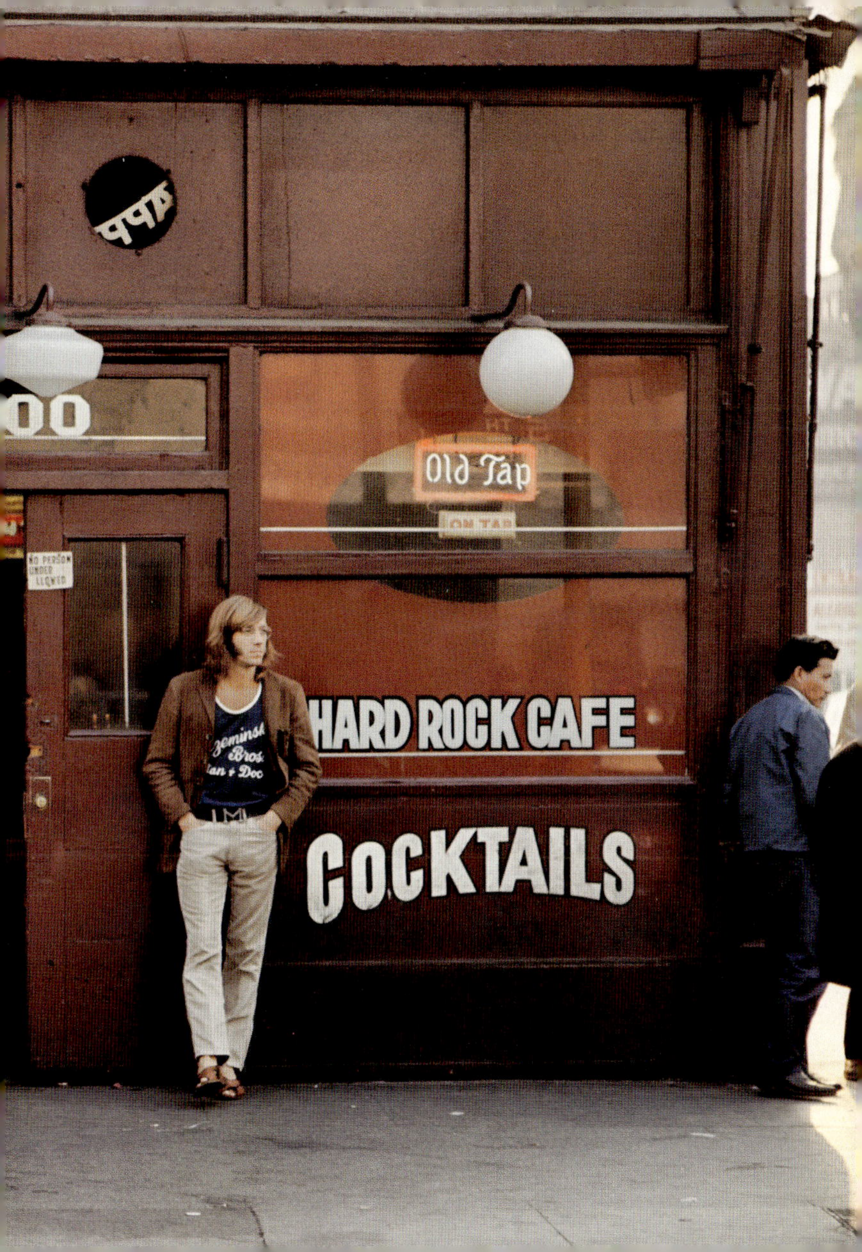
Old Tap
ON TAP
HARD ROCK CAFE
COCKTAILS

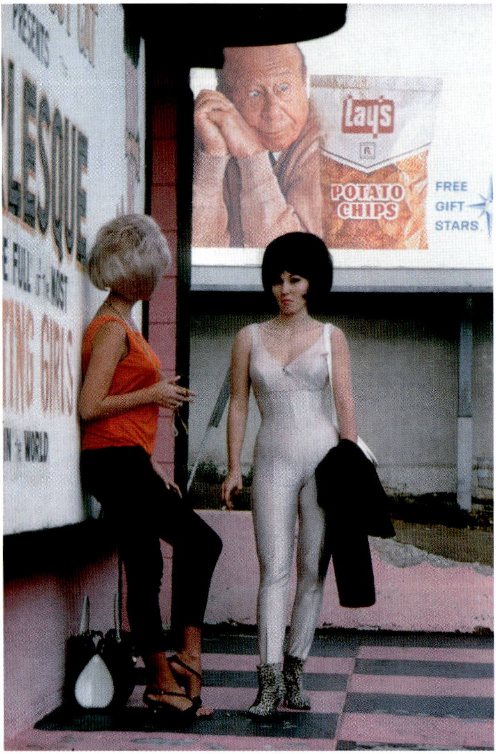

→
Dennis Stock
An alternative-press street vendor was an omnipresent fixture along boulevards frequented by cruising teenagers, 1968.

Auf sämtlichen Boulevards, auf denen Jugendliche unterwegs waren, gehörten die Verkäufer alternativer Zeitungen einfach dazu, 1968.

Les marchands de journaux alternatifs ambulants étaient omniprésents sur les boulevards fréquentés par les adolescents en vadrouille, 1968.

p. 164/165
Henry Diltz
The original Hard Rock Café, at 300 East Fifth Street, was the backdrop for a Doors photo shoot, 1969.

Das original Hard Rock Café in der East Fifth Street 300 dient als Kulisse für ein Fotoshooting mit den Doors, 1969.

Le Hard Rock Café original, au 300 Est de la 5e Rue, sert de toile de fond à cette photo des Doors, 1969.

↑
Burt Glinn
Streetwalkers prepare for an evening's work, 1965.

Prostituierte bereiten sich auf die Nachtschicht vor, 1965.

Des belles-de-nuit se préparent à une soirée de travail, 1965.

p. 168/169
Dennis Stock
Celebrating the summer equinox in front of the Pacific Ocean Park pier at the Venice Beach Rock Festival, 1968.

Feier der Sommer-Tagundnachtgleiche am Ocean Pier beim Venice Beach Rock Festival, 1968.

Célébration de l'équinoxe d'été devant l'embarcadère du Pacific Ocean Park lors du Venice Beach Rock Festival, 1968.

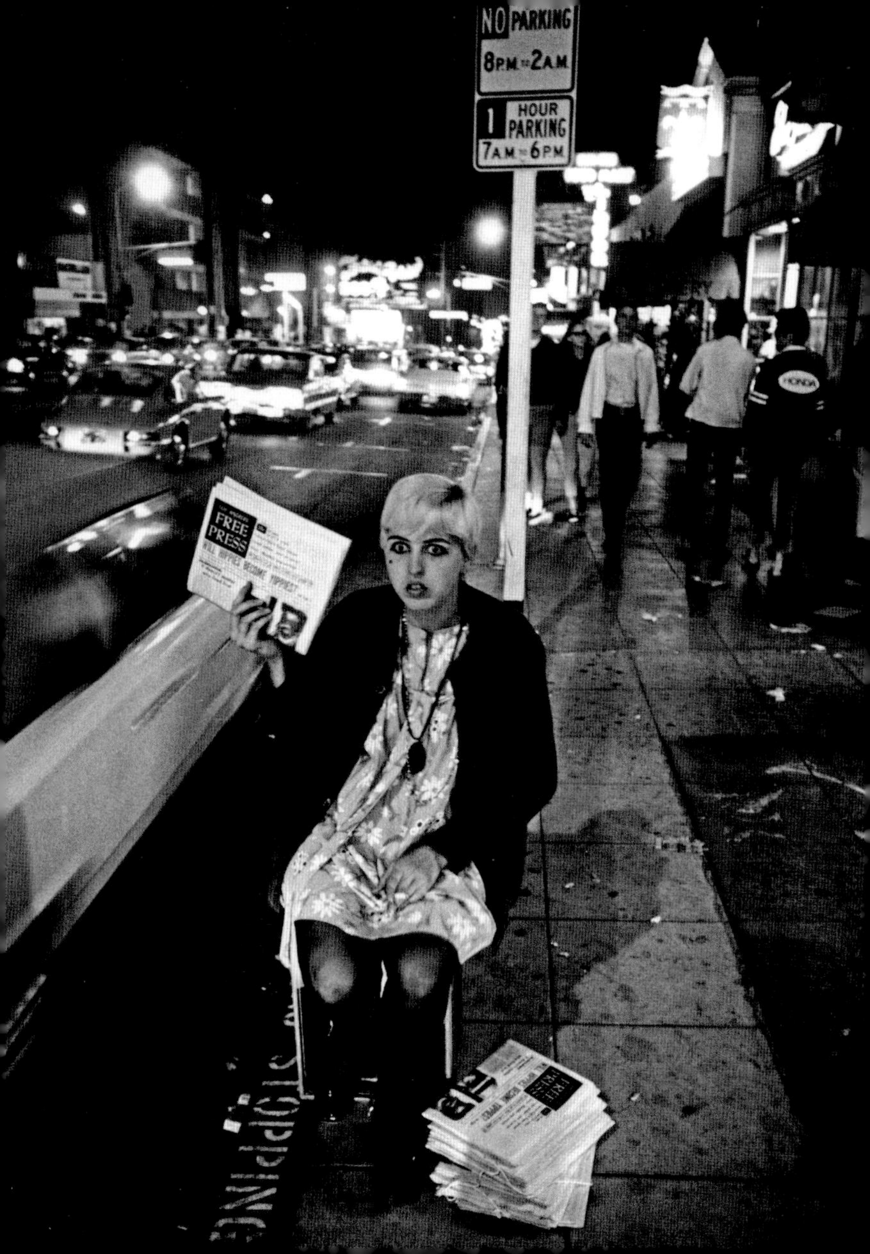
NO PARKING
8P.M. 2A.M.
1 HOUR PARKING
7A.M. 6P.M.
FREE PRESS
HONDA

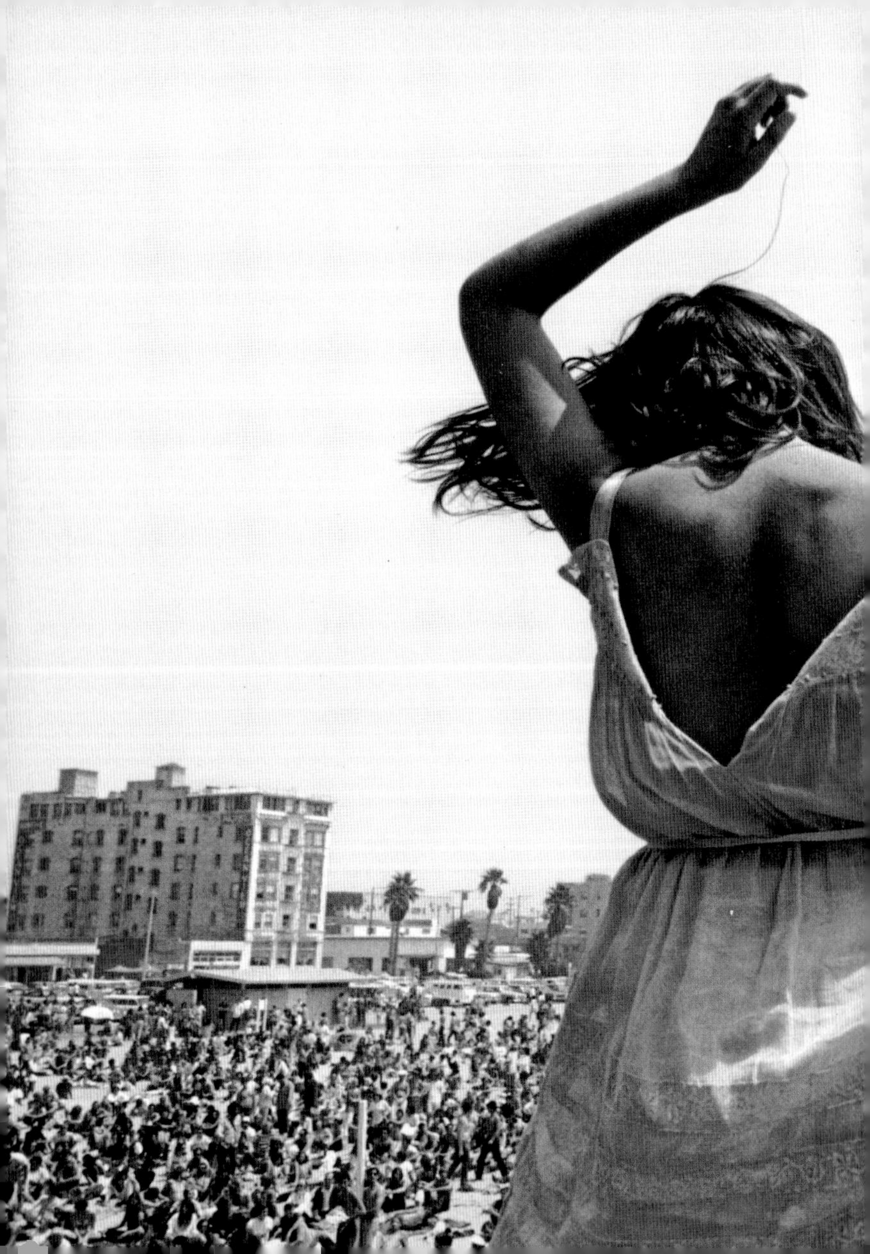

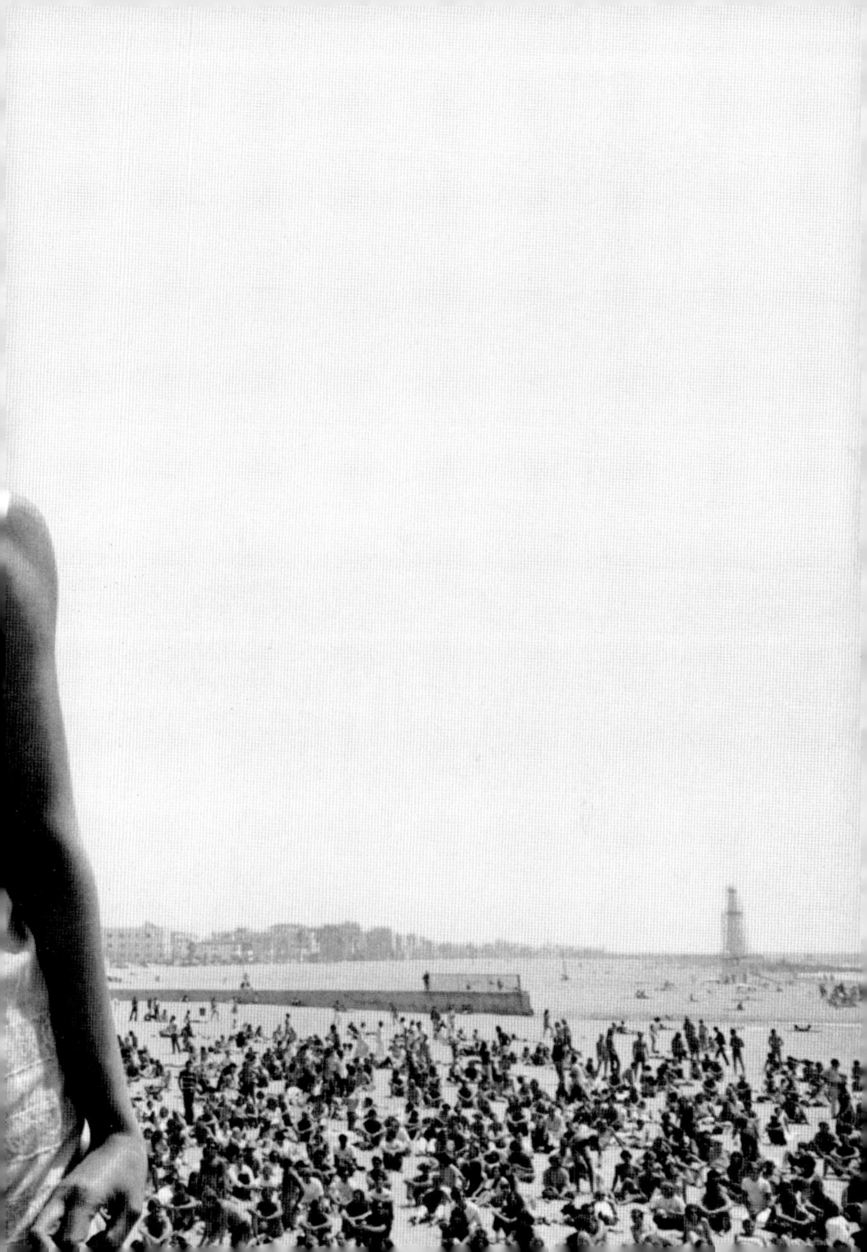

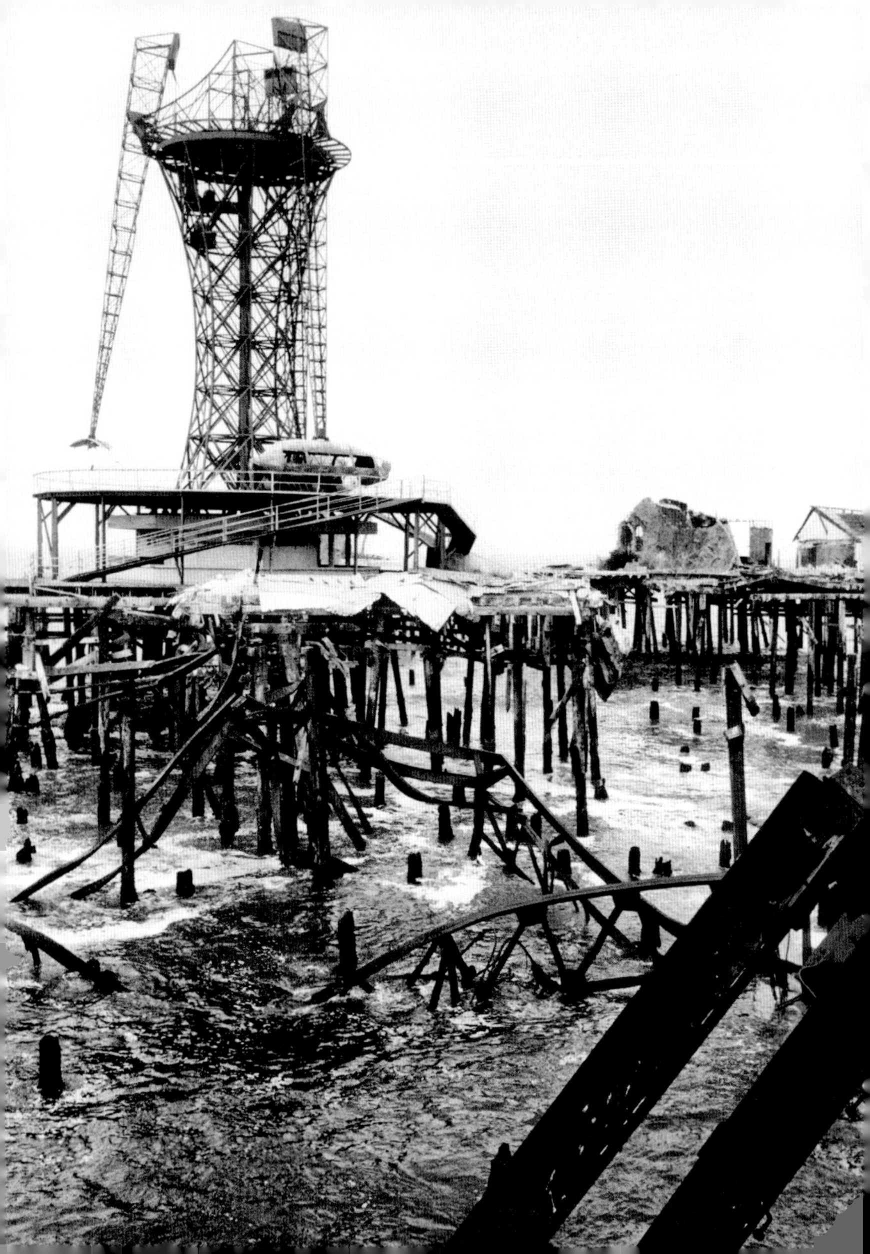

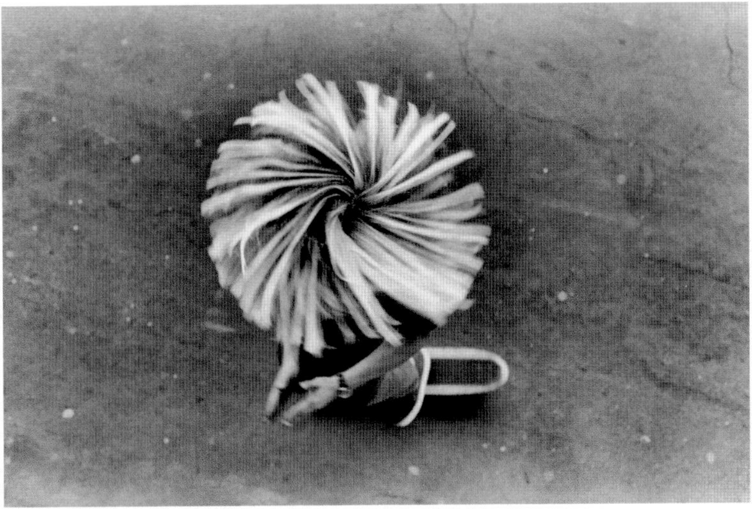

←

Anthony Friedkin

The remnants of Pacific Ocean Park pier after several fires laid waste to the decades-old pier, c. 1968.

Die Überreste des Pacific-Ocean-Park-Piers, nachdem der jahrzehntealte Pier durch mehrere Brände zerstört worden war, um 1968.

Les vestiges de l'embarcadère occupé par le Pacific Ocean Park après que divers incendies eurent détruit l'embarcadère vieux de quelques décennies, vers 1968.

↑

C.R. Stecyk III

A stylistic whirl of hair defines a freestyle and renegade skateboard culture, led by a local tribe of practitioners in Santa Monica called DogTown, c. 1972.

Das wirbelnde Haar wird zum Wahrzeichen der rebellischen Freestyle-Skateboardszene, angeführt von den DogTowns, einer Gruppe Skateboardern in Santa Monica, um 1972.

Cet élégant tourbillon de cheveux définit la culture skate freestyle *et rebelle, initiée par une tribu locale de pratiquants dans Santa Monica rebaptisée DogTown, vers 1972.*

Stingray

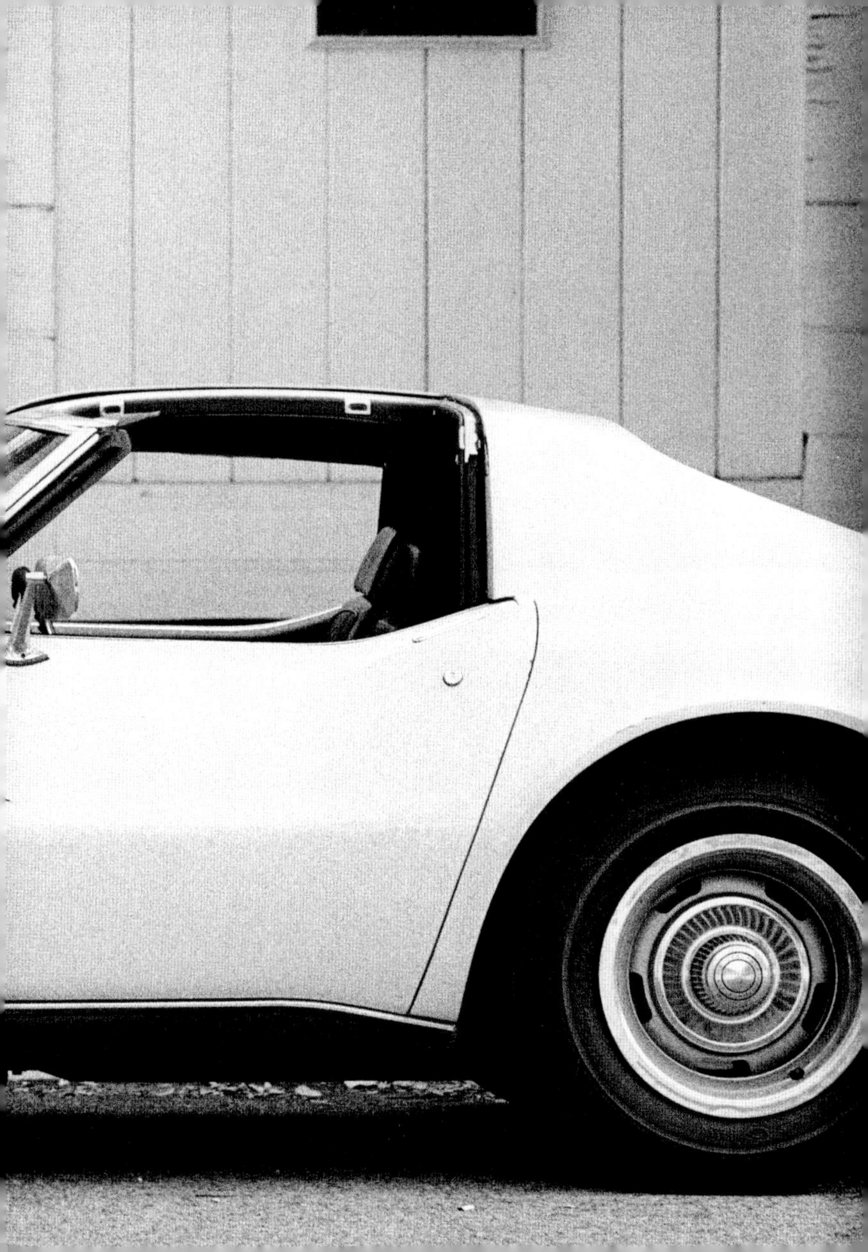

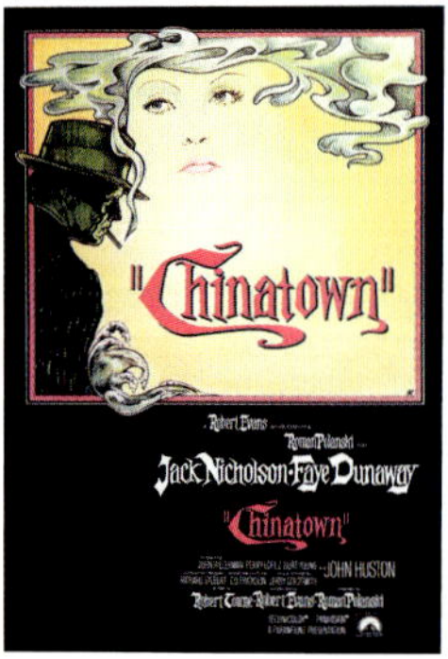

"Forget it, Jake. It's Chinatown."

„Vergiss es, Jake. Das ist Chinatown."

« Oublie ça Jake. C'est Chinatown. »

***Chinatown,* 1974**

p. 172/173

Julian Wasser

A California native, Joan Didion spent 20 years in Los Angeles with husband and fellow writer John Gregory Dunne observing and chronicling the region's cultural landscape, 1970.

Die in Kalifornien geborene Joan Didion lebte mit ihrem Mann John Gregory Dunne, der ebenfalls Schriftsteller war, 20 Jahre lang in Los Angeles und beobachtete und dokumentierte die Kulturlandschaft der Region, 1970.

Native de Californie, Joan Didion a passé vingt ans à Los Angeles avec John Gregory Dunne, son mari et compagnon d'écriture, à observer et tenir la chronique du paysage culturel de la région, 1970.

→

Steve Schapiro

Filming the climactic final scene of Chinatown, *1972.*

Beim Dreh der dramatischen Schlussszene von Chinatown, *1972.*

Le tournage de la scène finale paroxystique de Chinatown, *1972.*

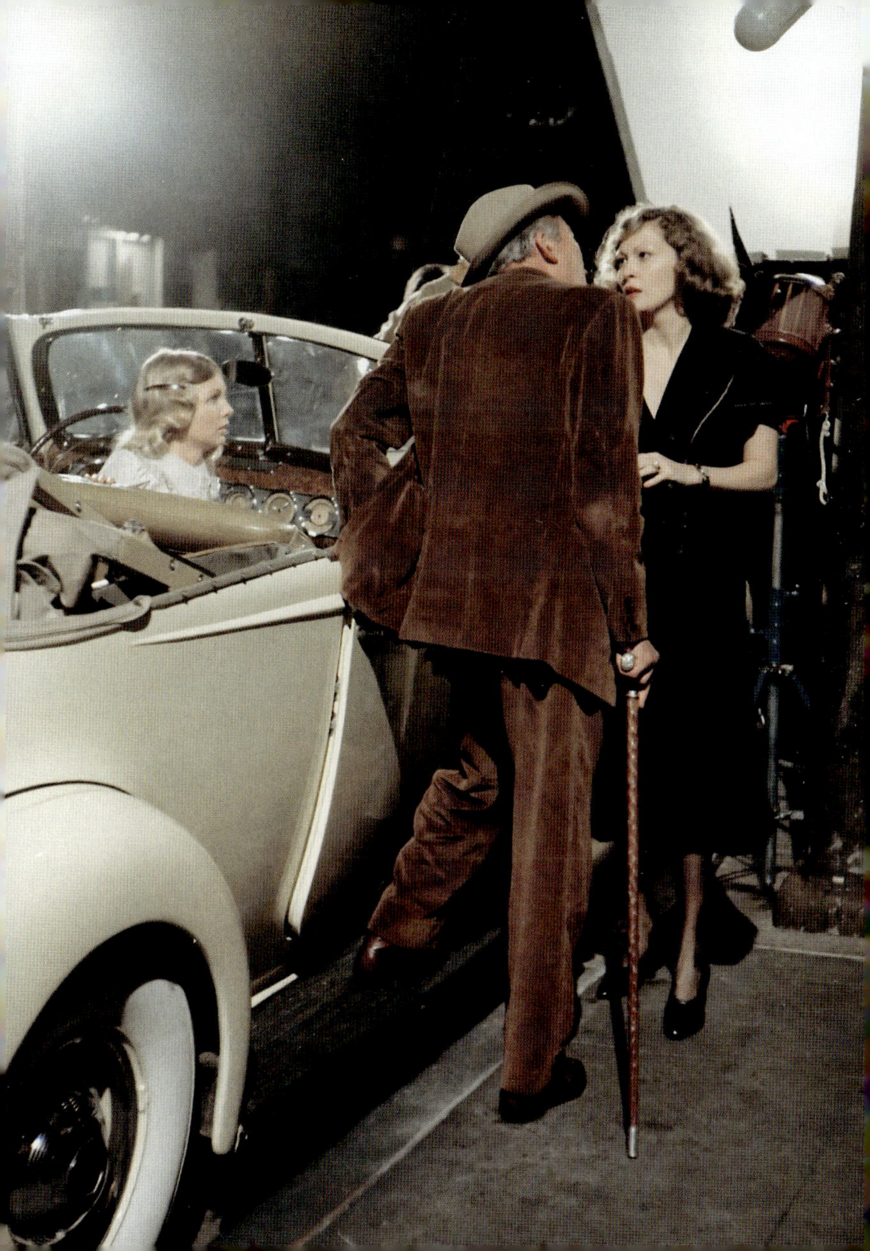

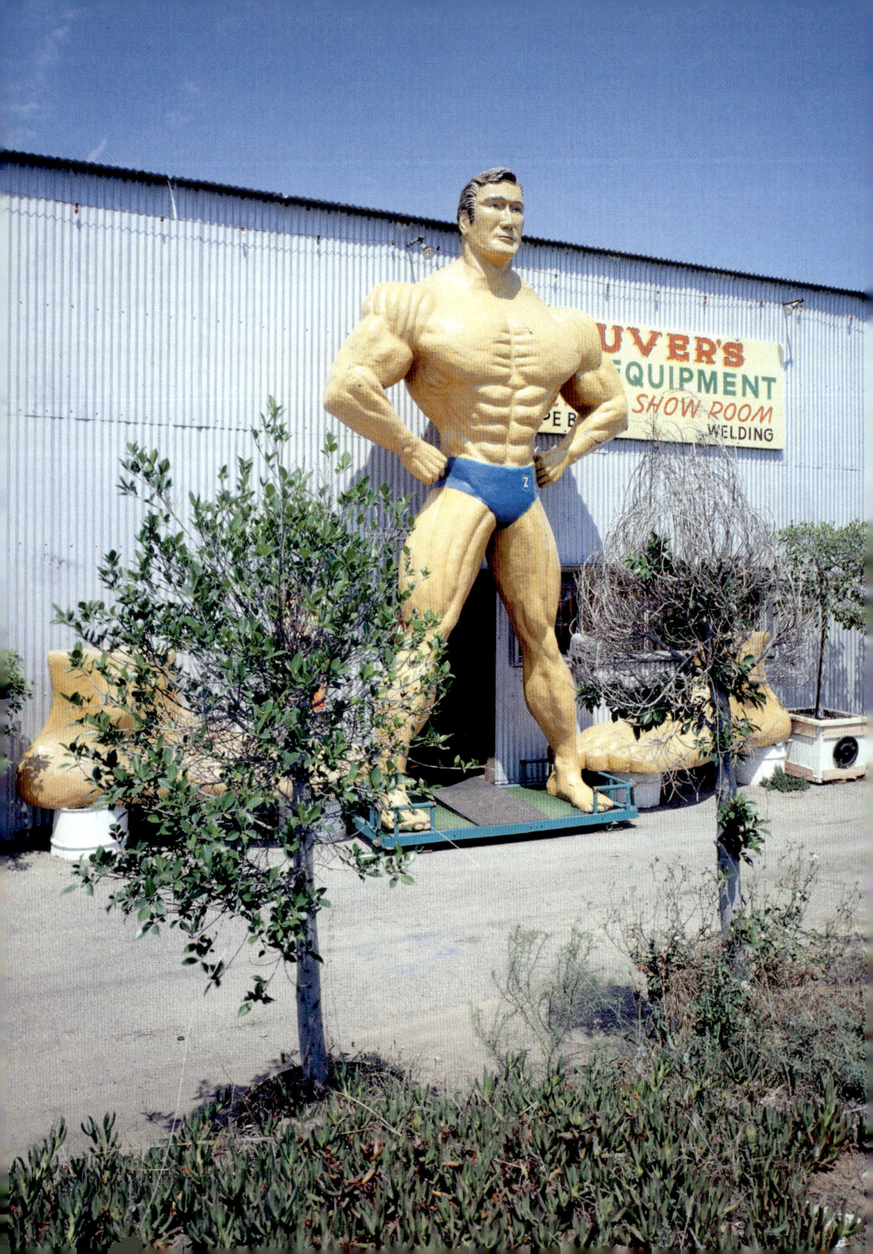
UVER'S
EQUIPMENT
SHOW ROOM
WELDING

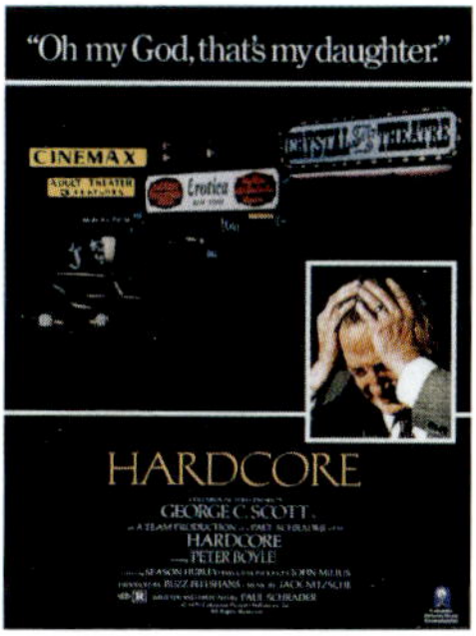

"A lot of strange things happen in this world. Things you don't know about in Grand Rapids. Things you don't want to know about. Doors that shouldn't be opened."

„Viele seltsame Dinge passieren auf dieser Welt. Dinge, von denen man in Grand Rapids nichts weiß. Dinge, von denen man nichts wissen will. Türen, die man besser nicht öffnen sollte."

« Beaucoup de choses étranges arrivent en ce monde. Des choses que vous ne connaissez pas à Grand Rapids. Des choses dont vous ne voulez pas entendre parler. Des portes qui ne devraient pas être ouvertes. »

***Hardcore*, 1979**

←

Douglas Hill

Kitsch imitates reality at a movie-prop rental shop, c. 1978.

Kitsch imitiert bei einem Filmrequisitenverleih die Realität, um 1978.

Le kitsch imite la réalité dans ce magasin de location d'accessoires de cinéma, vers 1978.

p. 178/179

Jim Heimann

With a bold and naive approach, as seen in this East Los Angeles muffler shop, businesses became sophisticated folk art as an increased Hispanic presence changed the way the city looked, 1987.

Mit gewagt-naiven Ladenfronten wie bei dieser Auspuffwerkstatt in East Los Angeles entwickelten Geschäfte sich zu aufwendigen Folkart-Kunstwerken, als die zunehmende hispanische Bevölkerung das Gesicht der Stadt veränderte, 1987.

Une présence hispanique accrue a changé l'aspect de la ville. Mêlant naïveté et audace, témoin ce magasin de silencieux pour pots d'échappements de East Los Angeles, les commerces sont devenus des œuvres d'art, 1987.

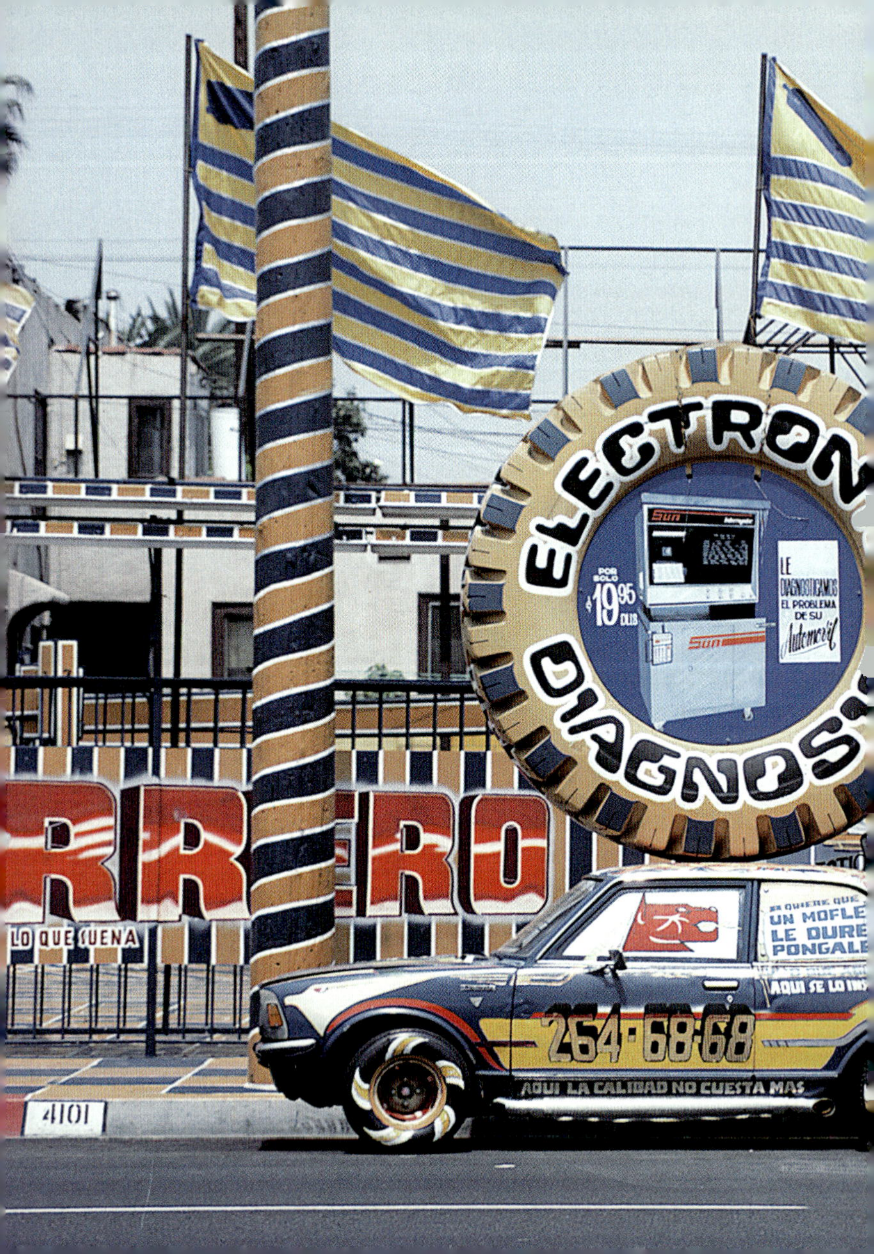
ELECTRON
DIAGNOS
POR SOLO $19.95 DLLS
Sun
LE DIAGNOSTICAMOS EL PROBLEMA DE SU Automovil
RRERO
LO QUE SUENA
UN MOFLE
LE DURE
PONGALE
AQUI SE LO INS
264-68-68
AQUI LA CALIDAD NO CUESTA MAS
4101

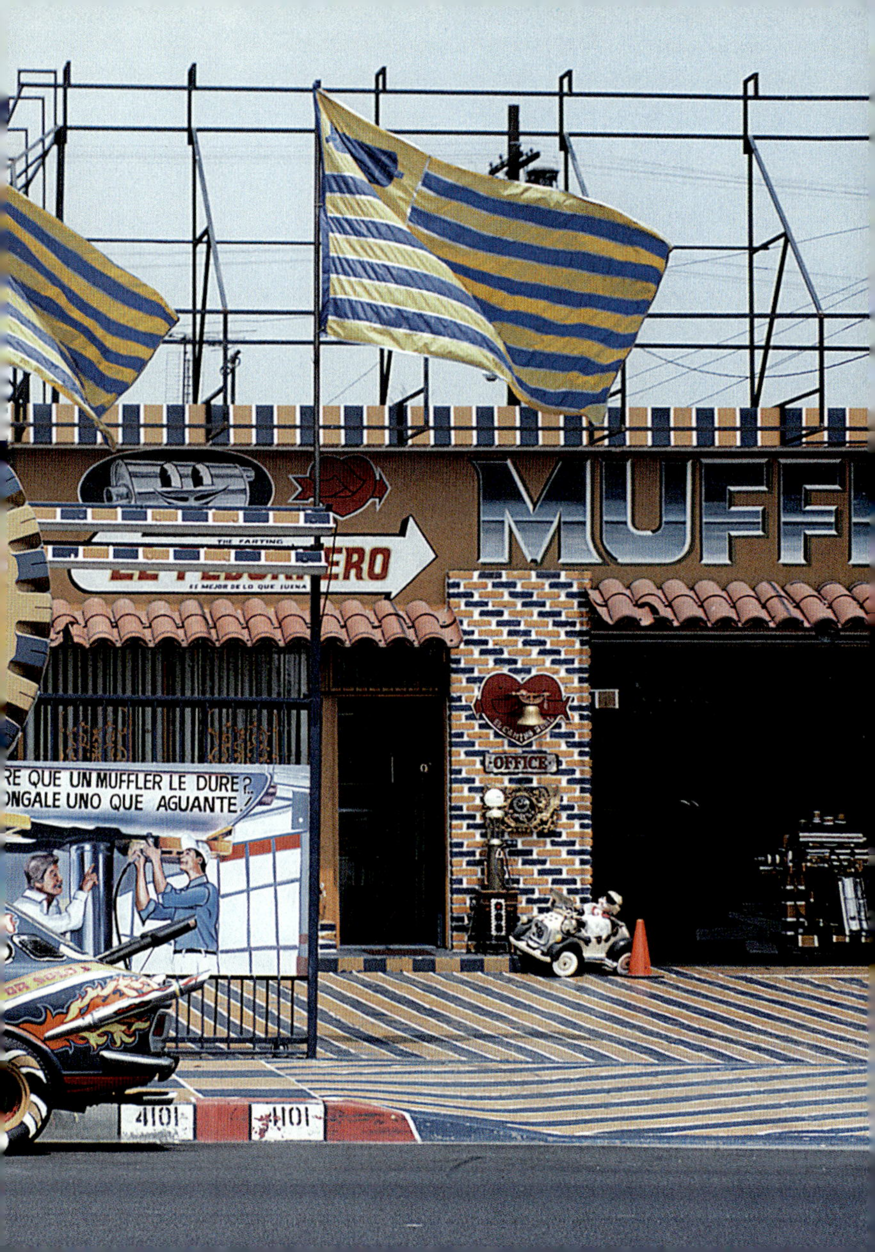
MUFF
THE FARTING
ERO
OFFICE
RE QUE UN MUFFLER LE DURE?
ONGALE UNO QUE AGUANTE
4101

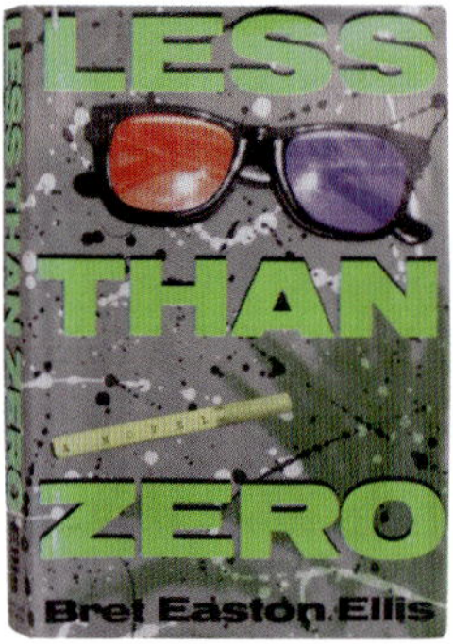

"After leaving Blaire … I stop at a Sambo's that's open all night …"

„Nachdem ich bei Blair's los bin … schaue ich bei Sambo's rein, das die ganze Nacht geöffnet hat …"

« Après avoir quitté Blaire… je m'arrête à Sambo's qui est ouvert toute la nuit. »

Bret Easton Ellis, *Less Than Zero*, 1985

→
Lennox McLendon

Officials remove the body of actor-comedian John Belushi from a bungalow at the Chateau Marmont, 1982.

Beamte holen die Leiche des Schauspielers John Belushi aus einem der Bungalows des Chateau Marmont, 1982.

Des fonctionnaires municipaux emportent le corps de l'acteur John Belushi d'un bungalow de l'hôtel Chateau Marmont, 1982.

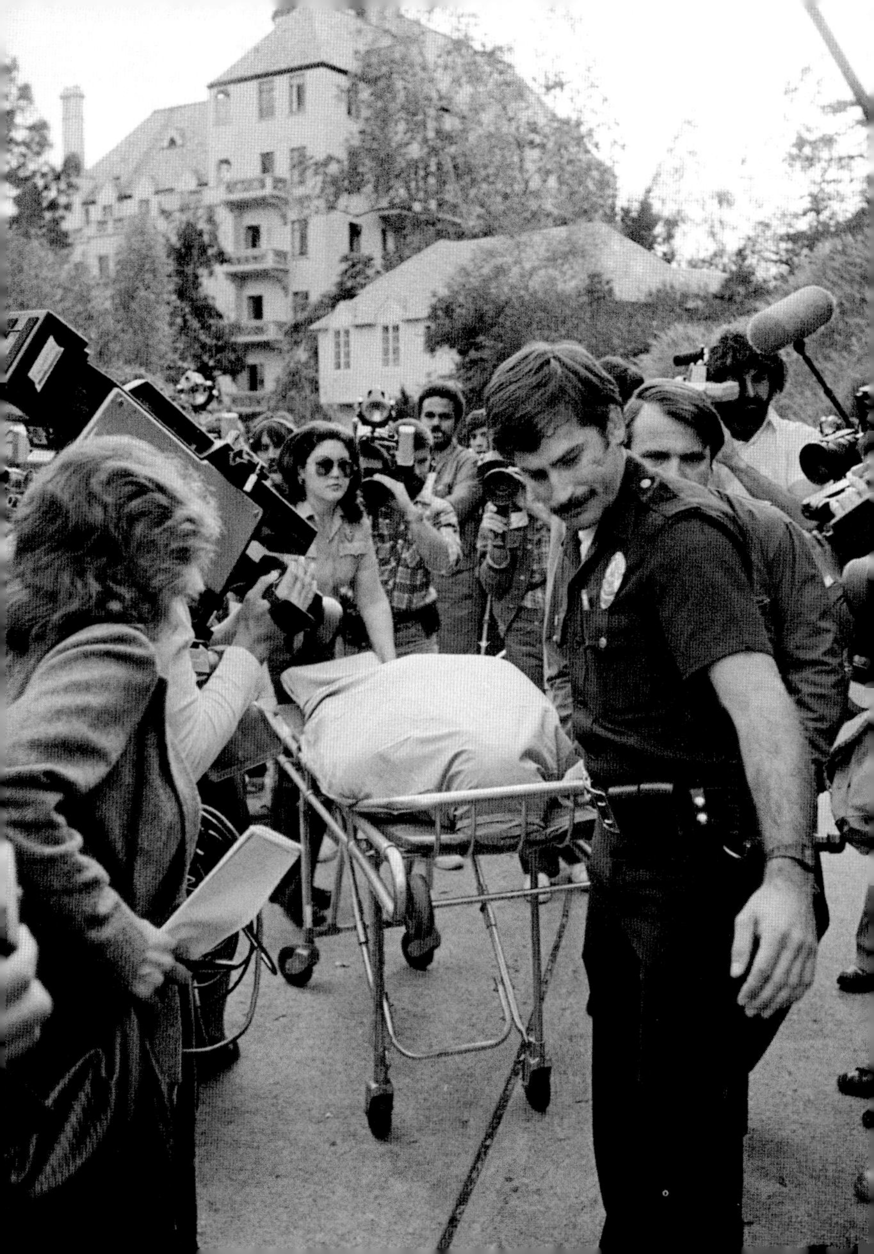

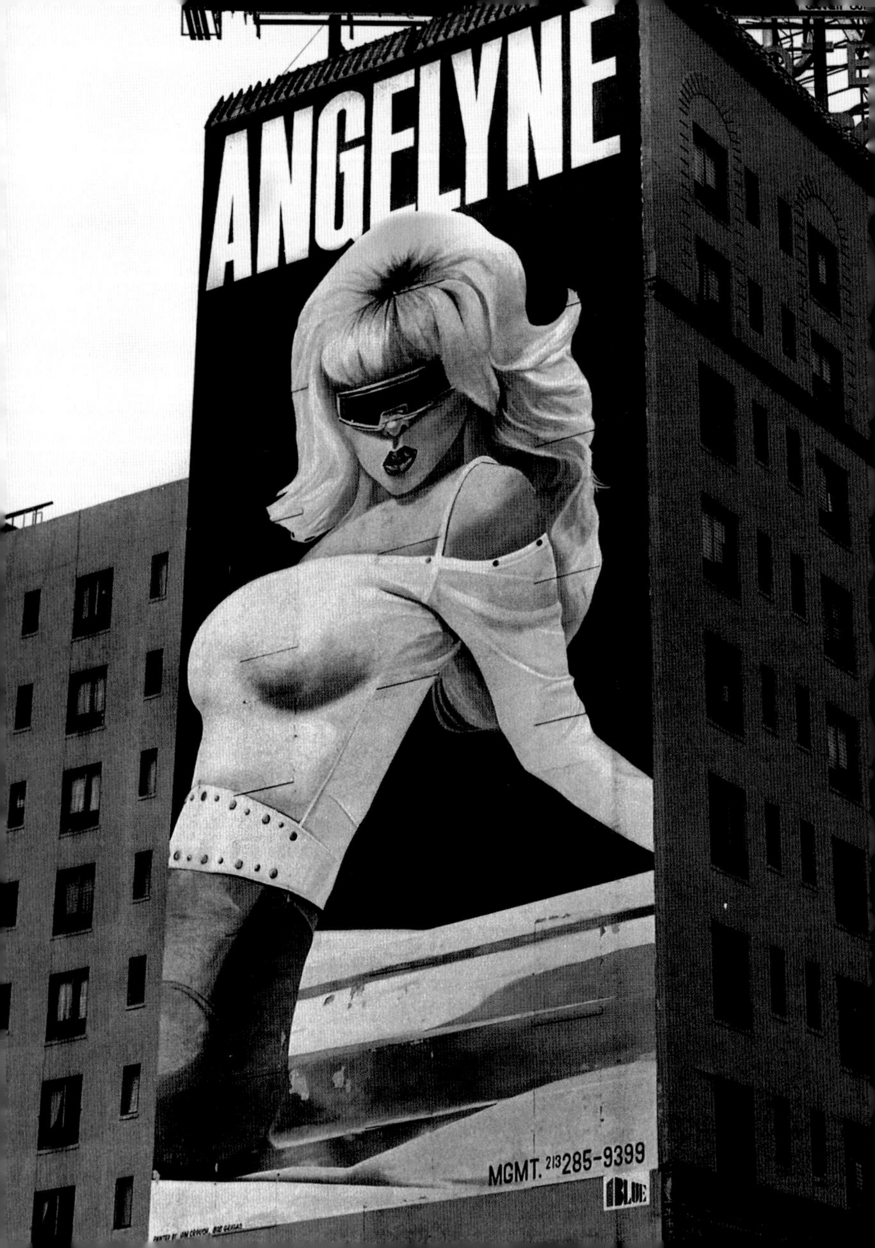
ANGELYNE
MGMT. 213 285-9399
BLUE

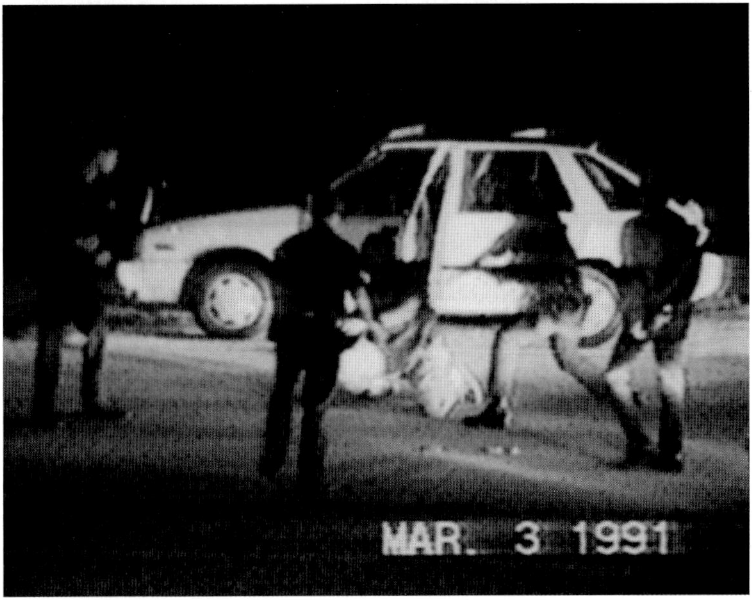

←
Dave Glass
Would-be Hollywood icon Angelyne emblazoned on one of her many self-promoting billboards, 1987.

Möchtegern-Hollywoodstar Angelyne auf einer überdimensionalen, von ihr selbst angemieteten Plakatwand, 1987.

Angelyne, aspirante à la gloire hollywoodienne, s'exhibe sur l'un de ses panneaux autopromotionnels, 1987.

↑
Anonymous
Videotape of the Rodney King beating instantly became a media phenomenon. The tape and the eventual acquittal of the involved police officers inflamed the African American community, 1991.

Die Videoaufnahme vom Angriff auf Rodney King wurde sofort zum Medienphänomen. Das Video und der spätere Freispruch der beteiligten Polizisten brachte die afroamerikanische Bevölkerung auf, 1991.

La vidéo amateur du tabassage de Rodney King devint un phénomène médiatique. La vidéo et l'acquittement final des policiers en cause enflamma la communauté afro-américaine, 1991.

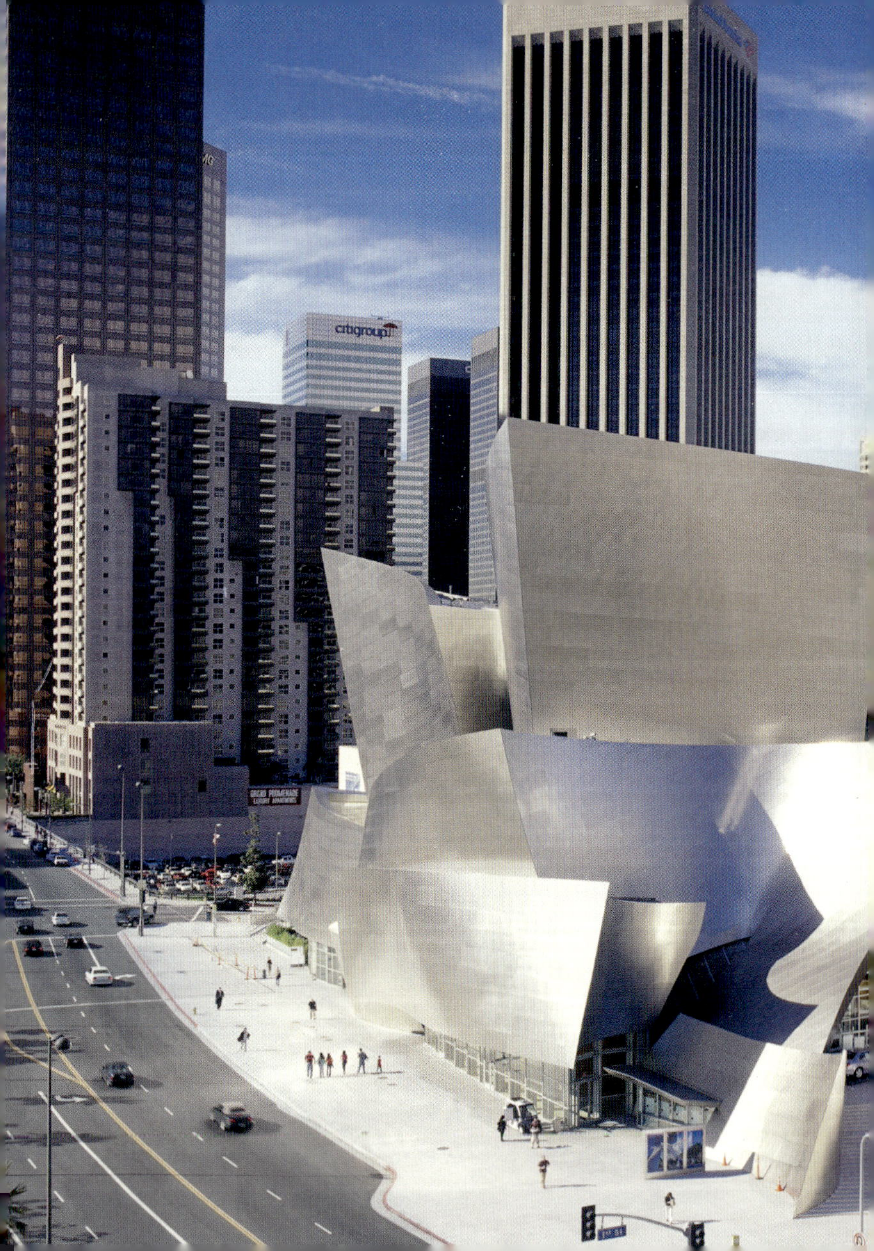
citigroup

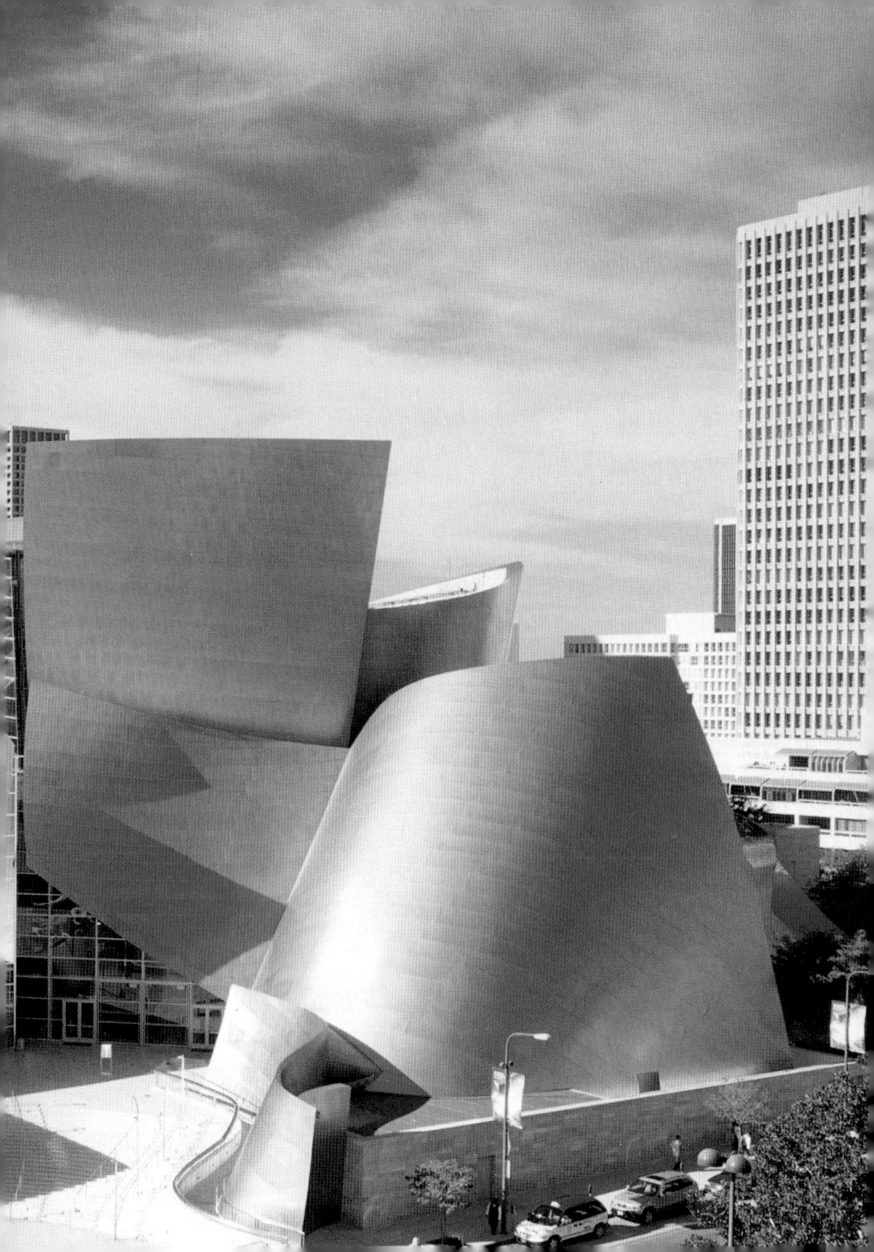

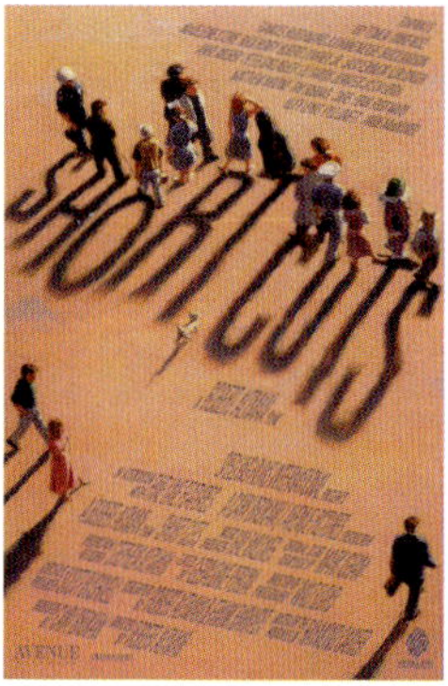

"I hate L.A. All they do is snort coke and talk."

„Ich hasse L.A. Hier wird nur gekokst und geredet."

«Je hais L.A. Ils ne savent que sniffer de la coke et parler.»

***Short Cuts*, 1993**

p. 184/185

Tim Street-Porter

The groundbreaking Disney Hall, by local architect Frank Gehry, became an instant landmark, c. 2002.

Die innovative Walt-Disney-Konzerthalle des in Los Angeles lebenden Architekten Frank Gehry wurde sofort zu einem Wahrzeichen der Stadt, um 2002.

L'époustouflant Disney Hall, par l'architecte local Frank Gehry, est devenu instantanément un des emblèmes de la ville, vers 2002.

→

Gary Leonard

Repeating an image from a century earlier, a palm is lifted into position in a new downtown residential district, 2005.

Wie als Echo einer vor 100 Jahren entstandenen Fotografie wird hier eine Palme in einem neuen Wohnviertel in Downtown in Position gebracht, 2005.

Répétant une image du siècle précédent, un palmier est transporté vers son emplacement dans un nouveau quartier résidentiel du centre, 2005.

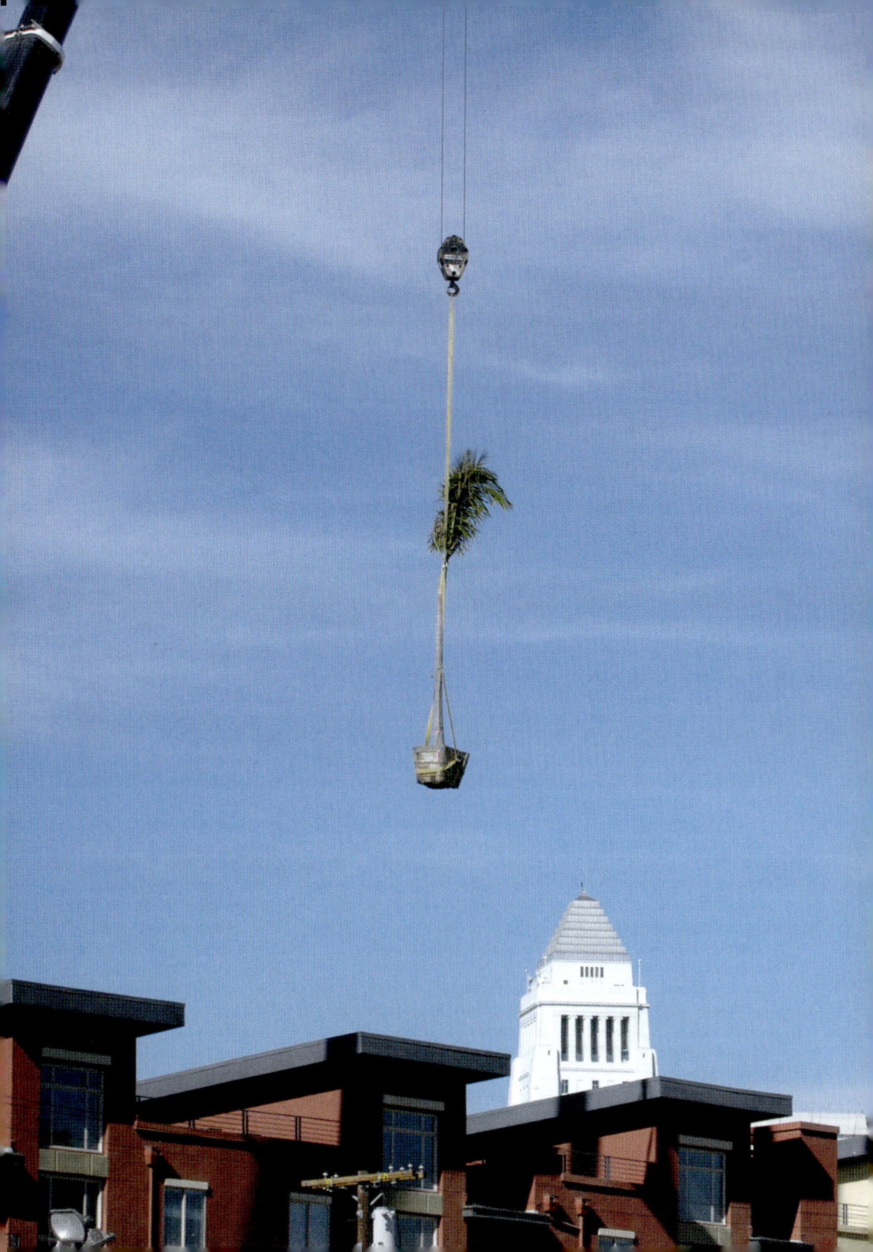

Photo Credits
Bildnachweis
Crédits photographiques

Any omissions for copy or credit are unintentional and appropriate credit will be given in future editions if such copyright holders contact the publisher. The publisher gratefully acknowledges the use of photographs provided courtesy of the following individuals and institutions:

Slim Aarons / Getty Images *2, 118–19, 144*
The Academy of Motion Picture Arts and Sciences *47, 65*
AP Images *181*
© Bettmann / Corbis *82, 109, 135*
Between the Covers Rare Books *33, 80, 102*
Bonhams & Butterfields Auctioneers *62, 128*
California Public Library, Mott Studios Collection *back cover, 70, 87*
© City of Los Angeles *130*
Ed Clark / Time & Life Pictures / Getty Images *129*
© William Claxton LLC / Demont Photo Management / Fahey Klein Gallery *148–49, 150*
© CNN *183*
Will Connell Collection, UCR / California Museum of Photography, University of California, Riverside *58, 59*
Corita Art Center Immaculate Heart Community *138–39*
Ralph Crane / Time & Life Pictures / Getty Images *112–13, 136, 153*
© The André de Dienes Archives LLC / OneWest Publishing *134*
© Henry Diltz / Corbis *164–65*
Dan DePalma *11, 40, 82, 42, 75*
J. R. Eyerman / Time & Life Pictures / Getty Images *120, 142*
© Ed Fox *29*
© Anthony Friedkin *170*
© J. Paul Getty Trust. Used with permission. Julius Shulman Photography Archive. Research Library at the Getty Research Institute (2004.R.10) *14, 115, 140, 141, 161*
© Dave Glass *182*
© LeRoy Grannis Collection *93, 158–59, 160*
Allan Grant / Time & Life Pictures / Getty Images *19, 133*
Jim Heimann Collection *30–31, 64, 66–67, 69, 72–73, 74, 78, 86, 88–89, 94–95, 96, 114, 121, 122, 137, 178–79*
© Douglas Hill *176*
The Burton Holmes Historical Collection *68, 79*
© Dennis Hopper *156*
The Huntington Library, San Marino, California *8, 60–61, 76–77*
Jack Laxer, Architectural Photography/Copyright, Pacific Palisades, CA *116*
© Gary Leonard *187*
Library of Congress, Prints & Photographs Division *36, 107*
Seaver Center for Western History Research, Los Angeles County Museum of Natural History *12, 37*
Los Angeles Public Library *100–101, 146*
J. Eric Lynxwiler *117*
© Burt Glinn / Magnum Photos / Agentur Focus *166*
© Dennis Stock / Magnum Photos / Agentur Focus *20, 167, 168–69*
Michael Ochs Archives / Getty Images *131*
National Geographic Society Image Collection *125*
Philadelphia Museum of Art, Archives: Gift of Jacqueline, Paul, and Peter Matisse in memory of their mother Alexina Duchamp *105*
The Reel Poster Archive *71, 87, 97, 174*
© San Diego Historical Center *56*
Walter Sanders / Time & Life Pictures / Getty Images *98, 99*
© Steve Schapiro *175*
Lawrence Schiller © Polaris Communications, Inc. *27*
Esther McCoy Files on Architects 1945–1989, Archives of American Art, Smithsonian Institution *53*
Seymour Rosen © SPACES — Saving and Preserving Arts and Cultural Environments *151*
C. R. Stecyk © 2013 *171*
© Tim Street-Porter *184–85*
Topical Press Agency / Getty Images *54*
Craig Krull Gallery © John Swope Trust *91, 103*
The Frank J. Thomas Archives *cover, 4–5, 124*
Collection Center for Creative Photography, University of Arizona © 1998 The University of Arizona Foundation *111*
R. M. Schindler papers, Art, Design, & Architecture Museum, UC Santa Barbara *52*
UCLA Charles E. Young Research Library Department of Special Collections, *Los Angeles Times* Photographic Archives, Copyright © Regents of the University of California, UCLA Library *83, 104, 106, 132, 147*
University of Southern California on behalf of the USC Special

Quotation Credits
Zitatnachweis
Crédits des citations

Collections *6, 32, 34, 35, 38, 39, 41, 43, 44–45, 48–9, 57, 63, 92, 126–27*

© Ellen von Unwerth / Trunk Archive *22*

Marc Wanamaker / Bison Archives *46*

© Julian Wasser. Courtesy of the artist and Craig Krull Gallery, Santa Monica, California *154–55, 162, 172–73*

Gregory P. Williams / The Cliff Wesselmann Collection *55, 81*

The Frank Lloyd Wright Foundation Archives (The Museum of Modern Art / Avery Architectural & Fine Arts Library, Columbia University) *51*

Tom Zimmerman Collection *84–85, 108, 145*

1 Will Rogers, *Washington Post*, May 17, 1964.

33 Helen Hunt Jackson, *Ramona* (New York: Grosset & Dunlap Inc., 1912), 60–61.

42 Charles F. Lummis, "In the Lion's Den," *Land of Sunshine*, December 1895.

50 F. Scott Fitzgerald, *The Last Tycoon: An Unfinished Novel* (New York: Charles Scribner's Sons, 1969), 70.

62 John Fante, *Ask the Dust* (Santa Barbara, CA: Black Sparrow Press, 1980), 27.

71 Janiss Garza, "Plot Synopsis." All Movie Guide, http://www.allmovie.com/work/hollywood-95435 (accessed May 14, 2009).

80 Horace McCoy, *They Shoot Horses, Don't They?* (London: Serpent's Tail, 1995), 16.

87 *What Price Hollywood*, directed by George Cukor: RKO–Pathé, 1932.

90 Upton Sinclair, *Oil!* (New York: Albert and Charles Boni, 1927).

97 *Sunset Boulevard*, directed by Billy Wilder: Paramount Pictures, 1950.

102 Kenneth Anger, *Hollywood Babylon* (San Francisco: Straight Arrow Books, 1975), 12.

110 Ross MacDonald, *The Drowning Pool* (New York: Knopf, 1950), 72.

121 Bing Crosby, "San Fernando Valley (I'm Packin' My Grip)," words and music by Gordon Jenkins, Mayfair Music Corp., 1943.

128 Raymond Chandler, *The Big Sleep* (New York: Alfred A. Knopf, 1939).

143 Joan Didion, *Play It As It Lays* (New York: Macmillan, 2005), 15.

152 Lawrence Lipton, *The Holy Barbarians* (New York: Julian Messner, 1959), 17–8.

157 The Beach Boys, "California Girls," from *Summer Days (And Summer Nights!!)*, Capitol, 1965.

163 The Doors, "L.A. Woman," from *L.A. Woman*, Elektra, 1971.

174 *Chinatown*, directed by Roman Polanski: Paramount Pictures, 1974.

177 *Hardcore*, directed by Paul Schrader: Columbia Pictures, 1979.

180 Bret Easton Ellis, *Less Than Zero* (New York: Vintage Books, 1998), 61.

186 *Short Cuts*, directed by Robert Altman: New Line Cinema, 1993.

Index

Numbers in italics refer to page numbers with images.

Aarons, Slim 2, *118–19*, 121, 144, 191
Aarons, Rita *2*, 191
Altoon, John *150*, 151
Angelyne *182*, 183
Anger, Kenneth 102
Ault, Julie *138–39*, 140
Beach Boys, The *157*
Becket, Welton 13, 147
Behme, Robert Lee 137
Belushi, John 180, *181*
Bengston, Billy Al *150*, 151
Blum, Irving *150*, 151
Bragg, Paul 75, *76–77*
Campbell, Naomi 21, *22*
Chandler, Harry 47
Chandler, Raymond 128
Claxton, William 147, *148–49*, 150, 151
Connell, Will 58, *59*
Crane, Ralph 110, *112–13*, 136, 137
Crosby, Bing 121
Cugat, Xavier 131
Dalí, Salvador *104*, 105
Davis, James "Two Gun" 54, *55*
Dean, James 135
Derrah, Robert V. 97
Didion, Joan 143, *172–73*, 174,
Dienes, André de *134*, 135
Diltz, Henry *164–65*, 166
Disney, Walt *184–85*, 186
Doheny, Edward 8, 16, 24
Doors, The 163, *164–65*, 166
Duchamp, Marcel 105, *154–55*, 157
Dunne, John Gregory 174
Eames, Charles *141*, 143
Eames, Ray *141*, 143
Edison, Thomas 9, 16, 25
Ellis, Bret Easton 180
Eyerman, J. R. *120*, 121
Fairbanks, Douglas 12
Fante, John 62
Fitzgerald, F. Scott 50
Fox, Ed 29
Freeth, George *56*, *57*
Friedkin, Anthony *170*, 171
Gehry, Frank 13, 21, 29, *184–85*, 186
Glinn, Burt 166
Grannis, LeRoy 93, *158–59*, 160
Grant, Allan 19, 132, *133*
Grant, Cary 163
Handler, Ruth 132
Hankey, Roy *146*, 147
Hefner, Hugh 147
Heimann, Jim 177, *178–79*
Hill, Douglas *176*, 177
Hilton, Conrad 13
Holmes, Burton 68, *79*
Hopper, Dennis *156*, 157
Hughes, Howard 109
Huntington, Henry 9, 17, 24
Jackson Five, The 27
Jackson, Helen Hunt 33
Jackson, William Henry *36*, 37
Jenkins, Gordon 121
Kennedy, Robert F. 11, 19, 27
Kent, Sister Mary Corita *138–39*, 140
Kienholz, Ed 11–2, 19, 28, 152, *153*
King, Rodney 13, 21, 28, 183
Kinney, Abbott 8, 16, 24
Kohner, Kathy (Gidget) 19
Lane, Abbe 131
Lautner, John 116, 140
Laxer, Jack 116
Leaf, Earl 131
Leonard, Gary 186, *187*
Lipton, Lawrence 152
Lugo family *37*
Lummis, Charles Fletcher 42
MacDonald, Ross 110
Mansfield, Jayne 132, *133*, 163
Manson, Charles 11, 19, 27
Martinez, Nicolas *32*, 33
Mascarel, José 34
Mayer, Louis B. 98
McCoy, Horace 80
McLendon, Lennox 180, *181*
McQueen, Steve 163
Merge, Mott *66–67*, 68, *69*
Miller, Richard C. *114*, 115
Monroe, Marilyn *134*, 135
Moses, Ed *150*, 151
Mott Studios *70*, 71, *86*, 87, 191, *back cover*
Mulholland, William 8, 16, 24
Neutra, Richard *53*, 87
Nichols, Alice 147
Northrop, John 12, 20, 28
Palmer, Alfred T. 106, *107*
Pendelton, James *118–19*, 121
Pendelton, Mary Frances *118–19*, 121
Pickford, Mary 12, 68
Pierce, C. C. 8, *32*, 33, 34, *60–61*, 62
Ray, Man 105
Rittenhouse, R. *130*, 131
Roberts, Joseph Baylor 125
Rodia, Simon 160
Rogers, Will 1
Rosen, Seymour 151
Ruscha, Ed 11, 19, 28
Sanders, Walter 98, *99*
Schapiro, Steve 174, *175*
Schiller, Lawrence 27
Schindler, Rudolph M. *53*, 87
Shulman, Julius 13, *14*, 53, 115, 140, *141*, 143, 160, *161*
Stackpole, Peter 116, *117*
Stecyk, C. R., III 171
Stock, Dennis 20, 166, *167*, *168–69*
Street-Porter, Tim *184–85*, 186
Swope, John 90, *91*, 102, *103*
Taylor Studio *40*, 41
Thomas, Frank J. *cover*, *4–5*, *124*, 125, 191
Ulin, David L. 3
Valentino, Rudolph 50
von Unwerth, Ellen 21, *22*
Warhol, Andy 151
Wasser, Julian *154–55*, 157
Wesselmann, Cliff 54, *55*, *78*, *79*, 80, *81*
Whittington, Dick 75, *76–77*, *88–89*, 90, 191, *192*
Woolf, John 121
Wright, Frank Lloyd 50
Yavno, Max 110, *111*

p. 2
Slim Aarons
Rita Aarons, wife of the photographer, floating in a pool festooned with baubles and a decorated Christmas tree, c. 1955.

Rita Aarons, Ehefrau des Fotografen, beim Baden im Pool, der mit Weihnachtskugeln und einem geschmückten Weihnachtsbaum dekoriert ist, um 1955.

Rita Aarons, épouse du photographe, nageant dans une piscine ornée de boules de Noël et d'un sapin décoré, vers 1955.

p. 4/5
Frank J. Thomas
Ocean Avenue in Santa Monica, c. 1955.

Die Ocean Avenue in Santa Monica, um 1955.

Ocean Avenue à Santa Monica, vers 1955.

p. 192
Anonymous
The customized mobile photo van of "Dick" Whittington Photography at Santa Anita racetrack, c. 1938.

Das Fotomobil, eine Sonderanfertigung für „Dick" Whittington Photography an der Santa-Anita-Rennbahn, um 1938.

La camionnette photo personnalisée de « Dick » Whittington Photography sur le champ de courses de Santa Anita, vers 1938.

Front cover / Umschlagvorderseite / Couverture
Frank J. Thomas
Muscle Beach, c. 1954.

Muscle Beach, um 1954.

Muscle Beach, vers 1954.

Back cover / Umschlagrückseite / Dos de couverture
Mott Studios
Opening of the Warner Theater, later the Wiltern, at Wilshire Boulevard and Western Avenue, October 7, 1931.

Eröffnung des Warner Theater, des späteren Wiltern, Ecke Wilshire Boulevard und Western Avenue, 7. Oktober 1931.

Inauguration du Warner Theater, qui deviendra le Wiltern, Wilshire Boulevard et Western Avenue, 7 octobre 1931.

To stay informed about upcoming TASCHEN titles, please request our magazine at www.taschen.com/magazine, find our app for iPad on iTunes, or write to TASCHEN, Hohenzollernring 53, D-50672 Cologne, Germany; contact@taschen.com. We will be happy to send you a free copy of our magazine, which is filled with information about all of our books.

Hohenzollernring 53, D-50672 Köln
www.taschen.com

Editorial coordination: Victoria Birch, Los Angeles; Kathrin Murr, Cologne; Nina Wiener, New York
Art direction: Josh Baker, Los Angeles
Design and layout: Anna-Tina Kessler, Los Angeles
Production: Frauke Kaiser, Cologne
German translation: Ronit Jariv, Cologne
French translation: Daniel Roche, Paris
Collaboration: Jonathan Newhall, New York

Printed in Slovakia
ISBN 978-3-8365-4515-0

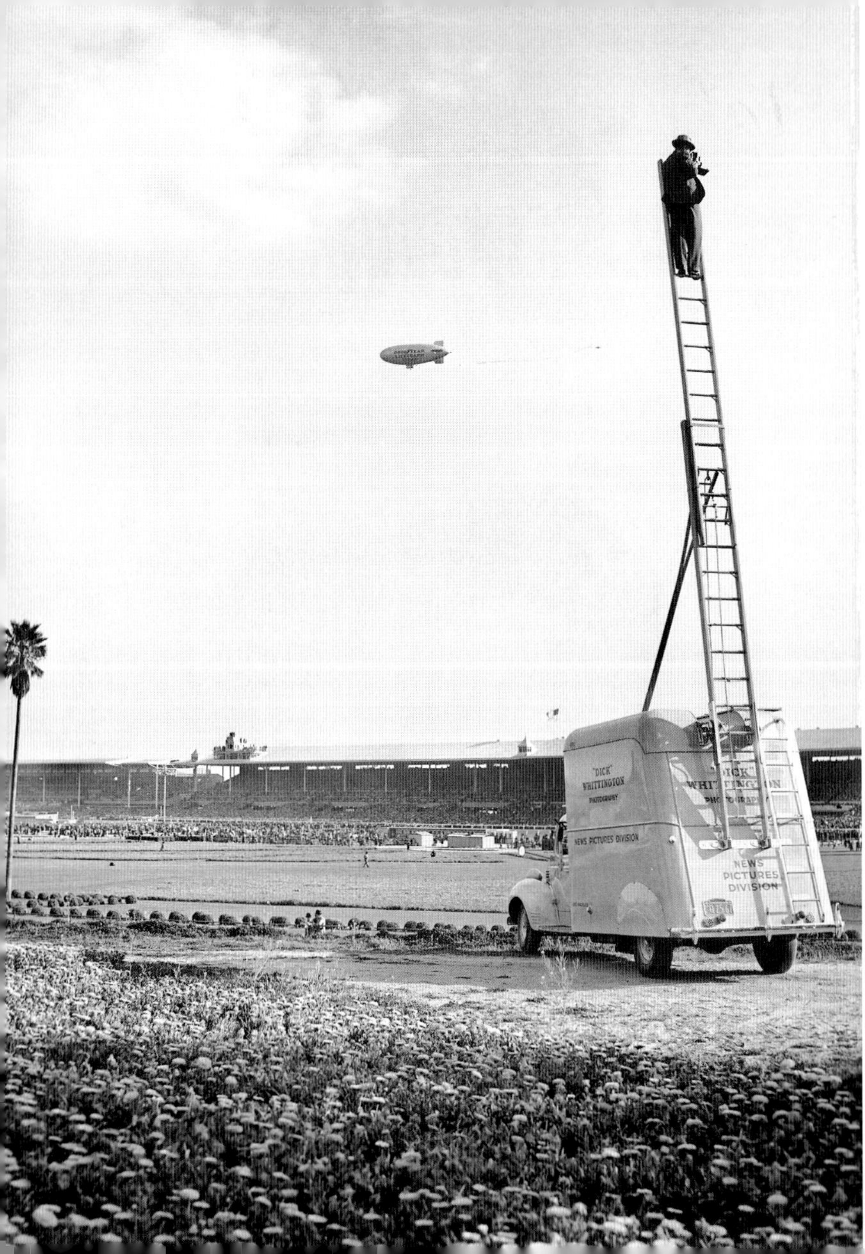
"DICK"
WHITTINGTON
PHOTOGRAPHY
NEWS PICTURES DIVISION
NEWS
PICTURES
DIVISION

Take your pick — or pick them all …

… the Piccolos are coming to town!

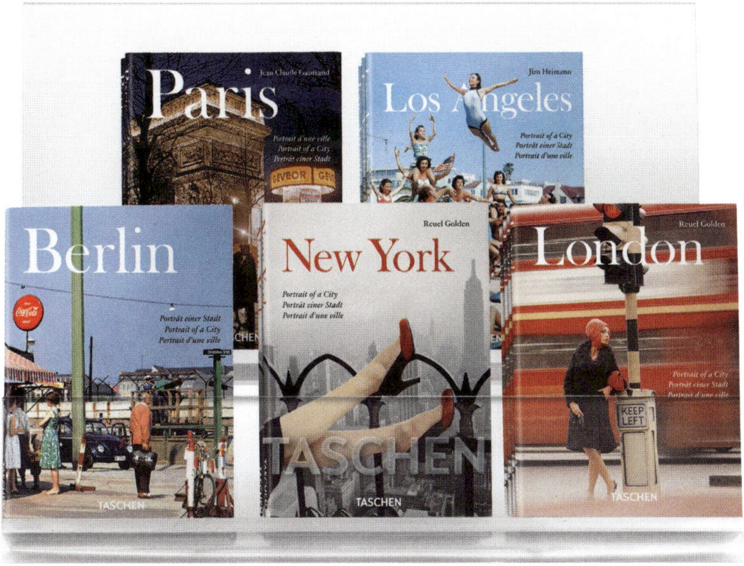

Our popular *Portrait of a City* series is now available in the new Piccolo format — 192 pages distilling the best of the originals into pocket-sized books that won't put a dent in your wallet.